Essential ICT

for AQA

A2 Level | Stephen Doyle

FD2828

United Kingdom: Folens Publishers, Waterslade House, Thame Rd, Haddenham, Buckinghamshire HP17 8NT.

www.folens.com

Ireland: Folens Publishers, Greenhills Road, Tallaght, Dublin 24.

Email: info@folens.ie

Editor:	Geoff Tuttle
Project development:	Rick Jackman (Jackman Publishing Solutions Ltd) and Claire Hart
Concept design:	Patricia Briggs
Layout artist:	GreenGate Publishing Services
Illustrations:	GreenGate Publishing Services
Cover design:	Jump To! www.jumpto.co.uk
Cover image:	Courtesy of Chris Harvey/Fotolia.com

First published 2009 by Folens Limited.

Every effort has been made to contact copyright holders of material used in this publication. If any copyright holder has been overlooked, we should be pleased to make any necessary arrangements.

British Library Cataloguing in Publication Data.

A catalogue record for this publication is available from the British Library.

ISBN 978-1-85008-282-8

Contents

Introduction to the A2 Units   vi

Introduction to the features in the student book   ix

Unit 3 Use of ICT in the Digital World

Topic 1: Future developments   1

1 Emerging technologies   2
2 Potential future uses of ICT   4
3 Implications of future developments and future use of ICT   6
4 Activity and Questions   10
5 Case studies   11
6 Exam support   13
7 Summary mind maps   15

Topic 2: Information and systems   17

1 Information needs in organisations   18
2 ICT supporting the activities of organisations   24
3 The types of ICT systems and their uses   26
4 Questions and Activities   31
5 Case studies   33
6 Exam support   36
7 Summary mind maps   38

Topic 3: Managing ICT   41

1 Managing ICT   42
2 Questions and Case study   45
3 Exam support   47
4 Summary mind maps   49

Topic 4: ICT strategy   51

1 ICT strategy   52
2 Questions and Case study   55
3 Exam support   56
4 Summary mind maps   58

Topic 5: ICT policies   59

1   ICT policies   60

2   Questions and Activity   62

3   Exam support   63

4   Summary mind maps   65

Topic 6: Legislation   67

1   The implications of legislation for ICT policies and organisational procedures   68

2   Questions and Case study   71

3   Exam support   72

4   Summary mind map   74

Topic 7: Developing ICT solutions   75

1   Factors that contribute to a successful development process   76

2   Factors that might contribute to the failure of a newly introduced system   78

3   Questions, Case study and Activity   80

4   Exam support   82

5   Summary mind maps   83

Topic 8: Development methods   85

1   The systems development life cycle   86

2   The need for systematic, formal methods   90

3   Development methodologies   92

4   Questions, Activity and Case studies   94

5   Exam support   96

6   Summary mind map   98

Topic 9: Techniques and tools for systems development   99

1   Investigating and recording techniques   100

2   Business process modelling tools   102

3   Data modelling tools   106

4   Techniques for testing   112

5   Questions   114

6   Activities   115

7   Exam support   117

8   Summary mind maps   119

Topic 10: Introducing large ICT systems into organisations — 121

1	Scale, reliability and testing	122
2	Installation	126
3	Backup and recovery	128
4	Maintenance	132
5	Questions and Case study	134
6	Exam support	136
7	Summary mind maps	139

Topic 11: Training and supporting users — 141

1	Internal and external users and their training requirements	142
2	Training and training methods	144
3	Support	146
4	Training and supporting customers	149
5	Questions	152
6	Activities and Case study	153
7	Exam support	155
8	Summary mind maps	157

Topic 12: External and internal resources — 159

1	Using external services and business support	160
2	Managing internal resources	162
3	Questions and Activities	164
4	Case studies	165
5	Exam support	167
6	Summary mind maps	170

Unit 4 Coursework: Practical Issues Involved in the Use of ICT in the Digital World — 171

1	Choosing a suitable project	172
2	Useful project advice, tips and assessment	176
3	How the project is assessed	178

Glossary	181
Index	184
Acknowledgements	187

Introduction to the A2 Units

Introduction to the A2 Units

There are two units for the A2 Information Communication Technology:

- Unit 3 The Use of ICT in the Digital World INFO 3
- Unit 4 Coursework: Practical Issues Involved in the Use of ICT in the Digital World INFO 4

For A2 level the balance of the marks for the two units is:

- Unit 3 The Use of ICT in the Digital World INFO 3 60%
- Unit 4 Coursework: Practical Issues Involved in the Use of ICT in the Digital World INFO 40%

Unit 3 The Use of ICT in the Digital World

Assessment for Unit 3 The Use of ICT in the Digital World

This consists of a question paper with answers written in an answer booklet which is marked externally by AQA. The written paper is of 2 hr duration.

There are two sections to the paper:

Section A

- All the questions from this section should be answered.
- Consists of structured questions.
- Questions are based on pre-release material.
- The pre-release material will be available on the AQA website prior to the examination and it will also be printed in the examination paper.

Section B

- All the questions from this section should be answered.
- Consists of questions requiring extended prose answers.

The organisation of Unit 3 The Use of ICT in the Digital World

Unit 3 is divided up into the following topics:

1. Future developments
2. Information and systems
3. Managing ICT
4. ICT strategy
5. ICT policies
6. Legislation
7. Developing ICT solutions
8. Development methods
9. Techniques and tools for systems development
10. Introducing large ICT systems into organisations
11. Training and supporting users
12. External and internal resources

1 Future developments

Predicting the future is almost impossible and it is very hard to pick out those emerging technologies in ICT that will shape the future. In this topic you will be looking at a range of emerging technologies, many of which concern working remotely using mobile devices. You will also be looking at the potential and future uses of ICT and how this might affect society and the way we run our lives.

One of the problems with ICT is the pace at which changes happen and this rapid development causes a number of social, legal, technical, ethical, economic and environmental issues which will be discussed in this topic.

2 Information and systems

In this topic you will be looking at the nature of organisations and the range of activities they perform. Within organisations there is usually a hierarchy of staff who use the routine information collected from the organisation's ICT systems in different ways. You will also learn that organisations have to deal with many outside organisations and that they often exchange information with these organisations. For this exchange to take place, there are a number of privacy, security and legal implications to consider.

Many organisations have very similar ICT systems because they need to, for example, pay staff, order goods and services, etc. You will be looking at these common functions and their information needs. You will also look at the systems, such as management information systems and decision support systems, which managers use to help them manage their area of the business.

3 Managing ICT

ICT is a resource and has to be managed just like any other resource such as human resources. In this topic you will be looking at how different organisations manage their ICT facilities. You will be looking at how organisations have an ICT strategy that will help them achieve their overall business objectives. This ICT strategy will be broken down into many different policies. You will also learn about the importance of the Chief Information Officer in a large organisation and how this role helps organisations ensure that all ICT developments are carefully considered and developed to meet business needs.

4 ICT strategy

ICT strategies set out where organisations want to go with their ICT developments. They are an overall vision of how ICT can support the changes needed to a business in order for it to remain competitive and achieve its business objectives. Strategy will include future proofing, dealing with developments in technology and procurement.

5 ICT policies

ICT policies are the detail of what needs to be done in order for the organisation to achieve its overall ICT strategy. In this topic you will be looking at security, training and procurement policies.

6 Legislation

There are many different laws that apply to the use of ICT and also to the way certain businesses are run. For example, financial systems are very heavily regulated, so organisations are not free to conduct their business however they want. In this topic you will look at some of the legislation and how this legislation has implications for ICT policies. You will also look at the way legislation impacts on the procedures within organisations.

7 Developing ICT solutions

In order for organisations to keep up with the business they are involved in they have to develop new ICT systems and these systems need careful development. There are many examples of systems that have been developed that do not bring about the hoped for benefits and are therefore a waste of money. In this topic you will be looking at the factors that contribute to a successful development process and those factors that could lead to the failure of the process.

8 Development methods

Some projects are successful and some are not. This topic seeks to look at the factors that contribute to a successful development process and will also look at the factors which can cause the failure of such a project. This topic also looks at the stages of development for an ICT project, including analysis and design, constructing the solution, testing, installation and conversion, and review and maintenance. Also covered is the fact that for systems to be developed effectively, the developer needs to use formal methods and that there are a number of such methods to choose from. Ultimately the choice of the method depends mainly on the type of project being undertaken and the experience of the developer.

9 Techniques and tools for systems development

Before a new system is developed, there is a period of investigating and recording that uses a variety of techniques. In this topic these methods will be looked at along with methods used for the modelling of business processes. Data modelling is an important tool that developers use to model existing systems as well as help design new systems, and the techniques of data modelling will be looked at. Both during development and once the system has been developed, testing needs to take place. The different types of testing will be looked at here.

10 Introducing large ICT systems into organisations

Organisations are widely different, with some running to just a handful of employees and others operating with tens of thousands of employees. In this topic you will look at those factors which need to be considered when introducing ICT systems. You will be looking at reliability and testing, installation, backup and recovery and maintenance.

11 Training and supporting users

ICT systems can be both external and internal to an organisation, so the training needed on systems may need to be presented differently. You will be looking here at the training requirements users have and the support they need after training has been given. You will be looking at how customers who have to use an organisation's ICT systems can be supported and how the interface is an important aspect in improving the usability of the system.

12 External and internal resources

Many organisations want to manage and do the things they are best at and leave some aspects of the business to other outside organisations. Many organisations now outsource certain aspects of their business such as customer support, network management, etc. In this topic you will look at using external ICT services for support and also what is involved in planning the management and control of internal resources.

Unit 4: Coursework: Practical Issues Involved in the Use of ICT in the Digital World

Assessment for Unit 4 Practical Issues Involved in the Use of ICT in the Digital World

This unit requires you to produce a project report based on your practical work/investigation. This involves creating an ICT-related system over an extended period of time. The main aim of the project is to develop your knowledge and understanding of the development of ICT systems through practical experience in using a variety of applications software in a structured way.

1 Background and investigation

This looks in detail at the organisation the project is being developed for and looks at the organisation itself and describes the current system and/or the environment the proposed new system will be in. The clients and users of the system will be identified, as will a business reason for the change to the system. You will then have to provide evidence that you have used relevant investigation techniques and that you have outlined the client requirements.

2 Analysis and deliverables

The scope of the project should be outlined by describing the internal and external constraints on the system, and the proposed system should be described in terms or the benefits and likely impact on the organisation. Processes should be identified and the users of the new system should be described. The evaluation criteria should be described in conjunction with the client, and deliverables should be agreed. Findings should be communicated to the client in a way that the client will understand.

3 Design and planning for implementation

This is the stage in which the evidence from the previous stage is used to create draft and final designs for the new system. A plan for the implementation, testing, and installation along with the relevant timescales should be produced. Training requirements for the new system are identified including documentation needed for training purposes. A testing strategy and test plan is included as preparation for the next stage.

4 Testing and documentation

In this section you will be required to produce evidence of testing as per the testing strategy outlined in the previous section. This testing needs to concentrate on the testing of complete processes and the system as a whole. There also needs to be evidence of client and/or user testing.

Comprehensive documentation of the solution is produced that would allow the solution to be used/maintained or developed further. The produced documentation has to be appropriate to the client/users.

5 Evaluation of the implemented solution

Included in this section is an evaluation of the implemented solution, which should identify strengths and weaknesses in your approach and how you might improve your performance should you have to complete a similar project in the future.

6 Project report

The completed work should be submitted in the format of a project report, which should be well structured and should make thorough use of the software packages. The project report should be well organised and include technically accurate textual and visual material for effective communication. The report should be well written as the standard of your communication will be assessed from the report.

Introduction to the features in the student book

Topic introduction pages

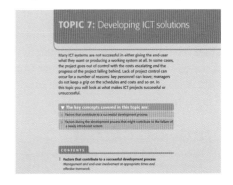

The philosophy behind the student book

This student book has been based on extensive research from schools and colleges on the different ways ICT is taught and this book has been developed with all the findings in mind. As this is a new specification, many students and teachers/lecturers will be finding their way and the aim of the book is to provide a depth of coverage for all the material for Units 3 and 4. This book covers all the material for the A2 level in ICT.

This book should be used by the teacher/lecturer in conjunction with the teacher support materials. Of course this book can be used stand-alone, but if you are a teacher then there are many resources in the teacher support materials to help your students succeed and maximise their marks. The Teacher Support CD-ROM contains the following non-digital resources: Answers to the Questions, Activities and Case studies and also provides additional Questions and Case studies.

The Teacher Support CD-ROM also includes a wealth of digital materials such as PowerPoint presentations, multiple choice questions, missing word tasks and free text tasks. These will all help your students consolidate their understanding of the topics.

The structure of the student book

The AQA A2 level consists of two units with each unit being divided into topics. In this book each topic has been further divided up into spreads. This allows division of each topic into bite-size easily digested chunks of material. For consistency and to make the student book easy to use, all topics are structured in the same way.

The first page of each topic consists of an introduction to the material in the topic and includes the following features:

Topic introduction: just a couple of paragraphs introducing students to the subject matter in the topic.

Key concepts: this lists the key concepts covered in the topic. These key concepts are identical to those in the A2 AQA specification.

Contents: the contents lists the spreads used to cover the topic and each spread covers key concepts.

Topic spreads

Introduction: introduces the content on the spreads.

You will find out: this tells you what you will learn from the content of the spreads.

The content: what you need to learn is presented in the content and this material has been written to give you the essential information in order to answer examination questions.

Cartoons: relevant cartoons drawn by the cartoonist Randy Glasbergen add a bit of humour and fun to the topics.

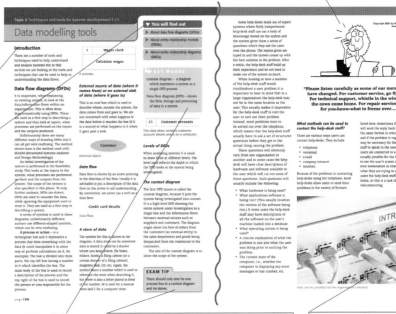

Key words: these are specialist terms used in the content spreads and it is important that you not only remember these words, but you can use them with confidence when describing aspects of ICT systems. There is also a glossary at the back of the book which can be used for reference.

Exam tips: useful tips based on the problems that students have when they answer questions on the topics.

Diagrams and photographs: bring the topic to life with relevant and carefully researched images.

Questions, Activities and Case study spreads

These are usually included at the end of the content spreads and are used to consolidate learning. There are some occasions where Activities or Questions are included within the content spreads. Each block of questions covers a certain number of pages and most of the time this will be a double-page spread. This allows you to look at the spreads and then practise the questions. The answers to all the questions are available in the teacher support materials, which are available separately on CD-ROM and complement the student text.

▶ **Questions 1**   pp. 2–9

1 Many technologies are combined in some devices such as mobile phones.
   Discuss the impact of mobile communication devices on:
   (a) Society (4 marks)
   (b) Individuals as consumers and as workers. (4 marks)
2 Many devices have revolutionised the way we work and play. Mobile phones are one such device.
   (a) Other than mobile phones, describe how a device or system has changed the way people work or play. (3 marks)
   (b) Briefly describe an emerging technology that is likely to change society. (2 marks)
3 Give **one** example of an ethical issue that has been brought about by the rapid development of ICT. (3 marks)
4 One of the problems with rapid development of ICT is that the problems it causes cannot always be anticipated. This means that laws to deal with the abuses have to be developed once the problems start. Give **two** examples of abuses of ICT systems and give the names of the pieces of legislation making the abuse illegal. (4 marks)
5 (a) Discuss the developments in ICT which have enabled remote and mobile working. (6 marks)
   (b) Despite the advances in ICT there are still limitations in remote and mobile working. Describe **one** such limitation. (2 marks)
6 When new ICT systems are developed, workers in organisations can feel threatened. Describe the reasons why staff may feel threatened. (4 marks)
7 ICT has an impact on individuals as consumers and as workers. Describe the impact new technology has had on individuals and as workers. You should illustrate your answer with examples. (20 marks)

Questions: are included at the end of each topic and refer to the content in the spreads and are clearly labelled so that you can either do them after each double-page spread or all in one go at the end of the topic. The questions are designed to be similar to A2 examination questions and have marks to give students the opportunity to understand how answers are marked.

The answers to the questions are included in the Teacher Support CD-ROM.

▶ **Activity 3: Entity relationship diagrams**

Draw entity diagrams to show each of the following relationships:
1 Classes consist of many students.
2 One customer has many orders.
3 One tutor lectures on many courses.
4 Each module is taught by one tutor.
5 Many students enrol on many courses.
6 Many customers order many products.

Activities: offer interesting things for you to do which will help add to and reinforce the material in the spreads.

▶ **Case study 1**   pp. 2–9

Wikipedia

Wikipedia was set up to empower and engage people around the world by collecting and offering free content which can be disseminated globally. It is a huge success story and has changed the way the Internet is used.

You will probably have already used Wikipedia but if not take a look at it now on:

www.wikipedia.com

Wikipedia is a charity and unlike most other free providers of content, it does not contain adverts and therefore gets no money from these sources. Instead it relies mainly on asking you and me to donate money or on revenue from grants. The money it obtains is used to buy hardware and also for hosting and bandwidth costs. People are not paid to add content – they do it for free!

Wikipedia is best described as an on-line encyclopaedia but it is different to other encyclopaedias in so much as it is made up from contributions by ordinary people.

You may think this is a bad thing. After all what if the information is wrong? It is easy to put in bogus information or information which someone believes is true but it isn't. Luckily other people can add information which corrects the information that is already there. The idea is that if enough people contribute, then the information is as good as that provided more traditionally.

1 One commenter on Wikipedia said: 'There is plenty of bogus information on the Internet. What we don't want is non experts making any old rubbish up on Wikipedia and then our children getting hold of it and believing it to be true.'
   Give a reason why this is less likely to happen than the commenter thinks. (2 marks)
2 You have been asked to give a brief description of what Wikipedia is to someone who has little knowledge of ICT. Describe Wikipedia in easy to understand non-technical language. You should make at least three main points in your description. (3 marks)
3 Wikipedia consists mainly of webpages containing text and images with links to other webpages. Describe **three** reasonably foreseeable future developments to Wikipedia that would improve it. (3 marks)

Case studies: real-life case studies are included that relate directly to the material in the topic. Case studies give a context in which you can answer the examination questions. Often examination questions on ICT ask not only for a definition or explanation but also an example. Case studies build up your knowledge of how the theory you learn about is used in practice.

Case study questions: will give you practice at answering questions which relate to real-life situations. The questions have been carefully constructed to be similar to the examination questions you could be asked and relate directly to the case study and other material contained in the content spreads.

If your teacher has the Teacher Support CD-ROM, they will have the answers to these case study questions.

Exam support

Worked example: is an important feature because it gives you an insight into how the examination questions are marked. At A2 level you can have the knowledge but still fail to get a good mark because you have failed to communicate what you know effectively. It is essential that you understand just what is expected of you when answering questions at A2 level.

Student answers: you can see an examination question which has been answered by two different students. For each student answer there is a corresponding Examiner's comment.

Examiner's comment: offers you an insight into how examiners mark student answers. The main thing here is to be able to see the mistakes that some students make and ensure that you do not make similar mistakes. By analysing the way answers are marked, you will soon be able to get more marks for the questions that you answer by not making common mistakes.

Examiner's answer: offers some of the many possible answers and an indication of how the marks are distributed between the answers. It should be borne in mind that there are many possible correct answers to some questions and that any mark scheme relies on the experience of the markers to interpret the mark scheme and to give credit for answers that do not appear in the mark scheme.

Summary mind maps

Mind maps are great fun to produce and a very good way of revising. They are included here to summarise the material contained in the topic. Sometimes there will be only one mind map and other times there will be several – it all depends on how the material in the topic is broken down.

As well as using these mind maps to help you revise, you should produce your own.

Why not produce them using the computer? There are many good pieces of mind mapping software.

Worked example 2

2 Describe **two** potential future uses of ICT and for **each** use explain how they are likely to benefit society. (4 marks)

Student answer 1

2 New modelling techniques can be used to model how drugs can attack cells. By understanding how drugs work, they can hopefully create new drugs that will target cancerous cells. Finding a cure for cancer will benefit the whole of society.
Greater use of speech recognition systems and speech synthesis systems will mean that the use of computers will not be limited by a person's need to use a keyboard. This will make computers easier to use which will widen their use further and benefit people with limited use of their hands. It will also benefit society because people will not develop RSI through repeated use of keyboards.

Examiner's comment

2 Both these future uses are acceptable answers. The second answer is only given one rather than two marks because speech recognition and synthesis systems have been around a long time and the answer fails to state why they are not more mainstream. Making them more accurate and capable of understanding speech that is not clear could have been mentioned. **(3 marks out of 4)**

Examiner's answer

1 One mark for a brief description of a use (this must be recent or future) and one mark for a clear statement of how it improves society. Typical answers could include: Flexible screens. Instead of having a small screen you can have a flexible screen that is folded out. This would be a big improvement when showing photographs or watching video clips on a mobile device as the device can still be kept small and light.

Student answer 2

2 The Internet will be used by people to vote at elections. This will mean that the country is more democratic, as ordinary people have more say in the way things are run. At present there are technical problems in doing this and the system is open to fraud. There will be more robots in the home. For example, robotic vacuum cleaners will clean the floors of your house at set intervals. Similarly, robot lawnmowers could mow the lawn while you were at work or on holiday.

Examiner's comment

2 The first answer is good and it clearly states the benefit to society (i.e., making it more democratic). The student has recognised that the system already exists by stating that technical problems need to be overcome.
The second answer talks about two types of robot which are already available and have been for a few years. If the device is already present then it is ok if the student talks about improvements to the device. This part of the answer is only given one mark. **(3 marks out of 4)**

Nanotechnology being used to make a shirt, which is capable of monitoring a patient's body while they go about their normal life.
Signals can be sent remotely to health care professionals if the readings start to fall outside acceptable ranges so they can be alerted and action taken. Such shirts can save lives and they also save money because patients can be sent home sooner after operations.

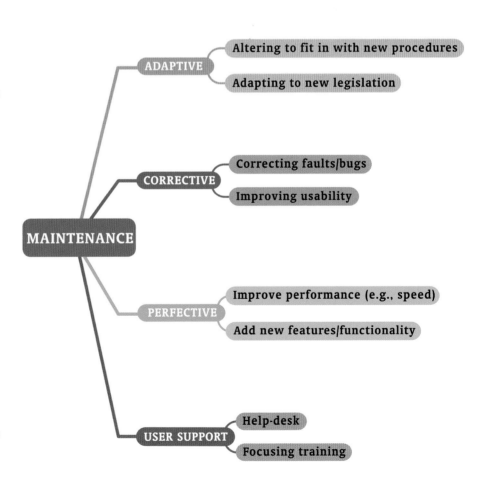

MAINTENANCE

- ADAPTIVE
  - Altering to fit in with new procedures
  - Adapting to new legislation
- CORRECTIVE
  - Correcting faults/bugs
  - Improving usability
- PERFECTIVE
  - Improve performance (e.g., speed)
  - Add new features/functionality
- USER SUPPORT
  - Help-desk
  - Focusing training

Mind map summarising the contents of Unit 3

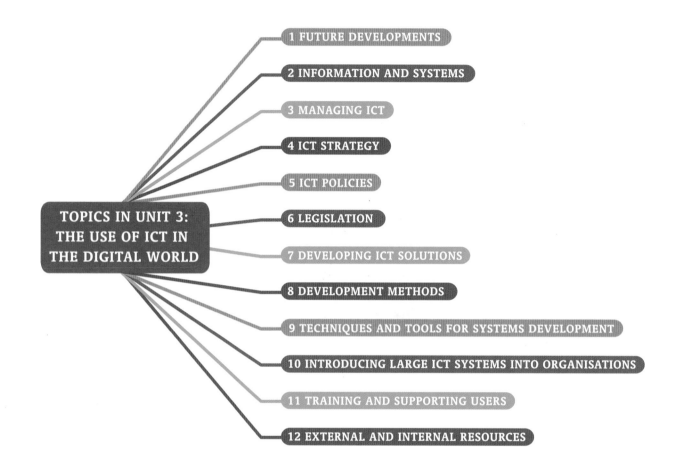

TOPICS IN UNIT 3: THE USE OF ICT IN THE DIGITAL WORLD

1 FUTURE DEVELOPMENTS

2 INFORMATION AND SYSTEMS

3 MANAGING ICT

4 ICT STRATEGY

5 ICT POLICIES

6 LEGISLATION

7 DEVELOPING ICT SOLUTIONS

8 DEVELOPMENT METHODS

9 TECHNIQUES AND TOOLS FOR SYSTEMS DEVELOPMENT

10 INTRODUCING LARGE ICT SYSTEMS INTO ORGANISATIONS

11 TRAINING AND SUPPORTING USERS

12 EXTERNAL AND INTERNAL RESOURCES

Mind map summarising the contents of Unit 4

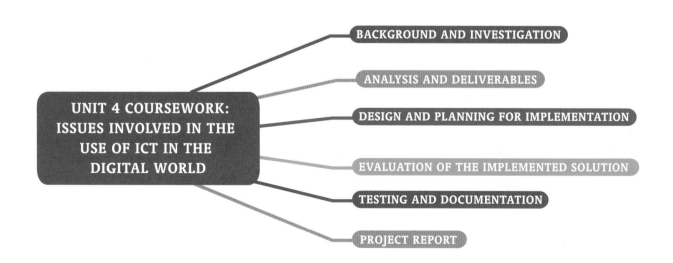

UNIT 4 COURSEWORK: ISSUES INVOLVED IN THE USE OF ICT IN THE DIGITAL WORLD

BACKGROUND AND INVESTIGATION

ANALYSIS AND DELIVERABLES

DESIGN AND PLANNING FOR IMPLEMENTATION

EVALUATION OF THE IMPLEMENTED SOLUTION

TESTING AND DOCUMENTATION

PROJECT REPORT

TOPIC 1: Future developments

In this topic you will be looking at emerging and future developments in ICT and the likely changes that these developments might bring to our lives. Trying to predict the future with any degree of accuracy is impossible, so in this topic you will be looking at developments which are emerging and you will soon see in everyday items.

▼ The key concepts covered in this topic are:

▶ Understand the emerging technologies and how they will bring business and leisure benefits

▶ Understand the potential future uses for ICT

▶ Understand the implications of future developments and future use of ICT

CONTENTS

1 Emerging technologies 2
Enabling devices for remote and mobile working (Bluetooth, BlackBerry®, mobile phones), nanotechnology, cognitive science, robotics and biotechnology.

2 Potential future uses of ICT 4
Wireless energy, novel user interfaces, flexible screens, Web 2.0 and smart cars.

3 Implications of future developments and future use of ICT 6
The impact on society, problems and abuses of new technology, the impact on the way organisations are run, the impact on individuals as consumers and as workers, the social, cultural, environmental, ethical, technical, legal, and economic issues surrounding the rapid development of ICT.

4 Activity and Questions 10

5 Case studies 11

6 Exam support 13

7 Summary mind maps 15

Unit 3 Use of ICT in the Digital World

Emerging technologies

▼ You will find out

▶ About enabling devices for remote and mobile working

▶ About the advances in technology that give business and leisure benefits

Introduction

It is impossible to predict the future but there is no doubt that the way we use ICT systems will change considerably over the next ten years.

Emerging technologies are those developments in technology that are likely to shape the future. Emerging technologies include nanotechnology, robotics, biotechnology, artificial intelligence and cognitive science. These will all be looked at in the following section along with other technologies that do not fall into this list.

Famous quotes from people as to the future of computers

Trying to predict the future of ICT is very difficult and here are some interesting quotations from people in posts of responsibility at the start of the development of computers who got it seriously wrong!

'Computers in the future may weigh no more than 1.5 tons.'
Popular Mechanics, 1949

'I think there is a world market for maybe five computers.'
Thomas Watson, Chairman of IBM, 1943

'I have travelled the length and breadth of this country and talked with the best people, and I can assure you that data processing is a fad and won't last out the year.'
The editor in charge of business books for publishers Prentice-Hall, 1957

'There is no reason anyone would want a computer in their home.'
Ken Olsen, president, chairman and founder of DEC, 1977

Emerging technologies

In this section you will be looking at the latest developments for remote and mobile working. Computers used to be confined to people's desks at work or at home, but now many people use ICT on the move, in hotel rooms, on flights and in coffee bars. The Internet can be accessed from almost anywhere using satellite links.

Mobile working

In this section you will be looking at the use of ICT for mobile working. Many workers now work more flexibly and this includes working while on the move (on planes, trains) or while waiting in cafes, bars, airport lounges, etc.

The way business is done has changed over the last few years, with more people working from remote locations using mobile devices such as mobile phones, laptops and PDAs. Business has changed in the following ways:

- Business can be done anywhere, anytime.
- It is much easier to do business internationally – businesses need to cope with the different time zones.
- Workers have more flexibility and can be more productive.
- Customers expect services to be available 24/7.
- There is improved communication between colleagues, customers and suppliers.

Many workers use mobile devices so they can work anywhere.

▶ KEY WORDS

Bluetooth – a standard for sending data using short-range radio signals

Bluetooth

Bluetooth is a standard for sending data wirelessly between devices. Bluetooth headsets wirelessly connect a mobile phone to an earpiece. They offer a hands-free solution to people who need to take calls whilst they are driving. This allows people to take and make phone calls whilst driving and stay within the law.

If Bluetooth circuitry is built into a device, the device can be networked with other devices such as phones, printers, digital cameras, laptops and headsets. This means that cables are not needed to link the devices in the network together.

Older computers may not support wireless networks but this device can be slotted into the USB port to enable wireless connection.

Many people now like to work wherever they are.

If you are listening to your iPod you may not hear your phone ring, so this Bluetooth set switches between the iPod and the phone when a call comes through.

BlackBerry®

A BlackBerry® smartphone is a personal digital assistant (PDA) and is a small device which is capable of being used as a phone, for e-mail, for web browsing, for text messaging, for Internet fax and it uses a small keyboard. Many mobile phones incorporate a global positioning system (GPS).

The BlackBerry® smartphone is very popular with business users as it is much smaller than a laptop but allows them to keep in touch wherever they are.

The BlackBerry® smartphone is a PDA with a small keyboard.

BlackBerry® 8820 smartphone

Mobile phones

Mobile phones are now more like PDAs as they are multifunction devices capable of a full range of functions such as voice, e-mail, web browsing, text messaging, call diverting, camera (still and video), music player and GPS.

Some phones now incorporate GPS.

Nanotechnology

Nanotechnology is a scientific technology which is still in its infancy and is set to transform our lives, like electricity or the internal combustion engine. New materials can be invented where standard sized particles can be reduced to sizes as small as a nanometre. A nanometre is about one-hundred-thousandths the thickness of a human hair. At these sizes materials start to exhibit strange properties. For example, gold melts at room temperature and carbon is 100 times stronger than steel.

Nanotechnology will have the following uses in ICT:

- personal computers with the power of today's computer centres
- chips containing films with over 1000 viewing hours
- miniaturised data storage systems with capacities equivalent to a whole library's stock
- flexible display technologies and e-paper
- printable electronic circuits.

Research sites

To find out more about nanotechnology try: http://www.nano.org.uk/news/newsarchive.htm

Cognitive science

Cognitive science is the study of the mind and it concerns how knowledge is obtained and used. Cognitive science embraces philosophy, psychology, artificial intelligence, neuroscience, linguistics, and anthropology. By understanding how the mind works, scientists can build computers which behave in a similar way.

Robotics

Robots have been widely used in manufacturing for years especially for painting and welding in car factories. Robots are also used for picking and packing goods in large warehouses. Robots have been developed for use on farms and these robots can perform a variety of farm tasks such as planting, weeding in-between crops, spraying crops and picking the crops.

Robots are used extensively by the military for neutralising unexploded bombs.

Robots have been developed that will do some of the tasks us humans hate to do such as mowing the lawn or vacuuming the floors.

Robots will eventually be seen in all homes – this vacuuming robot is already in the shops.

Mowing the lawn is a chore for many people, so this robot lawnmower is a useful device.

There are robots available for the home that will wash floors, clean gutters and clean swimming pools. The robots that are available at the moment in the home are usually capable of performing one task. In the future you will probably buy a single multifunctional robot capable of carrying out a range of different tasks.

Biotechnology

Biotechnology is technology based on biology. Biotechnology seeks to turn aspects of biology such as genetics, molecular biology, biochemistry, embryology and cell biology into useful forms of ICT or robotics.

Potential future uses of ICT

Introduction

There are a number of new technologies that are likely to change the use of ICT and will be used to develop new applications. In this topic we will attempt to get our crystal ball out and predict what the potential future uses of ICT might be.

Potential future uses of ICT

Here we will look at some developments which look promising but it is always hard to estimate what their impact will be.

Wireless energy

One main limitation of devices for remote and mobile working is that they can only be used for a certain amount of time without being connected to an electricity supply before needing charging.

Researchers in America have developed a method to power a device without the need for wires. Witricity, as it is called, could be used to charge up laptops, mobile phones and MP3 players.

Novel user interfaces

For devices to be mobile they need to be small. Using a small keyboard is not easy. Instead of using keyboard entry, some mobile devices, such as the Apple iPhone, use touch screen technology. This allows the screen to be made as large as possible because it can take up the space normally occupied by the keyboard.

Flexible screens

One limitation of mobile devices is that there is always a compromise between size, portability and ease of use. It would be nice to have a large screen on a portable device.

Flexible screens are being produced that are only a couple of millimetres thick and are very light. Because these screens are flexible they can be folded or even rolled up. An additional benefit

The touch screen interface on the iPhone allows you to make phone calls, send e-mail, browse the web and select music and video all using the multi-touch user interface.

is that unlike the LCD (liquid crystal display), they only need a small amount of power to operate. This is not only good for the environment – it enables devices making use of these screens to last longer on rechargeable batteries between charging.

It will be possible to download a picture to your mobile phone and then unroll your flexible screen and then view the picture on a good-sized screen.

Where could this go?

If you think of all the paper documents we use, then all could be replaced by a screen. The possibilities are almost endless. Here are a few ideas:

- e-newspapers with video adverts
- wearable computer screens
- electronic books
- thin screens for credit cards to show available balance and statements showing purchases.

"I'm still discovering cool stuff I can do with my smartphone. Today I sent a photo to my mom, bought some music, trimmed my sideburns, blended a smoothie, and neutered my cat!"

A smart car will use computer vision to recognise and track objects on the road for driver assistance and safety.

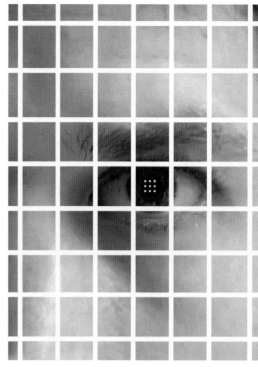

In the future there will be lots of face recognition systems.

Web 2.0

The Web has evolved considerably since it was first introduced owing mainly to vastly improved speeds of data transmission. Now that high speed Internet access is the norm you can have access to video, listen to radio using the Internet, make telephone calls, use webcams, share files, download music, etc.

Smart cars

Traffic accidents are mainly due to human error. Intel, the company who have a huge share of the market in the manufacture of microchips, are working on an ICT system for a smart car that will hopefully prevent many accidents.

The national DNA database

The national DNA database is a major tool in the fight against crime. This database is used to quickly identify offenders, make earlier arrests, secure more convictions and provide critical investigative leads for police investigations.

DNA samples are taken from the scenes of crime and also from suspects in custody as well as prevous offenders. The details of the samples are held in the national DNA database and samples from the scene of the crime can be matched with samples already held.

DNA is the genetic fingerprint obtained from blood, skin, hair, etc.

The use of this database has caused many privacy problems as the government would like the scheme to be extended further so that everyone has their DNA samples held. If this were the case then fighting crime and securing convictions would be made much easier.

Face recognition

One problem police have is identifying uninsured drivers. Although the car can be automatically identified by camera through the registration number, they also need to be able to identify the person driving the car. Face recognition cameras are being developed that can not only identify the driver of the vehicle but also the passengers as well.

Existing systems can tell whether a car is insured or not but they rely on the vehicle being correctly registered with the DVLA to trace the driver. With the new system the face could be compared with the photograph on the photo ID licence.

This is only one probable use of this system, but uses of such systems, not just in the fight against crime, are endless.

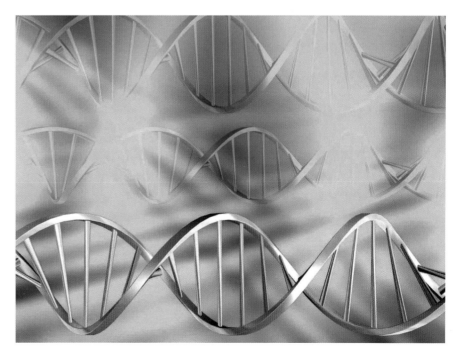

Implications of future developments and future use of ICT

Introduction

New developments in ICT cause changes in society for good and for bad. Developments also impact on the way organisations are run. For example, in the future more and more people will be able to work from home and people will not be constrained by having to live within commuting distance of the workplace.

The rapid development and use of ICT creates social, cultural, legal, technical, economic and environmental issues. These issues will be discussed in this section.

The impact on society

ICT brings a large number of benefits to society and these include:

- Higher standard of living – as workers are more productive with the use of ICT.
- More flexible working – higher expectations by customers that banking, shopping, etc., can be conducted at any time.
- Greater democracy – people may start to insist on voting for policy themselves rather than let MPs decide it.
- Improvement in health and life expectancy – use of ICT-controlled scanners can prevent serious illnesses.
- More intelligent systems in the home – such as robotic cleaning devices, lawn mowers, etc., take the drudgery out of some housework.

Problems and abuses of new technology

The people who create new technologies are often more influenced by the commercial benefits than worrying about any social problems that could be caused. Many of these problems and abuses could not have been envisaged at the time. For example, at the time of the development of the first computers, people did not envisage others would create viruses.

Here are some recent problems caused by new technology:

- Violent videos such as 'happy slapping' videos being posted on social networking sites.
- Use of encryption techniques allowing terrorists or criminals to have conversations which can be kept secret from the police and security forces.
- Illegal sharing of copyright material such as films and music.
- The ease with which people can sell stolen goods on Internet auction sites.
- Problems with addictions – people may become addicted to chat rooms, social networking sites, pornography, gambling, playing of computer games, etc.
- Irresponsible Internet sites – promoting terrorism, drug taking, etc.
- Loss of privacy – everywhere you go you are videoed by CCTV cameras.
- Risk of identity theft.
- Encourages a throwaway society – mobile phones and computers become obsolete after a short period of time.

The impact on the way organisations are run

Many organisations are run differently to how they used to be, due to the use of ICT.

ICT is used in organisations to reduce the administrative burden and to perform much of this administration automatically. ICT has also been used to expand organisations into other markets and to create new products and services.

Here are some of the ways ICT has had an impact on the way organisations are run:

- Customers like to buy goods and services using the Internet at any time of the day – this means that organisations must have a website with e-commerce capability.
- Customers expect goods to arrive within a day or so – this means organisations must have very efficient ICT stock control systems.
- Fast response times – means that there must be trading relationships with suppliers to ensure companies do not run out of stock.
- Remote working possible – some staff may be able to work remotely and in some cases from home.
- Flatter organisational structure – more staff are given the ability to work on their own initiative so fewer managers are needed.
- More data collection tasks are performed automatically – e.g., some electricity, gas and water meters are entered remotely using a terminal and the data is sent wirelessly to the ICT system for processing.
- The need for more training for staff – changes in ICT systems, changes in legislation, and changes in the business mean staff need to be trained.
- Greater opportunity for staff to misuse ICT systems – means organisations will need to introduce ICT policies to set out what staff can and cannot do using the ICT facilities.
- Need to ensure the security and privacy of personal data – more personal data being held and processed means organisations need to ensure that data protection laws are not being broken and that personal data is kept secure.

The impact on individuals as consumers and as workers

Disconnecting from work is very difficult for many employees, even when on the move, as there are so many ways a company can get hold of their employees. People are not only expected to attend meetings but they are expected to do other work while they are travelling or in their hotel room.

Problems caused:

- It is much more difficult to maintain barriers between work and play.
- Other people can be annoyed by constant interruptions.
- It can create friction at home when work places more demands on family life than your family.
- Passengers on trains and planes get annoyed by people having constant phone calls on their mobiles.
- Need to continually update skills.

ICT changes the way people communicate, for example:

- With the use of mobile phones plans are made later in the day – it is much easier to change arrangements.
- Conversations made using phones are briefer but more regular.
- Communication tends to be less formal.
- People can be contacted at any time.
- Global communication is much easier.

The impact on individuals as workers

ICT developments have led to huge changes in the way people work in the 21st century. Here are some of the changes workers typically have to face:

- **Changes to skills required and not required** – new ICT systems need new skills, and staff must be prepared to learn these skills. Old skills may not be needed so it is necessary for staff to go on courses to ensure that they do not become unemployable. When new systems are introduced, staff will need to be trained to use the new system. The increased use of ICT usually means that there is an increase in the number of skilled jobs (network managers, project managers, programmers, computer engineers, etc.) available, usually at the expense of less skilled jobs.
- **Changes to organisational structure** – when a completely new system is introduced into an organisation, many organisations will see it as an opportunity to alter the structure of their organisation so that it fits in better with the new system. The introduction of new systems frequently means that the boundaries between the functional areas become more blurred and staff will be asked to do a greater variety of tasks. For example, a customer may place an order with the sales staff and at the same time ask about the balance of their account, which would normally have been dealt with by the accounts department. The salesperson will probably do both activities. Staff may be dissatisfied as working groups may have to be split up and staff may have to adapt to working in a completely different way with different people.
- **Changes in work patterns** – with the increased use of computers and communications, many organisations now operate in global markets and have to be able to react to customer requests. This necessitates some operations having to run 24 hours a day. Flexibility can mean that more part-time work and work outside normal office hours is also available. This will suit some people, such as mothers with young children, but others may not get time off at the same time as their partner.
- **Changes to internal procedures** – staff members are often asked to take on more responsibility and do a wider variety of tasks when ICT systems are introduced. For example, some staff who previously would have performed a purely admin role, now get more involved directly with customers and they may be asked to sell goods or services. Since with the new ICT systems their traditional job may be completed in much less time, they now have time available to devote to more profitable activities.
- **Ways of doing things will have to be reviewed and changed if necessary** – since the systems analyst will not usually fit the ICT system around the existing system but will prefer to always consider the best method of performing the task. Working procedures frequently change and this can cause stress to some staff unless they are consulted about the changes and are properly trained to successfully deal with the new procedures. Many staff working with ICT systems have to obey a code of conduct that specifies what they can and cannot do with the ICT systems.

Workers often get reorganised when new ICT systems are introduced.

Implications of future developments and future use of ICT *continued*

The issues surrounding the rapid development of ICT

Social issues

- Changes in the way people spend their leisure time – less TV is being watched as more people spend time browsing the Internet, in chat rooms, downloading music, listening to radio, etc. This causes problems with advertisers who have to adapt to these changing patterns.
- Rise in obesity – many young people do not get enough exercise, as they spend too much time sitting surfing the net or playing computer games. There are other health risks associated with using computers for long periods.
- Changes in employment patterns – workers have to adapt to changes in employment patterns. Many jobs may be moved abroad, causing unemployment along with its corresponding social problems.
- Stress caused by change – many more people become stressed due to the number of new things they need to learn and things going wrong with ICT systems such as program crashes, viruses, identity theft, etc.

Cultural issues

- The way we buy and listen to music has changed – more and more people are buying music as downloads rather than physical CDs.
- The way we watch TV programmes has changed – people want to watch TV programmes when it is convenient for them. The BBC iPlayer allows you to catch up on TV and radio programmes over the previous seven days. Lots of people watch TV or listen to radio using the Internet.

- Viewing figures for TV are getting smaller – many more people are using the Internet in their leisure time.
- The use of ICT encourages globalisation – countries can lose their identity and culture.
- Many people use ICT for entertainment – playing games (not just the arcade type but games such as Scrabble, chess, etc.).
- Digital photography has become very popular – you are no longer limited by the cost of film and developing, so you can experiment using different techniques with your camera.
- Social networking sites/chat rooms, etc. – people can keep in touch with friends and family. This is an important use of ICT for people who are elderly or disabled and may be their only contact with the outside world.

Environmental issues

There are a number of environmental issues associated with the future developments and future use of ICT. These include:

- Production of ICT equipment has a high carbon footprint so it is essential to recycle old equipment.
- Less paper is used as e-mails and information on screens are not printed out. Bank and credit card statements can be stored and viewed on-line thus saving paper.
- Toner/ink cartridges are refilled rather than thrown away.
- Computer-controlled heating systems enable fuel to be used more efficiently thereby cutting down on carbon dioxide emissions.
- Telecommuting – means more people are able to work from home thus cutting down congestion and reducing carbon dioxide emissions.

Ethical issues

Ethics means behaving properly towards others. Here are some ethical issues associated with increased development of ICT:

- Increased monitoring by authorities – many people are concerned about the use of cameras to recognise people or their vehicles. Such systems are used to fight crime but they could be used for more sinister purposes.
- Monitoring of employees – employees can be monitored on their use of the Internet, how much work they get through, how long they spend on the phone, how long they are away from their computers and so on.
- Linking of databases – this enables government to check people are not claiming benefits they are not entitled to or ensure people are paying the right amount of tax.
- Control of the Internet – some countries censor what can be seen using the Internet in their country. This allows authorities to exert more control over the population.
- Lack of privacy when using search engines – some search engines record details of searches performed by a particular computer. This can be used to target advertising based on the searches performed but people are worried that this information is collected without their permission.
- On-line essay banks – these essay banks where students can buy essays on every subject and topic imaginable encourage students to cheat. Some people think such sites should be made illegal.
- Doing your own work in the organisation's time – many organisations have problems with staff wasting time doing tasks they should be performing in their own time. This includes sending e-mails to friends, on-line shopping, visiting social networking sites and chat rooms.

Technical issues

There will always be technical issues which will limit the way in which ICT can be used and these can include:

- Speed of transfer of data through communication channels – this is going up all the time and we now can watch TV programmes and video streamed over the Internet.
- Size of computers – the size of the microprocessors is decreasing all the time, allowing them to be used in portable devices.
- Storage capacity – everyone wants to store more music, more photographs, more video, etc. The demands are that users want the greatest amount of storage in the smallest possible space. Magnetic methods of storing data are limited, so new solutions are needed.
- More user-friendly interfaces – people want to communicate with computers the same way they communicate with other people. There are technical difficulties with the accuracy of speech recognition.
- Battery life – how long a battery lasts on a portable device before it needs recharging is dependent on the power of the device. A new series of microchips have been developed which use very little power, which means that laptops can be used for longer away from the mains power.

Legal issues

All organisations, including government bodies, must adhere to the law. Legal issues may therefore prevent some further or new uses of ICT.

Biometric input methods such as fingerprinting and retinal scanning are ideal for identifying a particular person. Biometric methods have the advantage that there is no card to forget and it is very fast.

There are problems concerning privacy. People are very concerned that Britain is becoming a surveillance society.

During the development of Terminal 5 at Heathrow Airport, the airport authority decided to use fingerprinting to identify passengers transferring to domestic flights. This would ensure

Fingerprints are used for identification in increasing numbers of ICT systems.

that the person who checked in at another airport was the same person who was transferring to an internal flight. Just as the new terminal was about to open they learnt that such fingerprinting could be illegal, so it had to be abandoned until they were sure it was legal.

The Information Commissioner's Office was concerned the fingerprinting could breach the Data Protection Act 1998. While the legality issues were sorted out, they reverted to the old method of using photographic evidence.

Changes to laws or regulations can sometimes help ICT developments. For example, the telecommunications regulator OFCOM has lifted the mobile phone blackout on UK-registered aircraft flying above 10,000ft in European airspace. The mobile phones have to be turned off during takeoff and you have to use the phone network on the aircraft. This will enable people to make phone calls and surf the Internet on their travels thus enabling

business users to be more productive. There are some legal issues associated with the development of ICT.

A person using a wireless internet connection without permission – unsecure wireless networks can be used by anyone to access the Internet. The other person is affected because their Internet connection runs slower because the bandwidth is being divided.

Economic issues

There is no doubt that the use of ICT improves the economy of a country, so the countries that are the most technologically advanced are also the wealthiest. In order to take advantage of new technology, the following economic issues must be in place:

- A government not afraid of the developments – many governments try to suppress their people's use of ICT, particularly use of the Internet.
- A highly skilled workforce – well-educated people are needed to use the new ICT systems.
- Investment in research and development – companies must be able to invest in new developments and they must be encouraged to take risks.
- Government which supports investment – research grants, investment in research in universities and tax incentives create a climate where new developments can flow.

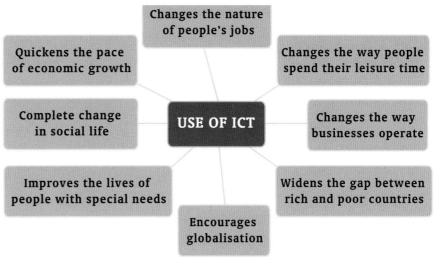
Uses of ICT.

Changes the nature of people's jobs

Quickens the pace of economic growth

Changes the way people spend their leisure time

Complete change in social life

USE OF ICT

Changes the way businesses operate

Improves the lives of people with special needs

Widens the gap between rich and poor countries

Encourages globalisation

Activity and Questions

▶ Activity: Planning what you are going to write about

Some of the examination questions on the A2 paper require an essay style answer and the top mark for this is around 20 marks. To get optimum marks you will need to produce a structured answer. You therefore need to plan it before you start writing.

ICT is evolving all the time. The way ICT has developed over the last ten years has shaped the way organisations are run.

Discuss the impact that ICT has had on the way organisations are run over the last ten years. (20 marks)

The quality of your written communication will be assessed in your answer.

You need to start off with a list of the developments you intend to discuss. You could produce a list of these or you might like to produce a mind map:

- Customers are more demanding in terms of level of service – they expect goods quickly – supply chains need to be automated.
- Centralisation of programs and data – use of networks.
- The use of e-mail for communication between staff and between the organisation and customers.
- Use of the Internet as the main vehicle to do business.
- Expanding globally – more markets reached by the use of the Internet.

- Greater ease with which it is possible to do business with people in other countries.
- Use of videoconferencing for communicating with staff in different branches/offices.
- Lower cost of hardware such as bar code readers, magnetic strip readers makes it possible to use these in small-scale applications.
- Fewer staff needed for the routine processing of data but more specialist staff are needed such as network managers, web designers, etc.
- Back office systems that will work with the ordering systems used on the Internet.
- Greater use of wireless to collect data and transmit it to a remote computer for processing.
- Mobile computing – more staff can work from remote locations using wireless and satellite communications.
- Greater use of management information systems means decisions are based on better information.
- Use of data mining tools to spot patterns in data and exploit the opportunities they present.
- Move away from physically obtaining software and music to downloading from websites.
- More legislation that organisations have to adhere to in order to cope with the many abuses that new developments in ICT create.

▶ Questions 1   pp. 2–9

1 Many technologies are combined in some devices such as mobile phones.
   Discuss the impact of mobile communication devices on:
   (a) Society (4 marks)
   (b) Individuals as consumers and as workers. (4 marks)
2 Many devices have revolutionised the way we work and play. Mobile phones are one such device.
   (a) Other than mobile phones, describe how a device or system has changed the way people work or play. (3 marks)
   (b) Briefly describe an emerging technology that is likely to change society. (2 marks)
3 Give **one** example of an ethical issue that has been brought about by the rapid development of ICT. (3 marks)
4 One of the problems with rapid development of ICT is that the problems it causes cannot always be

anticipated. This means that laws to deal with the abuses have to be developed once the problems start. Give **two** examples of abuses of ICT systems and give the names of the pieces of legislation making the abuse illegal. (4 marks)
5 (a) Discuss the developments in ICT which have enabled remote and mobile working. (6 marks)
   (b) Despite the advances in ICT there are still limitations in remote and mobile working. Describe **one** such limitation. (2 marks)
6 When new ICT systems are developed, workers in organisations can feel threatened. Describe the reasons why staff may feel threatened. (4 marks)
7 ICT has an impact on individuals as consumers and as workers. Describe the impact new technology has had on individuals and as workers. You should illustrate your answer with examples. (20 marks)

Case studies

 Case study 1 pp. 2–9

Wikipedia

Wikipedia was set up to empower and engage people around the world by collecting and offering free content which can be disseminated globally. It is a huge success story and has changed the way the Internet is used.

You will probably have already used Wikipedia but if not take a look at it now on:

www.wikipedia.com

Wikipedia is a charity and unlike most other free providers of content, it does not contain adverts and therefore gets no money from these sources. Instead it relies mainly on asking you and me to donate money or on revenue from grants. The money it obtains is used to buy hardware and also for hosting and bandwidth costs. People are not paid to add content – they do it for free!

Wikipedia is best described as an on-line encyclopaedia but it is different to other encyclopaedias in so much as it is made up from contributions by ordinary people.

You may think this is a bad thing. After all what if the information is wrong? It is easy to put in bogus information or information which someone believes is true but it isn't. Luckily other people can add information which corrects the information that is already there. The idea is that if enough people contribute, then the information is as good as that provided more traditionally.

1 One commenter on Wikipedia said: 'There is plenty of bogus information on the Internet. What we don't want is non experts making any old rubbish up on Wikipedia and then our children getting hold of it and believing it to be true.'
Give a reason why this is less likely to happen than the commenter thinks. **(2 marks)**

2 You have been asked to give a brief description of what Wikipedia is to someone who has little knowledge of ICT. Describe Wikipedia in easy to understand non-technical language. You should make at least **three** main points in your description. **(3 marks)**

3 Wikipedia consists mainly of webpages containing text and images with links to other webpages.
Describe **three** reasonably foreseeable future developments to Wikipedia that would improve it. **(3 marks)**

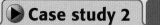 **Case study 2** pp. 2–9

A novel use for nanotechnology

The SmartShirt system uses a shirt that monitors an individual's heart rate, respiration and movement wirelessly and remotely. The shirt consists of a patented nanotechnology conductive fibre grid which is knitted into the material of the shirt. The shirt works by collecting signals from the wearer's body and then digitising them and sending them wirelessly to a base station. A computer can then be used to decide whether action should be taken on the basis of the readings it receives.

Potential uses of this technology include:

- monitoring patients who have just had operations
- monitoring elderly people living at home
- monitoring babies whose parents are worried about cot death
- monitoring truckers or other long distance drivers
- training for athletes.

One doctor spoke of the advantages of the system saying: 'This shirt system gives health care professionals early warning of abnormalities and access to the data they need to make smart decisions for their patients. These vital functions can be measured even if their patients are miles away.'

Topic 1 Future developments

Case studies *continued*

1 (a) Explain what is meant by the term 'nanotechnology'.
       (2 marks)
   (b) Explain how the use of nanotechnology with the
       SmartShirt system outlined in the case study works.
       (3 marks)
   (c) Describe **two** benefits that this system offers to
       society. (2 marks)
2 The rapid development of technologies such as the
   Internet and nanotechnology gives rise to a number
   of problems.
   Outline **one** problem caused by the use of
   nanotechnology. (2 marks)

3 Sensors have been available for years and it has also
   been possible to send data wirelessly from sensors.
   Describe **one** advantage that the SmartShirt system
   offers compared to the use of sensors. (2 marks)

▶ Case study 3   pp. 2–9

Virtual visitor

Irobot® ConnectR is a new kind of connection device
which can be used by busy parents and distant
grandparents seeking greater connection and involvement
with their children, grandchildren and pets.

By combining Internet connectivity and robotics the
device lets you remotely visit loved ones, relatives and
pets from anywhere. You can hear, see and interact with
them just as if you were there in person. You can move
the robot remotely around the home of the person you
wish to communicate with by using a keyboard or joystick
or a special remote control. You can see around the host's
house using the web camera on the robot. Speakers and
microphones can be used to communicate with the host.

The web camera can be
controlled remotely so you
can zoom in and out.

The Irobot® ConnectR
enables remote
communication.

1 The virtual visitor has a number of applications.
   (a) Explain how remote working has enabled this
       device to be produced. (2 marks)
   (b) Describe **two** different applications for the Irobot®
       ConnectR. (2 marks)

2 Discuss the privacy issues in using the Irobot®
   ConnectR. (2 marks)

Exam support

Worked example 1

1 Teleworking and videoconferencing are relatively new ways of working brought about by developments in ICT. Both of these developments have been brought about by the increased speed of communication using networks, including the Internet.

Describe **three** emerging technologies that enable people to work whilst they are away from their office and when they are travelling. For each of the technologies you describe, also explain the technological advances that have led to the ability to work remotely. **(6 marks)**

Student answer 1

1 The ability to use a mobile phone whilst on an aircraft. Engineers have found a way of allowing mobile phones to be used on aircraft without them affecting the aircraft's navigation equipment. This will allow people to make phone calls and use the Internet or other networks just as they would do if they were at their desk in their office.

One development which could revolutionise the mobile devices is the development of wireless power. This will allow devices such as laptops, to be powered without using a cable or a battery. This will be useful for people who are travelling for long periods of time, who are unable to recharge the batteries for their laptop computer. Another development is flexible screens that can be folded. This means it would be possible to have a large screen, which could be rolled into a tube. This would allow presentations to be shown to customers when on the move.

Examiner's comment

1 The ability to use mobile phones on aircraft is an emerging technology and a useful one. The student has clearly related their answer to business use on the move. Two marks are given for this part of the answer. Wireless power is an emerging technology and a very useful one for people on the move who are often restricted by the battery life of their computers. Two marks are given for this part of the answer.

Flexible screens are an emerging technology and the student has clearly described the technology and the benefits to someone on the move. Full marks are given for this answer. **(6 marks out of 6)**

Student answer 2

1 Nanotechnology will revolutionise ICT because storage devices will get much smaller and hold a lot more data than the storage devices we have at the moment. This will mean that whole film libraries can be stored in a very small space, which will mean that people on the move can have the choice of watching a whole range of films.

Advances in artificial intelligence and cognitive science will mean that computers will start behaving in a similar manner to the human brain. This will make them a lot more intelligent than they are at the moment. Computers will not need to be programmed as they will be able to learn from experience. This will enable computers to become experts in lots of different fields which will mean that everyone can consult an expert in the field for their opinion.

Examiner's comment

1 In this answer the student has clearly indicated the advances in technology that will give a clear benefit to society. Nanotechnology is certainly an emerging technology and one which is likely to yield huge benefits to society. This answer clearly states how the new technology might benefit someone on the move. Two marks are given for this answer.

For the second part of the answer the student has given a description of a valid emerging technology. They have, however, failed to relate this to a person on the move. Students must always read the question carefully to make sure they are answering the question and not the question they would have liked to have been asked. No marks are given for this part of the question. **(2 marks out of 6)**

Examiner's answer

1 Two marks for each application described. One mark for a brief statement of the application and two marks for a detailed explanation of the application.

Typical applications the students could cover include:

Flexible screens – so that someone who is using a laptop or PDA can use a larger screen and the device still be portable. Useful for giving ad hoc presentations in hotel rooms, bars, etc.

New low power chips (e.g. Atom chip) – means that portable devices such as mobile phones, PDAs and laptops can be used for longer before the battery runs down. This is useful for someone who uses these devices in remote locations without access to a power supply.

Improved human–computer interfaces making it much easier to communicate with computers using speech. This would make portable devices much smaller as they would not need a keyboard/keypad.

Worked example 2

2 Describe **two** potential future uses of ICT and for **each** use explain how they are likely to benefit society. **(4 marks)**

Student answer 1

2 New modelling techniques can be used to model how drugs can attack cells. By understanding how drugs work, they can hopefully create new drugs that will target cancerous cells. Finding a cure for cancer will benefit the whole of society.

Greater use of speech recognition systems and speech synthesis systems will mean that the use of computers will not be limited by a person's need to use a keyboard. This will make computers easier to use which will widen their use further and benefit people with limited use of their hands. It will also benefit society because people will not develop RSI through repeated use of keyboards.

Examiner's comment

2 Both these future uses are acceptable answers. The second answer is only given one rather than two marks because speech recognition and synthesis systems have been around a long time and the answer fails to state why they are not more mainstream. Making them more accurate and capable of understanding speech that is not clear could have been mentioned. **(3 marks out of 4)**

Student answer 2

2 The Internet will be used by people to vote at elections. This will mean that the country is more democratic, as ordinary people have more say in the way things are run. At present there are technical problems in doing this and the system is open to fraud. There will be more robots in the home. For example, robotic vacuum cleaners will clean the floors of your house at set intervals. Similarly, robot lawnmowers could mow the lawn while you were at work or on holiday.

Examiner's comment

2 The first answer is good and it clearly states the benefit to society (i.e., making it more democratic). The student has recognised that the system already exists by stating that technical problems need to be overcome.

The second answer talks about two types of robot which are already available and have been for a few years. If the device is already present then it is ok if the student talks about improvements to the device. This part of the answer is only given one mark. **(3 marks out of 4)**

Examiner's answer

2 One mark for a brief description of a use (this must be recent or future) and one mark for a clear statement of how it improves society. Typical answers could include:

Flexible screens. Instead of having a small screen you can have a flexible screen that is folded out. This would be a big improvement when showing photographs or watching video clips on a mobile device as the device can still be kept small and light.

Nanotechnology being used to make a shirt, which is capable of monitoring a patient's body while they go about their normal life.

Signals can be sent remotely to health care professionals if the readings start to fall outside acceptable ranges so they can be alerted and action taken. Such shirts can save lives and they also save money because patients can be sent home sooner after operations.

Summary mind maps

Enabling devices for remote and mobile working

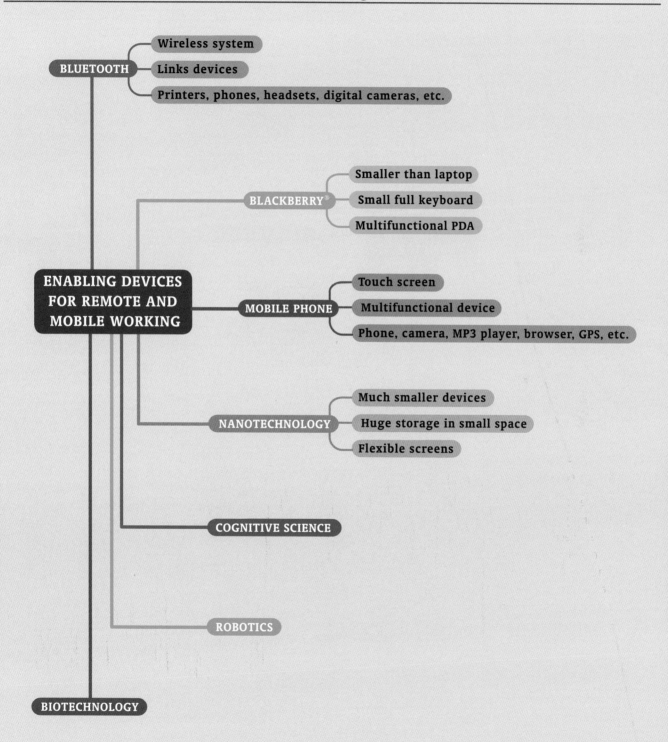

Summary mind maps *continued*

Potential future uses of ICT

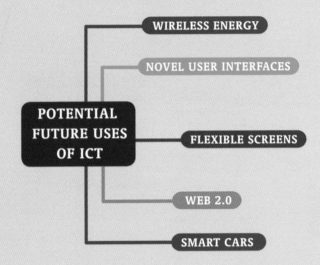

TOPIC 2: Information and systems

In this topic you will learn about the information needs of organisations and that different activities have different information needs. You will learn about the different levels of tasks performed by different levels of staff within the organisations and their special information needs. Organisations frequently exchange their information with external bodies and you will learn about issues such as privacy, security and legal compliance that this presents.

You will learn about how ICT management contributes to business strategy. Also covered in this topic will be how there is a need for information to be transferred both internally and externally.

The last part of this topic covers the various types of ICT system such as back office systems, transaction processing systems, management information systems, enterprise systems, etc.

▼ The key concepts covered in this topic are:

▶ Understand that different organisations have different information needs

▶ Understand that different activities within an organisation have different information needs

▶ Understand that different levels of tasks have different information needs

▶ Understand that different personnel have different information needs

▶ Understand that organisations have to exchange information with external bodies

▶ Understand that ICT systems support the activities of organisations

▶ Understand that ICT systems exist such as payroll, personnel and accounting

▶ Understand that there is a need for information to be transferred between ICT systems both internally and externally

▶ Understand the types of ICT systems and their uses

CONTENTS

1 **Information needs in organisations** 18
The different information needs of different organisations, the different information requirements of different activities, the information needs of different levels of tasks, the information needs of different personnel and the exchange of information with external bodies.

2 **ICT supporting the activities of organisations** 24
ICT supporting the activities of organisations, ICT systems such as payroll, personnel and accounting, the need for information to be transferred between ICT systems internally and externally.

3 **The types of ICT systems and their uses**...................26
Back office systems, transaction processing systems, management information systems, enterprise systems, decision support systems and e-commerce systems.

4 **Questions and Activities**...31

5 **Case studies**...33

6 **Exam support**..36

7 **Summary mind maps**..38

Unit 3 Use of ICT in the Digital World

Information needs in organisations

▼ You will find out

▶ About how different organisations have different information needs

▶ About how different activities within an organisation have different information needs

▶ About how different levels of task have different information needs

▶ About how different personnel have different information needs

Introduction

Organisations engaged in similar businesses have very similar information needs. So, for example, different supermarkets operate in very similar ways. Some organisations are larger and more complex than others, so their information needs will differ. In this section you will be looking at the information needs of organisations and the information that is needed to perform the wide range of activities necessary for the running of the organisation.

Most organisations have a hierarchy of staff with the directors at the top of the organisation to the managers who oversee the day-to-day running of their departments to the staff who do the routine work. The information needs of these different levels of staff are different and in this section you will be looking at how their information needs are different and how ICT systems can deliver this information.

Different organisations have different information needs

Organisations range from a few people on a single site to tens of thousands of staff spread widely on sites around the world. The information needs for these organisations are different but there are also some similarities. All organisations will have to comply with a whole set of laws which cover what they can and can't do, they will have to pay wages, manage, motivate and train staff, produce accounts and so on. The information needs are sometimes similar but on a much bigger scale.

There are three main types of organisation:

Commercial

In a commercial organisation either goods are purchased and then sold on to make a profit, or they supply services to customers. Examples of commercial organisations include:

- retailers
- wholesalers
- banks
- insurance companies
- website design companies
- accountants
- solicitors.

Commercial organisations are mainly driven by the need to make a profit on their activities and there are many ways ICT can be used to help do this.

Industrial

The main function of an industrial organisation is to manufacture products or process raw materials or be involved in construction. The main thing here is that they all produce a product or material or structure which can be sold to make a profit. Examples of industrial organisations include:

- car manufacturers
- house builders
- household appliance manufacturers
- chemical manufacturers
- quarries.

Producing chemicals is an industrial process.

Public service organisations

The main aim of a public service organisation is to provide goods and services from public funds. Producing a profit is not an aim of these organisations, although in some examples such as Her Majesty's Revenue and Customs, taxes are collected which are then used for purposes such as building roads, schools, hospitals, etc.

Their main aim is to obtain the maximum benefit for the public they serve and they are usually under pressure to do this in as efficient a way as is possible. ICT is therefore used widely in such organisations. Examples of public service organisations include:

- Her Majesty's Revenue and Customs for the collection of taxes such as income tax, VAT, etc.
- hospitals
- schools
- police service
- armed forces.

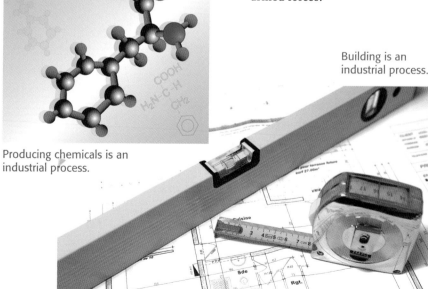

Building is an industrial process.

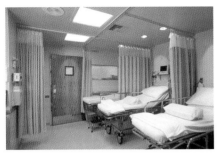

Health services are public services.

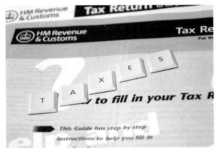

HM Revenue and Customs, who collect tax and VAT, are public services.

Schools are public service organisations.

Police forces are public sector organisations.

The armed forces are public sector organisations.

The scale of organisations

As well as classifying an organisation according to type, it can also be classed according to scale. Organisations are often classified by the number of staff they employ. For example, the following classifications can be used:

Small – 1 to 50 employees

- Generally informal structures
- Usually confined to a single site making use of local area networks (LANs)

Medium – Between 50 and 500 employees

- Uses formal structures
- Uses wide area networks (WANs) and local area networks (LANs)

Large – 500 or more employees

- Diverse range of products or services
- Can involve lots of separate companies/organisations
- Large number of staff usually in a hierarchical structure
- Examples include banks, car manufacturers, large retail multiples, etc.
- Can often have branches/ subsidiaries around the world
- Rely heavily on wide area networks (WANs) and local area networks (LANs)

Nature and management style

The nature of the organisation will often dictate the style of management used. There are four main styles of management:

- autocratic
- paternalistic
- democratic
- laissez-faire.

Autocratic

In this management style there is clear authority in the organisation and all the decisions are made by senior managers. Very little decision making is made lower down and workers are always told what to do and they do not work on their own initiative. Information is always channelled to the people at the top of the organisation in order for them to make the decision and communication tends to flow mainly from the senior managers downward. Autocratic styles of management make efficiently run organisations but staff are often de-motivated because they do not feel as involved in the organisation.

Paternalistic

Here the senior managers have authority but the decisions tend to be made more in the employees' interests than the business's interests. Management explain their decisions to the workforce and employees feel happy and as a result are loyal to their employers.

Democratic

In this management style employees take part in the decision making so no-one can complain if the decisions are bad. This type of management style is useful for ICT projects because project teams are usually made up of people with different specialisms such as networking, database design, programming, etc., and each person will see the project from a different, yet valid perspective. The decision making process is slowed down as meetings have to be arranged for decisions to be made.

Laissez-faire

This management style is the least formal and staff are expected to manage their own areas. Staff are at the same level and people work at their particular tasks. This type of management is good for professionals such as partnerships of accountants, solicitors and creative staff. There is very little communication between staff and this method can cause problems due to lack of leadership and focus.

Information needs in organisations *continued*

Ordering systems need to transfer information to other systems such as dispatch and stock control systems.

Different activities within an organisation have different information needs

Organisations perform many different activities such as paying staff, ordering goods and services, selling goods or services, accounting for the money used in the organisation, managing resources (people, staff, goods, etc.) and each of these activities will have information needs.

Here you will look at the information needs for two commonly used ICT systems: ordering systems and customer support.

Ordering systems

Ordering systems take a customer's order and process the payments and deliver the goods to the customer when available. Many ordering systems are computerised to reduce the costs and increase the efficiency of the ordering process and to be able to deliver the goods to the customer as quickly as possible.

Ordering systems basically:

- collect the order details from the customer. This could involve a member of staff keying in the details over the phone or from an order on paper or it could involve the customer keying in their own order using an e-commerce system
- check with the stock control system that the products are in stock
- process payments/link to customer accounts
- send order details to the warehouse for goods to be picked and packaged
- organise delivery with a delivery company.

Ordering systems also need to deal with:

- products out-of-stock
- substitution of similar products (where the original product is no longer available)
- returns of faulty or damaged goods
- refunds to customers
- multiple deliveries (where the goods are not all sent at the same time)
- customers changing their order.

Customer support

The purpose of customer support is to provide a service to customers who have bought products or services. For example, the staff might deal with payment queries, problems getting the product to work, organising repairs, etc.

For example, a bank customer support worker would deal with the following:

- enquiries about different accounts
- dealing with loan/mortgage applications
- queries over statements
- dealing with lost credit/debit cards
- dealing with forgotten pins (personal identification numbers)
- transfers of money between accounts
- opening of new accounts
- queries about credit/debit card transactions
- complaints.

For a manufacturer of products rather than services the customer support worker would deal with:

- customer complaints
- giving technical advice
- arranging for repairs to be made under guarantee
- sorting out problems the customer is having with the product
- dealing with payment problems
- assessing customer satisfaction with the product
- informing customers as to new developments with the product.

Technical help on computer problems is provided as part of customer support by hardware or software manufacturers.

The information needs of different levels of tasks

Staff in an organisation are usually levelled and this level determines the tasks they perform. Hence the tasks themselves can be thought of as being levelled.

The three levels in an organisation

From an organisational point of view in businesses employing lots of staff there are three levels which are:

- strategic
- tactical
- operational.

These levels can be defined in terms of the type of staff:

- strategic – directors, chief executives, executives, principal and vice principals in a college and heads and deputies in a school
- tactical – lower levels of managers, department heads, supervisors, etc.
- operational – accounts clerks, administration officers, teachers, lecturers, sales staff, etc.

They can also be defined in terms of their information needs:

- strategic – need high level overviews with little detail
- tactical – need summaries and reports to decide how to manage a problem
- operational – involved with information about day-to-day transactions such as problems with payments and customer orders.

They can also be defined in terms of the type of task and this is looked at in the following section.

Strategic tasks

Strategic tasks are completed by staff at the top of a company or organisation such as directors and chief executives. These tasks would include making decisions on the overall direction taken by the organisation. Here are some examples of strategic tasks:

- takeovers of other businesses
- decisions regarding expansions into new markets
- decisions about the introduction of new products or services
- decisions about major expenditure on new ICT systems.

Tactical tasks

Tactical tasks are completed by managers and these people look at how to achieve the objectives that the directors and chief executives set. They

also make decisions using operational information. For example, if a certain product they produce is not selling well, they can decide what to do.

Operational tasks

Operational tasks are those routine day-to-day tasks which keep the business or organisation functioning. The majority of operational tasks deal with all the transactions which take place when running an organisation. Examples of operational tasks include:

- paying wages
- ordering stock
- paying for stock
- keeping customer/client details
- attracting new customers
- obtaining payments for goods or services
- dealing with all the legal aspects of running a business
- dealing with customer/client queries
- accounts.

© Randy Glasbergen
www.glasbergen.com

"This call may be monitored or recorded because otherwise nobody would believe how stupid some tech support questions can be!"

Information needs in organisations *continued*

Different personnel have different information needs

Different personnel have different information needs which are determined by the task they perform and the area of the organisation in which they work.

All organisations have suppliers and commercial organisations will also have customers about whom information will need to be kept and exchanged. In addition all organisations will need to exchange information with official and legal bodies.

Suppliers

Suppliers are organisations which supply goods or services for another organisation. For example, your school or college has lots of suppliers such as:

- utility companies (gas, electric, water and telephone)
- maintenance (decorators, heating engineers, window cleaners, cleaning services, etc.)
- book suppliers
- software suppliers
- equipment suppliers (chairs, desks, computers, etc.)
- suppliers of supply teachers
- newspapers for adverts for teachers and other staff jobs.

Suppliers often have a very close relationship with their customers and help each other maximise each other's profits from the trading relationship. For example, if a drinks company has created a new product, they will promote it using TV and magazine advertisements. They can access the sales figures from the major supermarkets automatically because it is beneficial for the supplier and retailer to share this information. Customers and suppliers often make use of extranets to share information.

Customers

Customers are the people who place orders for products or services. If the customer was a large retailer then the orders would be placed automatically and also paid for automatically. In doing this both the customer and supplier benefit because both can take advantage of the savings made by reducing the administration costs.

Customers can be individuals who order goods and services using the Internet. These customers supply information in the form of their personal information as well as details of the goods or services ordered.

All the information on the customers and their orders can be

All organisations deal with Her Majesty's Revenue and Customs.

kept and this information is often used to help identify additional goods or services that the customer may be interested in, now or in the future.

Official and legal bodies

There are many official and legal obligations placed on organisations. For example:

- Most organisations own vehicles which means they have to supply information to: insurance companies; the Driver Vehicle Licensing Authority.
- Most organisations process personal data which means they have to register their use of personal data with the Information Commissioner's Office.
- Limited companies have to file their end of year accounts a certain way and send them to a government department called Companies House.
- In addition organisations have to deal with Her Majesty's Revenue and Customs and supply information to them about tax, VAT and National Insurance. They also have to deal with payments made to these bodies.

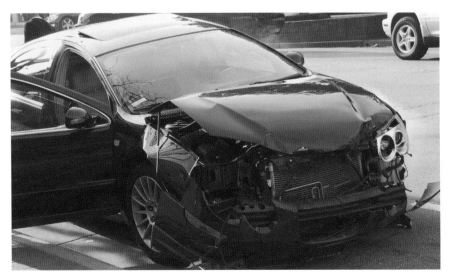

Insurance companies need information about all the cars owned by an organisation.

Organisations exchanging information with external bodies

In order for organisations to be as profitable and efficient as possible, it is necessary to agree how information is to be exchanged with their customers, suppliers, official bodies, etc. Organisations want to be able to supply data in a form that can be used by other organisations' ICT systems. This avoids keying in the information.

Some organisations such as the main supermarkets cannot trade with suppliers who still use paper-based systems. Instead they agree that their two systems should be able to communicate with each other thus supplying each other with information about sales, stock levels, marketing plans, orders and payments automatically. Most of these systems perform the routine transactions with little human involvement thus reducing costs.

When transferring information from one organisation to another there are a number of issues concerning the following:

- Privacy – both organisations must ensure the privacy of any personal information transferred. Methods of ensuring this include encryption, the use of private networks, the use of firewalls to prevent hackers, the use of private rather than public telecommunication channels, job-based access restrictions, etc.
- Security – much of the information being transferred between one organisation and another could be of use to competitors. It must therefore not fall into the wrong hands. Once the information has been transferred it must be kept safe, so both organisations need to have an ICT policy that is acceptable to the other.

Legal compliance implications

If personal information is being transferred then there is the requirement under the Data Protection Act that the information can only be transferred to those countries who have effective data protection legislation.

Organisations have to ensure:

- That they register the use of personal data with the Information Commissioner's Office and inform them of organisations they send the information to.
- They have sufficient security in place to ensure the privacy and security of personal data as required by the Data Protection Act 1998.
- That they do not break any copyright laws when transferring data. For example, many file sharing sites were found to be illegal.

Organisations need to ensure that confidential data/information passed between them is kept secure.

SECURE DATA

Organisations have to ensure they are compliant with the laws applicable in their business.

ICT supporting the activities of organisations

Introduction

ICT systems are introduced into businesses and organisations to support the activities the business or organisation has to perform. ICT systems support the activities of organisations by allowing them to reduce the administrative burden and hence reduce costs. ICT can also be used to widen the customer base of an organisation by using websites to advertise goods and services to a global audience.

ICT supporting the activities of organisations

There are many different activities involved in the running of organisations and all of these can be supported by the use of ICT. The main role of ICT is to improve the efficiency and effectiveness of business processes and it can do this in the following ways:

- By improving the accuracy of decision taking thus reducing risk and saving time, money and resources.
- By improving the efficiency with which resources are allocated.
- By reducing administration costs by automating many of the tasks that used to be performed by people.
- By using ICT to increase market share. Use of websites allows many more customers from around the world to buy goods and services.
- By using ICT to diversify into other markets.
- By using the electronic transfer of data between trading partners to increase the profitability of both the supplier and the customer.
- By improving the productivity of staff.

- By reducing wastage. For example, reducing goods stolen by better tracking of goods, reducing the amount of food products thrown away, etc.
- By being able to reduce wage costs by transferring administration abroad. For example, many call centres are located in India and other countries where the wage costs are much lower than in the UK.

ICT systems such as payroll, personnel and accounting

There are many ICT systems that are found in nearly every organisation and these include systems to help with the following tasks:

- payroll
- personnel
- accounting.

Payroll

All employees expect to be paid the correct amount and on time, so payroll processing is crucial to any organisation. Employees can be paid in different ways: for example, salaried employees have their annual salary divided by twelve to be paid monthly, whereas other staff have an hourly rate of pay and are paid weekly according to the number of hours they have worked. These hours may be at a basic rate or at an enhanced overtime rate for working weekends, bank holidays, etc. In addition to their basic pay, some employees may receive bonuses, commission and so on.

Not all employees get the same pay, even if they are doing identical jobs. Some may be given more pay because they have worked longer in the organisation. Some people's pay may differ because the amounts

deducted vary, for example the amount of tax. This depends on a person's tax code which in turn is determined by an individual's circumstances. Each employee is supplied with a detailed breakdown of the amount they are paid, including deductions, in the form of a payslip.

In addition to the money paid to employees, an organisation has to send money to many other organisations such as the Inland Revenue for income tax and National Insurance contributions, pension agencies for the payment of pension contributions, trade unions for the payment of subscriptions and so on.

Because of the security and cost problems of dealing with the transfer of large amounts of cash, most organisations use electronic funds transfer (EFT) using BACS (Bankers' Automated Clearing Services) to transfer the money between the organisation's bank account and the employees' accounts. They can also use the system to make payments to HMRC of income tax and National Insurance contributions that have been deducted from employees' pay.

Personnel

The personnel department, or human resources department as it is often called, holds personal details on all the employees such as employee number, name, address, telephone numbers, date of birth, next of kin, educational qualifications, references, appraisals, details of previous employment, position with the organisation and so on.

Training records need to be kept so that the organisation knows which employees are capable of doing certain tasks. They are also used to identify those employees who require further training.

The personnel ICT system will usually link to the training system and payroll system using the unique employee number, which is a number given to each employee when they join the organisation.

Accounts

Accounts will monitor and control the money coming into and going out of the business. All the other departments will have ICT systems which link to this important part of the business.

The need for information to be transferred between ICT systems internally and externally

Supply chain

A supply chain consists of organisations, people, resources, information and ICT systems that are involved in getting a product that has been ordered from the supplier to the customer.

A supply chain can be very long. For example, in the manufacture of a motor car, the metal has to be first obtained by digging the ore out of the ground and then refining it to produce the metal to make the car body, engine and other car parts. There are a huge number of organisations involved in the manufacture of the thousands of parts that make up a car. Car manufacturers therefore have a complex supply chain and ICT systems deal with all aspects of it.

Lots of different companies can be involved in the supply chain and they all rely on each other to produce the product and get it to the customer. Information needs to be exchanged between the different organisations in order to increase efficiency and reduce costs.

ICT systems are used for the management of the supply chain and these systems seek to make the best use of human resources, stock and other resources.

Without cooperation between all the organisations in the supply chain, each organisation would need to hold more stock so they do not run out of components, items, etc., and this would increase cost and reduce efficiency.

The ideal supply chain would be able to satisfy a customer's order instantly without the need to hold stock. This would mean that as soon as a customer placed an order, the order would be ready for delivery. This is impossible to achieve but supermarkets, in particular, are experts at what is called the just-in-time concept, where goods are produced and transferred to the shops precisely when required by a customer.

New systems interfacing with legacy systems

When a new system is introduced it still needs to interface with older systems (called legacy systems). So, for example, a firm may decide to produce a new human resources (personnel) system to improve knowledge about their employees and their training requirements. This system will include details about salaries and will need to interface with a payroll system so that if during a performance review by human resources they increase a person's salary, then the payroll details will be automatically updated.

Another example would be where a new order processing system is introduced. If the company is satisfied with the old accounts system then the new order processing and the accounts system (i.e., the legacy system in this case) will need to work together and transfer data between each other.

The supply chain involves the creation of a product and getting it to the customer.

The types of ICT systems and their uses

▼ You will find out

▶ About back office systems

▶ About transaction processing systems, workflow and document management systems and systems for collaborative working

▶ About management information systems (MIS)

▶ About enterprise systems and customer relationship management

▶ About decision support systems

▶ About e-commerce systems

Introduction

In this section you will be looking at the various ICT systems that are used in organisations apart from the usual systems such as payroll, personnel, etc., discussed in previous sections.

Back office systems

Back office systems are systems that run all the routine business administration processes and they often consist of an accounts package or a tailored database management system.

The back office systems:

- record the details of all the sales made
- record the details of all the purchases made
- update stock details
- generate any necessary paperwork such as invoices, receipts, packing slips, etc.

Transaction processing systems

Transaction processing systems process each transaction (i.e. bit of business) as it arises.

Examples of transactions include:

- an order being taken
- a customer paying for goods
- a flight or holiday being booked
- a payment being made to suppliers
- an employee being paid.

Workflow and document management systems

A document management system (DMS) is an ICT system which is used by organisations to keep track of electronically stored documents. Paper documents are often still used in many organisations, so in document management systems they will need to be digitised by scanning in.

Document management systems are used in lots of organisations where there is less control over the way the data arrives for entry into an ICT system. Insurance companies use document management systems for settling car insurance claims. Here are the main features of a claims system:

Paper documents arrive in many different formats:

Witness statements by letter, fax, e-mail

Photographs (film and digital)

Claims forms completed on-line or on paper

CAR INSURANCE CLAIMS DOCUMENT MANAGEMENT SYSTEM

Drawings/maps on paper

Documentation from solicitors

Quotes for repairs from garages on paper, by e-mail, or fax

Document management systems, such as this one for processing car insurance claims, need to cope with information arriving in different formats.

KEY WORDS

Transaction processing – processing of each transaction as it arises

Workflow – the scheduling of independent tasks using a manual or automatic system

Management information system – an organised collection of people, procedures and resources designed to support the decisions of managers

Workflow management systems

Different people in an organisation are responsible for different processes. For example, a person who is responsible for making orders with suppliers will not be the same person who is responsible for making the payments to the supplier. This means that work has to flow between different personnel in an organisation.

Workflow management systems provide automatic routing of documents to the personnel responsible for working on them. This means each person responsible for completing each step in a business cycle is given access to the data at exactly the right time for processing. Triggers can be given to managers to alert them if any of the steps are overdue.

Workflow management systems have the advantage that they do not depend on the manual flow of documents. People in organisations often keep hold of documentation for longer than they should do by putting off doing certain tasks. Workflow management systems automate the workflow by making use of databases and networks so that each user is given access to the data at exactly the right time. This means that the work is completed at the right pace and in the correct order.

Many document management systems have a built-in workflow management module and they are often referred to together as workflow and document management systems.

Systems for collaborative working

Collaborative working is where people work together on a task regardless of their location. They have to use the latest communications methods to keep in touch with each other and networks such as the Internet to pass work between people.

Collaborative working usually involves using some or all of the following ICT systems:

- videoconferencing
- file sharing
- e-mail.

Management information systems (MIS)

Managers in organisations have to make decisions about their area in the organisations and to make sure these decisions are good, they need to be based on information. It is the purpose of the management information systems to supply this information.

A management information system is an ICT system that is designed to take internal and external data

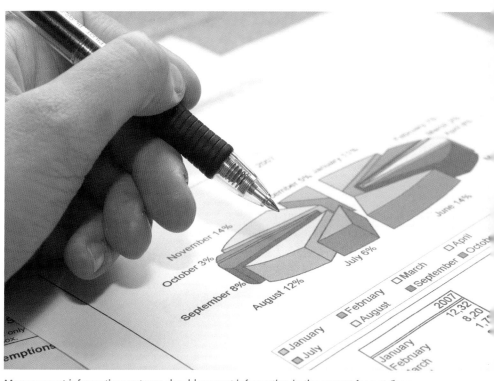

Management information systems should present information in the correct format (here charts and tables are used).

and turn it into information. This information is communicated in an understandable form that will enable managers at different levels in an organisation to make informed decisions.

Management information needs to be in an appropriate form to enable managers at different levels to make effective decisions for planning, directing and controlling the activities for which they are responsible. Management information systems are not a separate thing to information systems since they are really only part of them. Information systems are routinely used by all staff. Management information systems are designed primarily with the information needs of managers in mind.

One of the main problems with many managers is that they do not understand the role of information. To a manager, having lots of correct information reduces uncertainty when making decisions. These decisions can be reached quickly and with less worry because there is a much higher probability that the decision will be correct. If there was no uncertainty, then there would be no

need for information, since it would be possible for a manager to predict things accurately. Unfortunately, in reality things are not like this so it is necessary to gain as much management information that is relevant to the decision being made, as possible.

It is important to note that many managers have specific jobs and responsibilities and any management information needs to be tailored for the individual manager's needs. Historically the manager would contact the data processing department or database manager with a request for this information and they were frequently met with the reply that the system could not produce the information in the way that they requested it. Many large database systems were quite inflexible when producing these sorts of *ad hoc* reports even though they were capable of producing routine information gained during the organisation's data processing activities.

Now database systems are much more flexible and many managers are trained to be able to extract the information they need using a computer connected to the network.

The types of ICT systems and their uses
continued

Example of a management information system being used

In order to understand the importance of management information, let's look at an example based on a barbecue manufacturing company. This company employs eight representatives who are given an area in which they operate. Their work is to visit, promote and make sales in these areas. Suppose the sales manager who is responsible for the representatives tells the managing director that salesman X, who is responsible for the north western region, has made £100,000 worth of sales in the last month. That sounds good to the sales manager, but is it? How can he decide? The obvious way would be to look at the sales the other representatives had made in the same period in order to make a comparison. You could also compare these sales with the sales made for the same region going back several years. This might reveal a trend in that having barbecues is becoming more popular. Management information systems are popular because they make getting information such as this as easy as possible and they take away the need for specialist staff to extract the information from the computer system. There are clear advantages in letting the person who understands the business make the decision about the information they need to extract. Things are not quite that simple since quite a bit of training will be required before staff can extract the information in this way.

Other examples of management information systems

A chief executive of a supermarket chain may extract financial information about each supermarket in the chain in order to identify those which are making the least profits. This is so that they can be sold and the money used to open new supermarkets in areas that are likely to be more profitable.

A manager of a nationwide parcel delivery company uses the MIS to look at the distances each vehicle travels to make a decision on whether another depot is required.

Schools use MIS in various ways. For example, for long-term planning they would need to ensure they had the resources to cope with increases in the population. Internal information might include admission figures from previous years, details of brothers and sisters of existing pupils who will eventually start at the school, details of resources such as staff, rooms, desks, etc. External information sources could be figures from primary schools, census details (for indications of population), details of immigration, local authority data, etc.

The following diagram shows the sources of information and the information flows:

Customer relationship management systems

The better the relationship between a company and its customers then the more successful it will become. There are ICT systems available called Customer Relationship Management Systems that will help manage the day-to-day relationship with customers.

In the past, when a firm had an order from a customer, they fulfilled the order and then forgot about the customer. There was little contact with past customers until the next time they placed an order. Customers are more valued by companies now, as they know that if they are not looked after, they will go elsewhere, usually to a competitor.

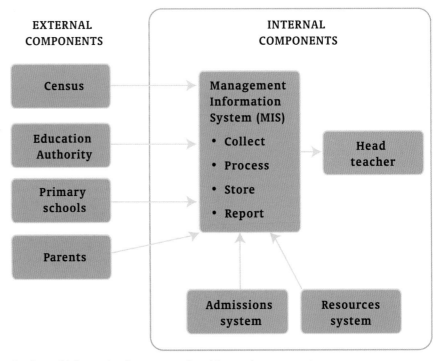

The flow of information from external and internal components of a management information system (MIS).

Here are some of the things customer relationship management systems do:

- They improve the effectiveness of communication between the organisation and its customers.
- They allow organisations to better understand each customer's value to the organisation.
- They allow the analysis of past orders that the customer has made, which allows the organisation to better advise them on what they might like to buy next.
- All communication with the customer is recorded so there is coordination between the web, e-mail and telephone.

It is much more expensive to find new customers, so CRM systems help keep previous customers from going elsewhere for their goods or services.

The main advantages of customer relationship management systems are:

- Sales are increased due to better timing due to anticipating when a customer is more likely to place an order based on their history of orders in the past.
- Customer needs are understood better, which means it is possible to understand which products or services the customer would be most interested in.
- You can cross-sell products by highlighting and suggesting alternatives or enhancements.
- Marketing can be targeted specifically at customer needs so money is not wasted on sending customers information about goods or services they do not need.

Enterprise information systems (EIS)

An enterprise is a large organisation so an enterprise information system is an ICT system that supports all the functions of a large organisation. Such a system needs to be able to deal with large volumes of data and allow an organisation to integrate and coordinate all its business activities.

Enterprise information systems:

- Mean that separate information systems are not needed as the enterprise information system provides all the information needs of the organisation.
- Integrate all the key business activities such as sales, accounting, finance, human resources, inventory (stock control) and manufacturing.
- Sometimes allow the system to link with suppliers, business partners and customers.

Decision support systems (DSS)

A decision support system is a type of information system that supports the decision-making process. For example, if there are three possible ways of making a business more profitable each with different levels of risk, it can help a manager choose which one would be best by supplying them with the appropriate information. Decision support systems can be used to extrapolate figures to provide forecasts (e.g., for future sales).

Here are two examples of applications for decision support systems:

Helping bank managers to make loan decisions

The manager of a bank could use a decision support system to evaluate whether a person should be given a loan to expand a business or not based on their previous banking history, their outstanding commitments, their profits, etc.

Decision support systems do not actually make decisions: they simply give the manager more information about the decisions they are proposing to make.

Helping companies decide whether to market their products abroad

A company producing products might want to start selling its products abroad but first wants to find out if this is a good idea. The company could use a DSS to gather information from its own ICT systems to determine if expansion into other areas is possible. It also uses data from external sources such as information from competitors, market research, etc., to see if there is a demand for the products. The DSS will collect the information from these sources and present it in a way that makes it easy for managers to understand and so make their decision.

A decision support system (DSS) gives information as to which path to take. It supports decision making.

The types of ICT systems and their uses
continued

What is e-commerce?

Commerce means all those activities needed for the successful running of a business. Commerce would typically involve the following:

- buying
- distributing
- marketing
- selling
- paying.

If some, or all of the activities listed above are performed using electronic systems such as the Internet or other computer networks, then the business can be said to be involved in e-commerce. E-commerce is not just about the selling of products, it also involves the selling of services.

E-commerce systems

E-commerce systems are Internet stores or sites where customers can browse products/services and order and pay for goods/services. Most e-commerce stores contain:

- a database of products
- shopping cart software
- check-out software for payment processing and delivery information.

All these are what the customer sees, so this system acts as the storefront or web-based front end. In order for a business to function, it is necessary to also keep records of all transactions and this business administration is performed by the back office system. This is the part the customer does not see, hence the name.

With most e-commerce systems, the on-line store and the back office system are integrated, which means that they are able to communicate with each other. All the details from the back office are available to the storefront and vice versa. This is important as it could, for example, let a customer know when an out-of-stock item is likely to be in stock again. Here the storefront would need to get the information from the part of the back office system where orders to suppliers are made.

Integration of the web-based front end system and the back office system means that whenever a customer places an order on-line, the web store and back office treat the sale as one. This means the on-line system accepts the order and then relays the order details back to the customer, whilst the back office system records the transaction and adjusts stock levels, generates an invoice and fulfils the order.

Licence applications: an example of e-commerce

The DVLA (Driver and Vehicle Licensing Agency) is a government organisation that checks that all vehicles and drivers are properly licensed. They are also responsible for the recording of licence details of all people allowed to drive.

In the past, if you wanted a tax disc, you would have had to take the form (sent by post) to the Post Office along with your payment, current insurance certificate and MOT if the vehicle is over three years old. You would then usually have waited in a lengthy queue until a member of staff checks your documents, collects the payment and issues the tax disc. With the development of on-line ordering, many people saw this as a tedious waste of their time. It is therefore not surprising that the DVLA looked at the creation of an e-commerce site which would enable people to pay their vehicle tax on-line without leaving their home.

The driver is sent a reminder by post in the usual way. Once the user has entered the site they are required to enter a 16-digit reference number on the form and their registration number to access their record. Once this has been done, the system will check the database of MOT certificates to ensure there is a current one for the vehicle being registered. The system also checks that there is a current certificate of insurance in force using information supplied by insurance companies. Payment is then made using credit or debit card and the tax disc is produced and sent by post to the driver.

> ▶ **Activity Which type of organisation?**

Here are some organisations. You have to decide whether each organisation is commercial, industrial or public service.

- **NHS Hospital**
- **Building Society**
- **Local Area Health Authority**
- **Oil Company**
- **Computer Manufacturer**
- **College**
- **Insurance company**
- **Dating Agency**
- **Website design company**
- **Garden centre**
- **Supermarket**
- **Internet Service Provider**
- **Private Nursing Home**
- **Council Tax Department**
- **Insurance company**
- **Quarry**
- **Airline**
- **Car manufacturer**
- **Construction company**

The DVLA e-commerce site can also be used to apply for driving licences and for having vehicle or driver details changed. The site can also be used to book your driving theory and practical test.

It would be a good idea for you to take a look at this site at:
http://www.dvla.gov.uk
Anyone who has a TV or who watches TV on their computer should have a valid TV licence for the property where they reside. Applying for or renewing a TV licence can be performed on-line. Once you are on the licensing site and you have entered the details and made payment, an e-mail is sent to you with a link which you then follow to confirm your identity, where you can then view and print your TV licence.

Ticket reservations: an example of e-commerce

There are many on-line booking systems for booking holidays, flights, trains, theatre, cinema and concert tickets. These systems enable a user to first browse and then book and pay for the tickets using a credit or debit card.

Many of the systems enable tickets to be printed on your own printer rather than the tickets having to be collected or posted.

Questions and Activities

▶ Questions 1 | pp. 18–30

1 A school uses an ICT system to help manage all the tasks involved in the running of a school such as timetabling, keeping pupil records, keeping accounts, processing attendance details, supplying management information and so on.

There are three groups of staff in the school and they can be divided into the following:

   Senior management – the head teacher and their deputies, the bursar and governors

   Managers – heads of departments

   Teaching staff and admin staff.

   (a) Most schools operate in a hierarchical management style. Explain with reference to a school what this means. (2 marks)

   (b) In organisations there are three levels of staff:

      Strategic

      Tactical

      Operational.

      Using an identified person in the school at each of these three levels, explain their particular information needs. In your answer you need to explain how their information needs are different depending on their level. (9 marks)

2 Using a suitable example you have come across to illustrate your answer, explain how people work at different levels in an organisation and how their information needs differ. (9 marks)

3 (a) Staff in organisations can be divided into those staff who are operating and those staff who are managing.

   Explain the differences in the tasks that these two groups of staff perform. (4 marks)

   (b) Different staff have different information needs. Describe how the information needed about suppliers and customers differs depending on whether the member of staff is involved in operating or managing.

   You should mention a suitable example in your answer. (4 marks)

4 There are three levels at which information can be communicated in an organisation. Give the names of these three levels. (3 marks)

5 At which of the three levels would the following information/tasks most likely be dealt with? (1 mark each)

   (a) Information about the costs and profitability of a number of garden centres that a large supermarket chain is thinking of buying.

   (b) A department head has been given a spreadsheet to help them reduce the costs associated with running their department.

   (c) A large organisation is thinking of merging with a competitor to strengthen both companies and they are looking at information on the political implications of this.

   (d) Customer services have just received a complaint about a damaged item.

   (e) An administration officer receives information from a customer informing them that they have changed address.

   (f) A junior accounts manager has received a list of customers with their credit card details who are over two months behind with their payments and has to decide what to do.

   (g) A company is thinking of relocating its large head office away from London and the directors need information about grants available, availability of suitably qualified staff, etc.

   (h) A manager needs to get information in order to get the best price for a fleet of company vehicles for the sales staff.

   (i) The directors of a supermarket chain need to reduce costs and need information about the profitability of each store in order to decide which ones to close.

   (j) Information is needed about the charges from different delivery companies so that one can be chosen for a new e-commerce business.

6 (a) Organisations frequently have to exchange information with external bodies.

   A manufacturing company making office furniture exchanges information with external bodies. Explain an example of the information that would be exchanged externally with each of these three bodies:

      Suppliers

      Customers

      Official and legal bodies. (6 marks)

   (b) Discuss the privacy, security and legal compliance issues involved in the transfer of information to external bodies. (6 marks)

7 Many large organisations make use of an enterprise system.

   Explain what an enterprise system is and describe how it can be used. (4 marks)

▶ Questions 2 | pp. 24–26

1 ICT is used to support the activities of organisations. Explain, by giving suitable examples, how ICT can improve the efficiency and effectiveness of business processes. (6 marks)

2 Some ICT systems are used in nearly every type of organisation.

Describe how ICT is used to help support the following tasks:
Payroll
Personnel
Accounts. (6 marks)

▶ Questions 3 | pp. 26–30

1 (a) Describe what is meant by a management information system (MIS) and give an example of a task where a management Information system is used. (3 marks)

(b) Explain why most organisations make use of management information systems. (3 marks)

2 Decision support systems are often used in organisations. Explain what a decision support system is and give an example of how it might be used in an organisation. (3 marks)

3 Management are the people who have the responsibility in organisations for the making of decisions. Management information systems go hand in hand with data processing systems but are used for different purposes.

(a) By giving a suitable example for each, explain the difference between a data processing/transaction processing system and a management information system (MIS). (4 marks)

(b) Management information systems are used in most organisations such as hospitals and schools.

Describe, by giving a relevant example in each case, a use to which a management information system can be put in each of these organisations. (4 marks)

4 (a) Most organisations make use of a management information system (MIS).
Explain the purpose of a management information system. (3 marks)

(b) Explain why an MIS is particularly useful to managers. (2 marks)

(c) Give an example of one MIS that you have come across and explain briefly how it was used. (3 marks)

5 Many organisations use e-commerce to help make them more efficient.

(a) Describe the advantages that e-commerce offers to organisations. (4 marks)

(b) E-commerce can only work successfully if it is supported by back office systems.
Describe what is meant by a back office system and explain the sorts of task the system would perform to support the e-commerce system. (4 marks)

▶ Activity 1: Setting up an e-commerce business

Have you seen the TV programme Dragons Den? Here budding entrepreneurs demonstrate their new product or service.

You need to think about a product or service which you think you can sell using an e-commerce site. You are going to produce a PowerPoint presentation of your proposed e-commerce business. Although the product or service is important, this presentation needs to focus more on how you can develop the e-commerce site and make it as easy as possible for the customer to use.

As your business is only in the development stage, the Dragons, your teacher and the rest of your group, will need to know how the e-commerce site that you will develop will address the following:
Accept payments including payments from people who do not have access to a credit card.
How all the likely security issues in running an e-commerce business can be overcome.

Case studies

▶ Case study 1   pp. 18–30

SIMS (Schools Information Management System)

Running a school or college is very complex as there are many people and events to manage. It is not surprising that there are management information systems available for them to do this and the most popular one is called SIMS.

The SIMS system is able to produce information at different levels from information needed by the head teacher at a strategic level to tactical information needed by managers to operational information needed by teachers and schools administration staff.

Schools information management systems help schools in many ways:

They reduce the workload in every area of work in the school by automating many of the tasks undertaken by teachers and support staff.

Tactical managers such as heads of department can use the system to plan what is taught in their department.

The head has to make strategic decisions about staffing. The management information system can help them do this by being able to analyse what impact an additional teaching assistant might have on the budget, the class size, and the pupil's achievement, based on what has happened in the past. They can then make the decision more easily because it is based on facts.

Teachers can supply operational information about pupil's good or bad behaviour in lessons and this can be used by staff to identify patterns of behaviour.

Strategic staff such as the head and assistant heads can use the management information to plan timetables making the best use of staff and resources.

At an operational level, classroom teachers can reduce the time it takes to write pupil reports by using a comment bank where a wide selection of comments can be selected and used to produce the report.

The head can plan long-term and short-term finances and make informed budget decisions.

Heads of years can strengthen school-home links by sharing information about pupils using the reporting tools and by sharing this information with parents using text messaging and e-mails.

1 There are three levels of staff in a school:
   - Operational
   - Tactical
   - Strategic.

For each of the following staff, explain which of the three levels is most appropriate for them. (8 marks)
   - Head teacher
   - Classroom teacher
   - Teaching assistant
   - School office clerk
   - Head of department
   - Head of year
   - Deputy or assistant head
   - Caretaker.

2 Schools and colleges make use of management information systems (MIS). Different levels of staff have different requirements from the system.
   (a) Explain what is meant by a management information system (MIS). (3 marks)
   (b) Describe, by giving an example, a task that a head teacher would use the MIS for at a strategic level. (2 marks)
   (c) Describe, by giving an example, a task that a head of department/manager would use the MIS for at a tactical level. (2 marks)

▶ Case study 2   pp. 29–30

Decision support systems helping to decide which new drugs to develop

New drugs to treat illnesses are being developed all the time, but it is a risky and expensive business. A new drug can take 10 years and hundreds of millions of pounds to develop.

Because of the huge cost and the resources required, drug companies cannot take forward all the drugs they discover. This means that the companies have to choose which drugs to develop and this is very hard. This is where an ICT system called a decision support system comes in.

The DSS takes internal and external data and uses it to compare the costs and resource requirements of each proposed new drug and produces information on which managers can base their decision. This means the managers can get information on a series of proposed new drugs and choose the one offering the greatest chance of success and profitability.

Using a DSS in this way reduces the risk of developing a drug that may not succeed in the market.

1 (a) Describe what is meant by a decision support system. (3 marks)

… questions over the page.

(b) Explain **one** advantage in a drug company using a decision support system to decide which out of a choice of drugs to develop. (2 marks)

2 Decision support systems use both internal and external data.
   (a) Explain what is meant by internal and external data. (2 marks)
   (b) Give one example of internal data and one example of external data that the drug company would need in order to make an effective decision as to which drug to choose to develop. (2 marks)

3 Decision support systems are not single applications because they use data from many other applications. Briefly explain what this statement means. (3 marks)

▶ Case study 3   p. 30

easyJet

easyJet, the low frills and low cost airline, was one of the first businesses to make full use of the Internet. Costs and hence fares are kept low by:

- Using the Internet to reduce distribution costs – over 95% of seats are sold using the Internet.
- Ticketless travel – customers receive an e-mail containing their travel details. This helps eliminate many of the problems with traditional tickets (e.g., producing, posting, altering, collecting, etc.).
- Paperless operations – simplified working practices using computers rather than paper. All the ICT systems used by the airline can be accessed through secure servers anywhere in the world. Orders are placed with suppliers and paid for automatically without any paperwork.

1 easyJet is a low cost airline which makes extensive use of e-commerce.
   Access the easyJet site at www.easyjet.com and answer the following questions:
   (a) Explain how easyJet uses ICT to manage the relationship it has with its customers. (5 marks)
   (b) easyJet has back office systems that support its use of e-commerce.
       Explain the meaning of the term back office and give two tasks that a back office system would typically perform. (4 marks)

2 Explain how the use of the Internet and ICT networks has enabled easyJet to offer lower fares compared to other airlines. (3 marks)

3 Describe the typical steps involved, from an e-commerce point of view, in the booking of a flight. (5 marks)

The importance of the Internet to the easyJet business is reflected in the web address on all its aircraft.

TNT Express

TNT Express is a large package delivery organisation that transports packages from business to business. The organisation delivers packages around the world and it delivers 200 million consignments each year using 50,000 people, 19,000 vehicles, 42 aircraft and 1000 depots. The processing requirements for this number of consignments are huge.

One of the problems that TNT Express had is that when parcels are sent to and from other countries, the parcels have to pass through customs. This is so that any duty which is due is identified by Customs and Excise and this can be charged to the sender.

In order to pass a parcel through customs several pieces of paperwork need to be completed. One of the main problems is that these papers can get separated from the packages and this can delay delivery. TNT then decided to forward the 'paperwork' electronically so that the paperwork arrives before the parcels. Sending this information electronically minimises the risk of losing it and also speeds up the delivery.

TNT decided to use a document management system to control the movement of the documents between the depots. Because of the importance of this system, TNT have decided to develop the system using its own IT staff and they have made sure that the system is scalable and therefore will cope with any future expansion.

The document management system allows customer paperwork to be scanned at the collection depot. This means that all the documentation for the parcels is in electronic format so it can be sent electronically using a secure network to the destination in time for the parcel's arrival. Using this system has meant that the time taken for a package to clear through customs has been cut by between 4 and 8 hours. In addition to this there is no paper document that needs copying or storing and this has enabled TNT to reduce the administration costs.

There is also improved workflow because people do not need the parcels to arrive in order to receive the paperwork. This means that the work can be carried out smoothly at airports rather than it all being concentrated soon after the arrival of the parcels on aircraft.

1 TNT Express is a large global organisation. There are four main management styles used by organisations:
   - autocratic
   - paternalistic
   - democratic
   - laissez-faire.

   State the management style TNT Express is most likely to use and give a reason for your answer. **(3 marks)**

2 (a) Describe what is meant by a document management system. **(2 marks)**

   (b) Explain why TNT Express have decided to implement a document management system. **(3 marks)**

   (c) The document management system also incorporates a workflow management system. Give an example of how this company makes use of their workflow management system. **(3 marks)**

3 People at the strategic, tactical and operational levels of TNT Express will have different information requirements from the document management system.

   (a) Identify a person at each of the three levels and briefly describe what information they might need from this system and how they would use it. **(9 marks)**
   (i)   Strategic
   (ii) Tactical
   (iii) Operational.

   (b) Give one reason why the environmental implications of the new system are an improvement on the previous system. **(2 marks)**

www.tnt.com

Exam support

Worked example 1

1 The directors and executives operate at the highest level of an organisation. They perform strategic tasks and make strategic decisions and have very particular requirements from an information system.
 (a) Give **one** example of an information system that would be appropriate for managers at this level and explain how it would be used. (1 mark)
 (b) State **two** other levels of task within an organisation. (2 marks)

Student answer 1

1 (a) An information system that tells the boss who has not paid their bills so that they can be taken to court for the money.
 (b) Strategic
 Operational

Examiner's comment

1 (a) The student has not appreciated that the question is about the use of information systems at a strategic level. The task mentioned here would be made at a more junior level and does not need a strategic decision.
 No marks for this answer.
 (b) The student has not read the question as it asks for 'two **other** levels of task'.
 One mark for the answer 'Operational'. **(1 mark out of 3)**

Student answer 2

1 (a) A management information system to enable the directors of a business to decide which shops in a chain of supermarkets are the least profitable and should be closed in order to cut costs and plough the money into the other profitable stores
 (b) High level tasks
 Low level tasks

Examiner's comment

1 (a) The student has named an information system and given an indication that it is used at a high level (i.e., by directors of the organisation). They have also explained how and why it is used. Full marks for this section.
 (b) This is not an acceptable answer. Only the answers Tactical (Implementation) or Operational are acceptable so no marks for this section. **(1 mark out of 3)**

Examiner's answer

1 (a) One mark for the name of an information system such as Management Information System (MIS), an Executive Information System (EIS) or Decision Support System (DSS). For the one mark the student must mention which type they are discussing and include a description where the information is being used for a task at a strategic level such as planning or decision making for the other two marks.

Suitably detailed examples are included here:
Executive Information System (1) could be used to identify where it would be best to locate a number of distribution centres (1) based on their location near key customers to reduce the cost in getting supplies to customers as cheaply as possible (1).
A Sales Management Information System (1) that will allow a director to decide how best to organise the sales and marketing operations (1) of a large company based on the location of the most profitable customers (1).
A Decision Support System (1) which will enable a board of directors to look at the financial risks and benefits (1) involved in buying competitors in order to increase their market share (1).

 (b) One mark each for two of the following:
 Tactical (Implementation)
 Operational

Worked example 2

2 (a) Many companies make use of a management information system. Describe what is meant by a management information system. **(2 marks)**

(b) Give **two** reasons why the managers in an organisation would use a management information system. **(2 marks)**

(c) Another type of ICT system, called a decision support system (DSS), is often used by organisations. Explain what a decision support system is and, by giving a suitable example, explain how one would be used. **(3 marks)**

Student answer 1

2 (a) A system that managers use to supply them with information in order to make decisions.

(b) To use the information gained to make effective decisions.

(c) A bank manager could use a DSS to help make a decision as to whether or not a large company should be given a loan. The system can use internal data such as information about accounts held, loans paid back in the past and external data from credit reference companies.
The system supplies the manager with the information she could use to make the decision.

Examiner's comment

2 (a) This is an example of a student using the information in the question and simply repeating it in the answer. You must make sure that you do not do this in your answers. The answer here gains no marks.

(b) This is one valid reason and is worth one mark.

(c) Here the student has explained an example of a DSS and also explained fairly well how it would be used. They have failed to explain what a decision support system is. This part is only worth two out of the three marks. **(3 marks out of 7)**

Examiner's answer

2 (a) One mark each for explanations similar to the following:
A management information system is an ICT system which takes data from internal and external sources and processes it to produce information (1). This information is produced in an appropriate form and used by managers at different levels in the organisation (1).

(b) One mark for each reason to a maximum of two such as:
To enable managers at different levels in an organisation (1)
to use the information produced by the MIS (1)
to give them the information they need to make more accurate decisions (1).

(c) One mark for a suitable definition such as:
A type of information system that supports the decision-making process.
Two marks for a brief description of the context with marks allocated in the following way:

Student answer 2

2 (a) A management information system is a system that managers use that takes data from internal and external sources and turns it into information in a suitable form that will enable them to make decisions.

(b) To enable the managers at different levels in the organisation to obtain the information structured in a way so it can be used to make decisions about the business.

(c) A decision support system is used by managers when they have a choice of actions to take. The DSS enables the managers to make the best choice based on the information from the system.

Examiner's comment

2 (a) This is a good definition of an MIS and contains the three main points. Full marks are given for this part.

(b) Two of the reasons are covered, so two marks here.

(c) A good definition but the student has failed to give and discuss an example of a DSS. Only one mark is given (for the definition). **(5 marks out of 7)**

One mark for a statement as to who it is that uses the system.
One mark for what it would be used for.
A medical diagnosis system to assist doctors (1 mark for who) in making clinical decisions as to the best course of action in treating a patient. For example, a patient may just be treated using drugs or by having an operation and the system allows the doctor to choose by using the system to report on the treatment of similar patients with similar conditions (1 mark for what it is used for).
Other examples of decision support systems (DSS) they could discuss include:
Using the system to work out which shares to buy on the basis of past and present performance.
A rail track company uses a DSS to work out which sections of worn track to repair first to reduce the chance of derailments and reduce the delays to journeys.
Marketing in financial services where a product is to be chosen from a number of products. The decision support system allows information on potential customers for each of the products from the existing customer base to determine the size of the potential market for each product. This will allow the best product to be chosen.

Summary mind maps

Types of ICT system

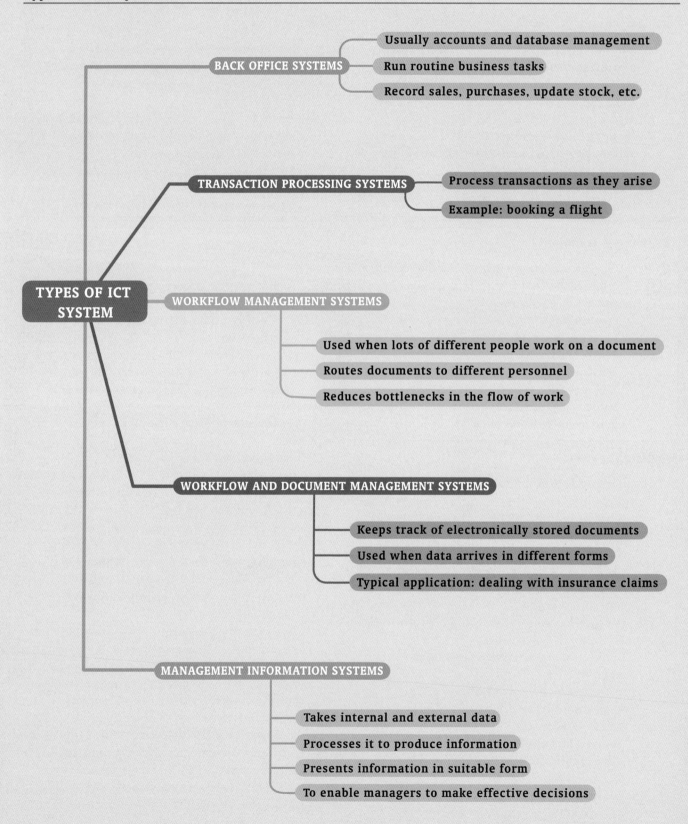

BACK OFFICE SYSTEMS
- Usually accounts and database management
- Run routine business tasks
- Record sales, purchases, update stock, etc.

TRANSACTION PROCESSING SYSTEMS
- Process transactions as they arise
- Example: booking a flight

TYPES OF ICT SYSTEM

WORKFLOW MANAGEMENT SYSTEMS
- Used when lots of different people work on a document
- Routes documents to different personnel
- Reduces bottlenecks in the flow of work

WORKFLOW AND DOCUMENT MANAGEMENT SYSTEMS
- Keeps track of electronically stored documents
- Used when data arrives in different forms
- Typical application: dealing with insurance claims

MANAGEMENT INFORMATION SYSTEMS
- Takes internal and external data
- Processes it to produce information
- Presents information in suitable form
- To enable managers to make effective decisions

Types of ICT system cont'd

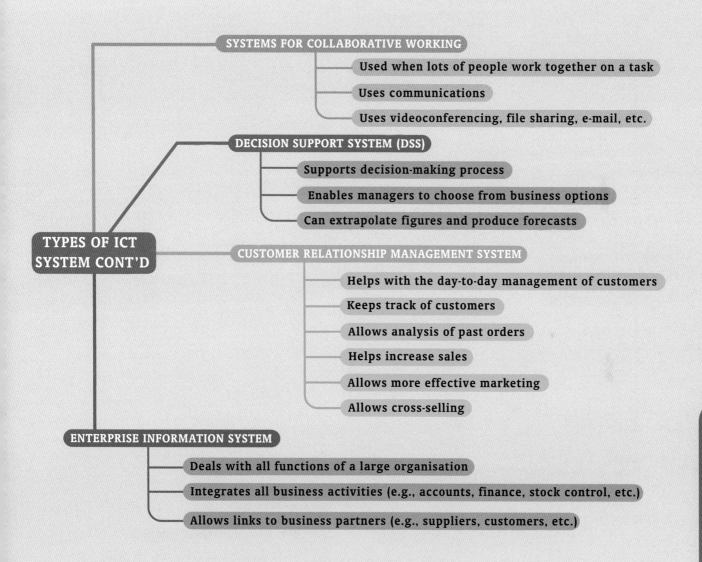

TYPES OF ICT SYSTEM CONT'D

SYSTEMS FOR COLLABORATIVE WORKING
- Used when lots of people work together on a task
- Uses communications
- Uses videoconferencing, file sharing, e-mail, etc.

DECISION SUPPORT SYSTEM (DSS)
- Supports decision-making process
- Enables managers to choose from business options
- Can extrapolate figures and produce forecasts

CUSTOMER RELATIONSHIP MANAGEMENT SYSTEM
- Helps with the day-to-day management of customers
- Keeps track of customers
- Allows analysis of past orders
- Helps increase sales
- Allows more effective marketing
- Allows cross-selling

ENTERPRISE INFORMATION SYSTEM
- Deals with all functions of a large organisation
- Integrates all business activities (e.g., accounts, finance, stock control, etc.)
- Allows links to business partners (e.g., suppliers, customers, etc.)

Classifying organisations

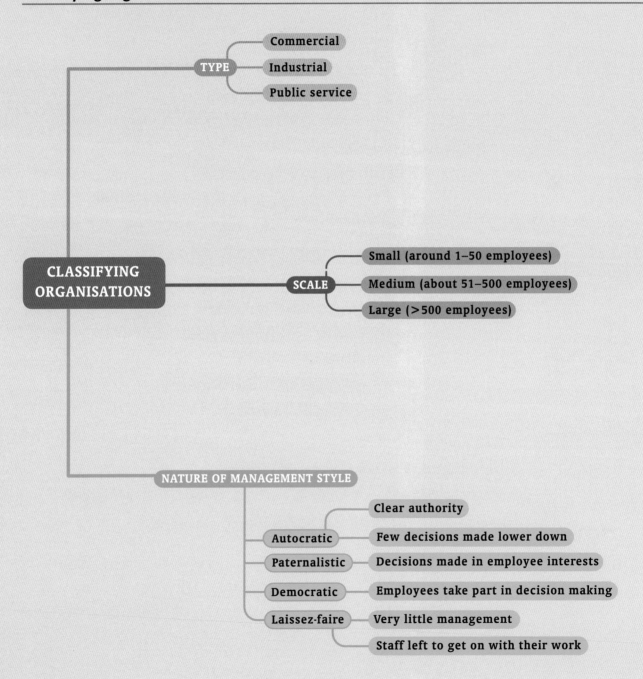

TOPIC 3: Managing ICT

Like any other function of a business, ICT needs to be managed and the way this is done depends to a large extent on the size of the organisation. Large organisations have clearly defined roles for each member of staff involved in ICT, with closely defined chains of management. Smaller organisations need more flexibility and if one member of staff is off then others often have to cover their area of work if needed.

In this topic you will look at how ICT is managed in small and large organisations and see how an ICT strategy is developed in order to meet the long- and short-term aims of the organisation. You will also look at how people at the highest level of ICT management can help plan business strategy.

▼ The key concepts covered in this topic are:

▶ How the size of an organisation affects the degree of formality with which ICT is managed

▶ Matching the ICT strategy to the long-term aims of the organisation

▶ How ICT policies outline how a strategy would be put into operation

CONTENTS

1 **Managing ICT**..**42**
How the size of an organisation affects the degree of formality with which ICT is managed, matching the ICT strategy to the long-term aims of the organisation, how ICT policies outline how a strategy would be put into operation and the contribution of ICT management to business strategy.

2 **Questions and Case study**...**45**

3 **Exam support**..**47**

4 **Summary mind maps**...**49**

Managing ICT

Introduction

All organisations making use of ICT will need to have their ICT resources managed. ICT makes a major contribution to the success of most organisations and all organisations must plan and properly manage it.

In this topic you will look at how ICT can be managed and how it needs to support business aims.

How the size of an organisation affects the degree of formality with which ICT is managed

ICT departments can range from a single person to several hundred people. For example, the company TNT Express, which you came across in the case study in the previous topic, employs 500 ICT staff. There is a huge difference in the way a small ICT department is managed compared to a large one.

Someone employed in a large organisation will have a specific role and will not usually be asked to do anything outside this role. Someone employed in a small organisation will usually work flexibly and have to undertake a whole range of ICT-related tasks as and when required.

The size of an organisation usually affects the degree of formality with which ICT is managed. Large ICT departments tend to have an autocratic style of management and a hierarchical management structure. This means that there are formal systems for the management of ICT. Small ICT departments have a democratic structure where all employees are involved in ICT decisions and management. Such staff do not need formal systems and the management of ICT tends to be informal.

▶ KEY WORDS

Policy – a deliberate plan of action to achieve certain desirable goals or outcomes

Matching the ICT strategy to the long-term aims of the organisation

What is an ICT strategy?

All organisations have an aim, which is what they would like to achieve in the future. For example, the aim of a retailer might be to increase their market share. In order to realise this aim the retailer will have to introduce a successful e-commerce site which offers the customer a better experience than competitors. In order for this to happen it would be necessary to have an ICT strategy which supports this aim.

ICT strategy issues are those issues connected with how the organisation can best achieve its aims and objectives using ICT resources.

The ICT strategy is therefore the overall direction in which the organisation should be going. It is therefore necessary for the managers involved in ICT to have ICT policies which will help achieve the overall strategy.

All organisations have a series of long-term aims and the ICT strategy must support these. Here are some of the ways the aims can be supported by the ICT strategy:

▼ You will find out

▶ About how the size of an organisation affects the degree of formality with which ICT is managed

▶ About matching the ICT strategy to the long-term aims of the organisation

▶ About how ICT policies outline how a strategy would be put into operation

▶ About the contribution of ICT management to business strategy

All organisations should have an ICT strategy to support their business aims.

strat•e•gy
(strāt' ə-jē) *n.*
1. Plan of action designed to achieve a particular goal.

Aim	ICT strategy
To increase market share	To use database marketing to target customers more efficiently To introduce an e-commerce site To improve communication with existing customer base Use decision support systems to use the sales and marketing budget more effectively
To reduce costs	Greater use of automatic data entry Use smaller offices by allowing some staff to work from home Admin should be performed automatically by back office systems To reduce the mistakes made with orders
To reduce the delivery time to customers	To introduce an ICT system that will allow customers to track the progress of their orders using the Internet To exchange order information with suppliers so that goods do not go out of stock To make more efficient use of own vans
To improve the way the organisation is managed	To introduce management information systems to allow managers to get information that will help them make decisions To use project management software to better manage projects Use decision support systems to supply information that will help choose between different courses of action
To improve the security of the data stored	To use on-line backup of the data held so that data is stored off-site To provide training to make users aware of problems with hackers, viruses and other threats To produce administrative procedures that will protect the organisation against fraud by employees

EXAM TIP

Do not get confused between a strategy and a policy. A strategy is an overall aim and is worded in general terms. Policies are the fine detail of a strategy and set out how the strategy can be achieved.

How ICT policies outline how a strategy would be put into operation

All organisations that make use of ICT should have a series of policies which set out how the use of ICT will be developed within the organisation. For example, an ICT policy might be that all computers in the organisation must be networked and capable of Internet access, whether they are used inside the offices, on the move or at home.

Strategies give the overall direction for the organisation and policies add the fine detail.

ICT policies cover the different aspects of the use of ICT such as security, training and procurement (i.e., buying). In some cases an organisation will look at what policies it needs in the short term and in the long term.

Most organisations have policies covering the following:

- Security policy – covering access to information resources, use of networks, hackers, viruses, physical security, logical security (e.g., usernames, passwords, access rights, etc.) and lists of risks and prevention.
- Use of Internet and internal mail systems – covering use for company business, confidentiality, prohibited activities, illegal activities and security.

- Personal information policy – covering adherence to regulations (e.g., Data Protection Act 1998), training, encryption, protection of laptops and other portable devices.
- Password policy – covering password management, account lockout and enforcement.
- Environmental policy – covering the shredding and recycling of paper, the re-filling and re-use of printer ink, the recycling of old computers and the reduction in the electricity used by ICT hardware, the reduction in the use of paper, etc.

Security policy

The security policy will set out a series of rules and regulations designed to ensure the security of ICT systems and data.

The security policy will lay out those things that will help the detection of misuse and also those things that will prevent misuse along with outlining the penalties should the misuse come from employees of the organisation.

Normally the security policy will contain documentation concerning the following:

- physical security
- the prevention of misuse
- the continuous investigation of irregularities
- logical access – establishing procedures for accessing data such as log on procedures, firewalls

- personnel administration
- operational procedures
- staff code of conduct and responsibilities
- disciplinary procedures.

Procurement policy

The procurement policy sets out the arrangements for the purchasing of ICT equipment and services. Procurement is important because efficient procurement will deliver good quality, value for money services and supplies.

Normally the procurement policy will contain requirements and documentation concerning the following:

- For small amounts of expenditure, staff must show they have achieved value for money and must supply evidence of this if asked.
- Expenditure over a certain amount must be subject to competition. For example, a few different suppliers would be asked for a quote for a network and the best one in terms of expertise, service and price would be chosen. This is called tendering.
- The purchase of hardware – such as it must be above a certain specification.
- The purchase of software – such as it must be capable of running using the existing operating system.
- The purchase of services from contractors – must be subject to the standard contract used by the organisation.

The use of swipe cards to access ICT network facilities may be documented in the security policy.

Managing ICT *continued*

KEY WORDS

Chief Information Officer – the person at executive level responsible for making all of the strategic ICT-related decisions, including the management, implementation and usability of all ICT in an organisation

Training policy

Staff with skills and knowledge matched to the tasks they perform is essential if an organisation is to meet its business aims and objectives. Most organisations have a training policy which will ensure staff are:

- correctly and appropriately matched to the job they perform
- knowledgeable about legal issues (copyright, misuse of computers, data protection, health and safety, etc.)
- properly trained in new hardware, software and new procedures introduced.

The training policy will usually stipulate the following:

- All staff must have their skills and knowledge assessed at yearly intervals.
- After assessment, human resources will assess the training needs of the member of staff.
- Any new rules and regulations that staff must adhere to must result in training for all staff involved.
- Staff must receive training when any new hardware, software, systems and procedures are introduced.

The contribution of ICT management to business strategy

ICT is used in organisations because there are business benefits in using it. Organisations use ICT to help manage their business strategy. For example, if the business strategy of a company manufacturing a certain product is to expand into new markets, then ICT resources must be able to deal with the increase in business, dealing with payments in other currencies, dealing with international shipments and customs regulations and so on.

The Chief Information Officer (CIO)

Many organisations have a post called the Chief Information Officer, or CIO for short, whose job is to be in overall charge of ICT resources. Because of the importance of ICT resources in an organisation, the Chief Information Officer operates at the strategic level and is at executive or board level.

Many government departments have CIOs because they need very experienced ICT staff in order to avoid the many costly mistakes with ICT systems bought in the past that were abandoned part of the way through the project or did not live up to expectations.

The job of a Chief Information Officer would typically include the following:

- Being responsible for the overall technological direction of their organisation.
- Being involved in the strategic business plan as part of the executive (i.e., the people at the top of the organisation).
- Being knowledgeable about administrative procedures such as budgeting, recruiting staff, taking on contract workers and supervision.
- Responsibility for budgets for projects and programs.
- Making decisions regarding staff training.
- Making decisions about the purchase of hardware, software and ICT services.
- Providing organisations with the vision to use ICT as a competitive tool.

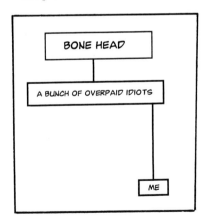

"Who was put in charge of making the new organizational chart?"

Training is essential if organisations are to get the most out of their most important resource: people.

Questions and Case study

▶ Questions 1   pp. 42–44

1 Organisations can be divided by size such as small, medium and large and will have a different style of management based on this size. Discuss how the size of an organisation affects the degree of formality with which ICT is managed. (6 marks)

2 By giving a suitable example relevant to ICT, explain the difference between formal systems and informal systems. (2 marks)

3 Ideally the ICT strategy should reflect the long-term aims of an organisation.
  (a) With reference to an organisation you have come across, explain what the aims of the organisation are. (4 marks)
  (b) Explain with reference to the same organisation mentioned in part (a) what the ICT strategy could include in order to meet the aims of the organisation. (6 marks)

4 A company making high performance loudspeakers has the following aim: to increase the company's market share for loudspeakers.
  With the above aim in mind, state and explain two ICT strategies that would be needed. (4 marks)

5 Explain the differences between an aim of an organisation and an ICT strategy. (4 marks)

6 Many large organisations have a Chief Information Officer as a member of the executive.
  Describe why organisations have a Chief Information Officer and describe **three** tasks they would typically perform. (8 marks)

▶ Case study 1   pp. 42–44

All organisations have long-term aims and the following are the long-term aims of the Hampshire Fire and Rescue Service:
- reduce deaths and injuries from accidental fires by 30% by 2010
- reduce the number of deliberate fires by 20% by 2010
- reduce the number of fires by 20% by 2010
- work with others to reduce deaths and serious injuries on the road by 2010
- be in the top 10 performing fire and rescue services in the country by 2010.

Like most organisations, Hampshire Fire and Rescue have an ICT strategy.

In order to achieve the above, the Hampshire Fire and Rescue Service need to manage the following resources:

- human resources (i.e. people)
- physical resources (buildings, equipment, etc.)
- information communication technology resources
- financial resources.

ICT is mentioned separately in the above list but it can be used to help manage all the other resources in the list. For example, ICT can be used to identify which staff need specialist training or to organise a staff rota.

Hampshire Fire and Rescue Service invest significantly in ICT to provide an efficient and cost-effective service. They do this by making use of telephones, computer workstations, radios, pagers, mobile phones, electronic mail, and a host of business applications including access to the Internet for all staff including staff who are out and about in the course of their duties.

The ICT department are responsible for the development and maintenance of a network that enables staff to communicate and share information across Hampshire and beyond. The ICT department also provide facilities that allow communication with external bodies using technologies such as electronic mail and videoconferencing.

The ICT department consists of 21 staff who provide technical and user support including 24/7 emergency call-out cover, management of contracts with suppliers, a help-desk service and training.

▶ Case study 1 (continued) PP. 42–44

ICT Strategy

- A new wide area network (WAN) is to be set up to provide a communications infrastructure to support the growing needs for ICT systems and to meet external demands from central government.
- The introduction of VOIP (Voice over Internet Protocol) which will enable voice and data networks to be combined. This will reduce operating costs.
- The removal of legacy systems. There are some old database systems which will be decommissioned in favour of modern database management systems which will integrate better with other applications.

- A web content management system will be introduced that will enable departments to manage their web content more easily.
- A new training/human resources system. This will replace the existing legacy system for training which does not integrate well with the human resources system. This will improve workforce management.
- To make more use of mobile working. This fire service wishes to take advantage of emerging technologies that can be safely integrated into the other systems.

1 The Hampshire Fire and Rescue Service have an ICT strategy and ICT policies.
   (a) By giving suitable examples, describe the differences between an ICT strategy and an ICT policy. (4 marks)
   (b) The case study mentions the term 'legacy system'. Explain what is meant by a legacy system and why such systems often have to interface with newer systems. (3 marks)

2 Explain, by giving suitable examples, how the aims of the Hampshire Fire and Rescue service are supported by the ICT strategy. (6 marks)

3 Explain how the use of remote and mobile working can improve the efficiency of this fire and rescue service. In your answer you should mention the technologies that can be used and the benefits they bring. (5 marks)

4 By looking at the items listed in the ICT strategy for the Hampshire Fire and Rescue Service, write down a list of four ICT policies and describe why they are needed. (8 marks)

5 A large organisation has a Chief Information Officer as a member of the company executive.
   Describe the role of the Chief Information Officer and describe some of the tasks they are likely to perform. (8 marks)

Exam support

Worked example 1

1 (a) **Compare and contrast how ICT would be managed in a large organisation compared with a small organisation. (4 marks)**

(b) **Explain, by giving a suitable example, how the ICT strategy should match the long-term aims of an organisation. (3 marks)**

(c) **Describe the role of the Chief Information Officer in an organisation and explain why it important that the person in this role is a member of the company executive. (3 marks)**

Student answer 1

1 (a) A small organisation would not have an ICT department as such but instead one employee would be in charge of the network. Users would be expected to do more of the ICT work for themselves such as installing new software, running virus checks and backing up their own data.

In a large organisation they would have an ICT department with systems analysts, programmers, website developers, testers, network managers and administrators, engineers and help-desk staff. They would all have their own roles and would not be expected to do a bit of each job as in the small organisation.

(b) The aims of an organisation are the general direction the organisation would like to go in. For example, they may have the aim of being the largest on-line clothes retailer. The ICT strategy would need to reflect where the company wants to go by putting suitable ICT policies in place.

(c) The Chief Information Officer is the person responsible for all the information resources in the business. They make all the decisions and are in charge.

Student answer 2

1 (a) ICT in a large organisation would be managed formally with a hierarchical structure. The ICT staff would have clearly defined roles and responsibilities and would work together as a team each contributing their own expertise.

(b) Long-term aim – to conduct more business using the Internet ICT strategy would be to put in place a website with a back office system that supports the operations such as order processing, stock control, payments, etc.

ICT strategy would be to minimise the amount of time from customer order to the order being delivered.

ICT strategy would be to facilitate order being placed from countries around the world.

(c) The Chief Information Officer is the person at executive level responsible for making all of the strategic ICT decisions. They are responsible for the management, implementation and usability of all ICT in an organisation. They need to be at the executive level in an organisation because they need to advise on ICT direction at a strategic level so that costly ICT decisions are not made without sufficient knowledge.

Examiner's comment

1 (a) The student here has failed to realise that a small organisation can still employ quite a lot of employees and their answer seems to reflect that the small organisation they are talking about only employs a handful of employees.

Although they have not mentioned the hierarchical structure necessary in large organisations, they have clearly understood that there are clearly defined ICT roles in the large organisation. Two marks are given here.

(b) Although the student has correctly understood and stated what an aim might be for an organisation, they have not given any precise examples of strategies. This answer is worth only one mark.

(c) This is the sort of definition most people could make up from the title Chief Information Officer and is therefore worth no marks. **(3 marks out of 10)**

Examiner's comment

1 (a) The student has understood the way that ICT is managed in a large organisation but they have failed to contrast this with the way ICT is managed in smaller organisations so this part is only worth 3 of the 4 marks.

(b) The student has correctly identified an aim for an organisation and has mentioned four items in broad terms that would be part of the ICT strategy. Full marks for this section.

(c) The student has identified correctly that the CIO is a member of the executive and makes strategic ICT decisions. They have identified some of the tasks they perform and have identified a reason why large organisations have a CIO. Three important and distinct points have been, so full marks are given for this section. **(9 marks out of 10)**

Examiner's answer

1   (a)   Two marks for two points relevant to a small organisation and two marks for points relevant to a large organisation.
Example points include:

Large organisation:
Clearly defined roles and responsibilities
Less flexibility needed
Hierarchical structure
Many tiers of management.

Small organisation:
Flatter structure
Fewer tiers of management
ICT staff act more on their own initiative
More flexible approach to the tasks staff do.

(b)   One mark for a statement saying that the ICT strategy is in place to support the business aims/objectives for the organisation.
One mark for a statement outlining the business aim, e.g. to sell more goods internationally.
One mark for saying how the ICT strategy could support the business aim, e.g. by setting up and publicising an e-commerce site that supports on-line ordering of goods.

(c)   One mark for a definition of the CIO's roles such as:
The person at executive level responsible for making all of the strategic ICT decisions.
One mark for further detail on the role such as:
They are responsible for the management, implementation and usability of all ICT in an organisation.
One mark for an explanation as to why they are at executive level.
To use their considerable experience to ensure the viability and success of large, expensive ICT projects.

Summary mind maps

How the size of an organisation affects the formalities with which ICT is managed

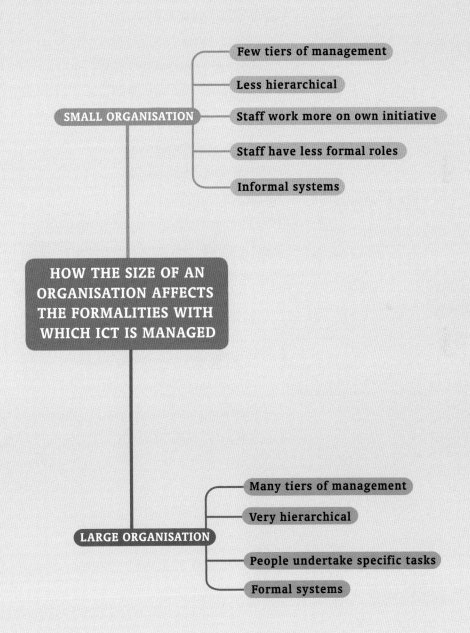

SMALL ORGANISATION
- Few tiers of management
- Less hierarchical
- Staff work more on own initiative
- Staff have less formal roles
- Informal systems

HOW THE SIZE OF AN ORGANISATION AFFECTS THE FORMALITIES WITH WHICH ICT IS MANAGED

LARGE ORGANISATION
- Many tiers of management
- Very hierarchical
- People undertake specific tasks
- Formal systems

Topic 3 Managing ICT

ICT policies outline how a strategy would be put into operation

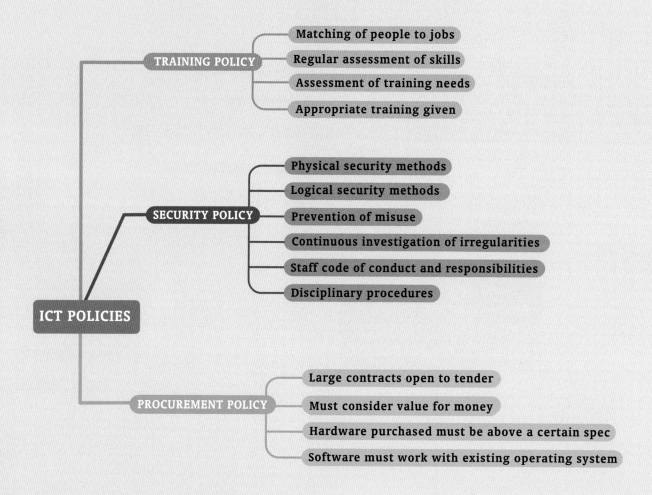

TOPIC 4: ICT strategy

You will already know from the last topic the reasons why organisations should have an ICT strategy that supports the short- and long-term aims of the organisation. To develop a streamlined and efficient ICT system, management need to set out with a long-term view of what they want to do and then put all the pieces in place over a period that is consistent with this approach.

Many organisations have now decided to outsource their ICT to a facilities management company using the argument that these companies provide a cheaper and more efficient service than running the ICT facilities in house. Although the nature of ICT changes with time, without a coherent ICT strategy, the organisation might develop systems that are incompatible with other existing systems and the whole management of the resources would be a nightmare.

In this topic you will look at ICT strategy in more detail.

▼ The key concepts covered in this topic are:

▶ Factors that influence an ICT system strategy within an organisation

▶ The management of information assets over time

▶ The need for a corporate strategy covering technology for ICT systems in large organisations

▶ Standards exist that may affect strategic choices

CONTENTS

1 ICT strategy 52
Factors that influence an ICT system strategy within an organisation, the management of information assets over time, the need for a corporate strategy covering ICT systems in large organisations, and standards that exist that may affect strategic choices.

2 Questions and Case study..55

3 Exam support...56

4 Summary mind maps...58

Unit 3 Use of ICT in the Digital World

ICT strategy

Introduction

Strategies are ways that organisations can realise their aims and objectives. For example, the aim of an organisation may be to become the largest on-line retailer of CDs and DVDs. The various strategies would set out how this would be achieved. Usually strategies consist of broad details of what will be needed and it is the actual policies that give the fine detail.

In this topic you will look at ICT strategies and the factors that affect them.

Factors that influence an ICT system strategy within an organisation

The ICT system strategy of an organisation looks at how the organisation can best achieve its overall objectives using ICT resources.

Internal factors influencing an ICT system strategy

Some of the factors in the diagram below are internal factors which are determined by the organisation itself. Internal factors include:

- Business goals – what the company would like to achieve in the short and long term. For example, a company may want 30% of their employees to work from home in order to reduce office costs and also to reduce their carbon footprint. Whatever the business goals are, ICT systems will need to be put in place to support them.
- Available finance – organisations have to operate within certain financial limits. Projects have budgets attached to them and it is necessary to develop ICT systems within these budgets. The benefits of any new system have to outweigh the costs of development.
- Legacy systems – it is rare that new systems completely replace all the

old systems. What usually happens is that there is a mixture of old and new systems and this creates a problem because the systems often have to interface together. This means that the systems have to be capable of using each other's data. Because of this, the older system (called the legacy system) places constraints on the development of the new system.

- Geography of clients and business fulfilment – where customers/ clients are located determines the ICT systems strategy and the way that the customers/clients receive the goods or services is also a factor. For example, if customers are situated all around the world, then an e-commerce site would need to be developed, and to save on administration costs, a system of tracking could be used where customers are able to track the progress of their orders and deliveries using the Internet. Having clients all over the world will increase the complexity of the ICT system used.

External factors influencing an ICT system strategy

Some of the factors in the diagram are external factors which are determined by other bodies outside the organisation.

External factors include:

- legislation
- compliance.

The ICT systems developed by an organisation must ensure that the way they are used complies with certain laws and regulations. There are many laws and regulations in the UK which govern the way data or information is presented or can be used. Compliance means ensuring that the ICT systems being developed do not break any of these laws or regulations.

An organisation may also need to comply with the rules set by other organisations for the exchange of data between them. For example, HMRC (the tax and VAT organisation) stipulate the way data is passed to them.

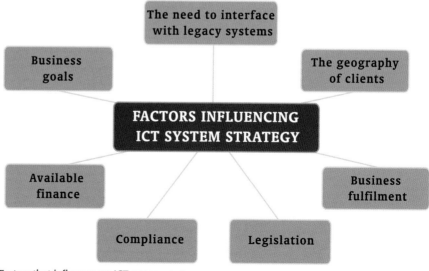

Factors that influence an ICT system strategy.

Legislation

The laws must be obeyed and any new system developed must not break these laws. The main laws applicable to ICT systems are:

- Freedom of Information Act 2000
- The Data Protection Act 1998
- The Copyright, Designs and Patents Act 1988
- The Computer Misuse Act 1990.

Compliance

This means conforming to a specification or policy, standard or law that has been clearly defined. For example, as well as obeying the laws listed above, there are many regulations that organisations must adhere to as set out by organisations such as the Financial Services Authority (FSA), HM Revenue and Customs, Trading Standards, the Environmental Protecton Agency and so on.

Many industries, such as financial services and the health service, are highly regulated and it is a full-time job for someone to ensure that whatever the organisation does is within the law.

The management of information assets over time

In business and most organisations information needs to be kept for a long period of time. For example, self-employed people are required by HM Revenue and Customs to keep financial records of their income and expenses for at least six years.

Organisations need to keep records for long periods of time, so it is important that any ICT system being developed has plenty of spare capacity to cope with an increasing volume of data. For example, many organisations store much more information about customers and their orders than they did a few years ago because it allows them to extract useful information which can be used for marketing. Supermarkets and other retailers who make use of loyalty schemes hold huge amounts of data about their customers including details on everything they buy from the store and how they pay for them.

In addition, organisations store details about voicemails, e-mails, internal memos, etc. You may wonder why such information is kept. Many organisations store this information in case there is ever any need for it as evidence in a legal case.

Not only do organisations need to store all the data, they need to keep backup copies of it as well.

The increasing volume of data not only creates storage problems but it can create a nightmare if someone is asked to produce some documents or e-mails recorded 10 years ago. Finding such information takes time and can be very expensive. Many organisations have systems that can be used to search all the archived data.

The need for a corporate strategy covering technology for ICT systems in large organisations

To keep up with the latest developments in ICT resources means to take advantage of the commercial benefits it offers. All organisations will review new developments from time to time to see what advantage can be gained from them.

Software is regularly upgraded or improved upon and the organisation will probably want to take advantage of the increased functionality. However, too much change in an organisation can be bad as staff have to constantly learn new things and they may feel that it is not worth learning one piece of software thoroughly if there is another release soon.

Upgrading may also be done when an old piece of hardware starts to become unreliable and the maintenance costs start to increase. It is a bit like having a washing machine at home that regularly needs repairing. Eventually you get fed up with the hassle and the unexpected repair bills and decide to replace it with a new one.

Older computer hardware, which many companies still use, may have expensive maintenance agreements and since the hardware producers are the only people who can repair it, this can be very expensive and some maintenance contracts can cost in the region of several hundred thousands of pounds annually. This is probably now more than the cost of new up-to-date hardware.

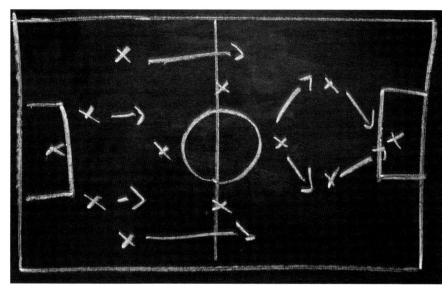

Just like the manager of a football team will have a strategy, the ICT function of an organisation needs a strategy.

> **KEY WORDS**

Business goals – the long- and short-term objectives the business would like to meet

Legacy system – an old system or piece of hardware/software that continues to be used because the organisation does not want to alter or replace it

ICT strategy *continued*

Many organisations keep huge quantities of historical data.

Future proofing

Whenever ICT systems are developed, they need to be future proofed. A new ICT system developed today will need to be able to cope with the ever increasing demands of business over many years.

Future proofing is difficult because it is hard to foresee potential developments in the business but here are some ways ICT systems can be future proofed:

- Scaleable networks – where it is easy to add extra servers and terminals.
- Applications that are independent of the operating system used – this means if operating systems change, the application can run on the new operating system.
- Data stored is separate to the database programs used to manipulate it – this means that different applications can use the data.
- Large amounts of storage – large amounts of storage capacity can be purchased initially to cope with the ever increasing amounts of data stored from year to year.
- Higher processing power than needed at the time – to cope with more demanding applications.

Developments in technology

New developments evolve rapidly in ICT and organisations have to move quickly to adopt them in order to take advantage of the benefits they bring. If they do not do this, their competitors will and could gain market advantage.

The ICT strategy should not be so rigid that it cannot be changed in the light of new developments.

Procurement

Procurement means the purchasing of goods and services. Procurement would typically involve:

- researching suitable providers of hardware, software and services

- tendering (asking for quotes from different companies to compare costs)
- collating all the relevant information
- choosing companies or individuals for providing hardware, software and services
- setting up contracts.

The ICT strategy will specify procedures for doing this. This is mainly to make sure that the purchasing decisions are soundly based and not simply giving the business to a friend or relative irrespective of the price charged.

Technology life cycle

There are four phases in the technology life cycle and these are:

- Research and development – new systems are investigated and then built. This phase costs money for resources such as staff, equipment, hardware, etc.
- The ascent phase – here the costs of the new system have been recovered (by reduction in admin costs, improved efficiency, less wastage, etc.). The savings start to rise above the costs of research and development.
- The maturity phase – where the ICT system works well and helps to make savings for the company or helps generate more income by providing better access to quality information.
- The decline phase – this is where the ICT system starts to become out-of-date and the costs of maintaining the system rise and the benefits from the system fall. The system is old and needs replacing.

In the technology life cycle the cycle is started all over again with the research and development of a new ICT system.

Information management

Information is a valuable corporate asset that must be available to anyone

in the organisation who needs it and is allowed to access it. In order to extract information on an *ad hoc* basis, systems need to be in place which use data from other ICT systems such as order processing, stock control, payroll, etc., and produce management information that enables decisions to be made. The availability of information and systems such as management information systems to extract the information needs to be a corporate resource and the ICT strategy must specify the importance of this and put policies in place to provide this information.

People considerations

As the technology changes, people need to gain new skills, or new people must be recruited with expertise in the new area. There may be reorganisations to cope with the new technology and people may work in a new place or even work from home.

The ICT strategy covering technology will need to ensure that the staff and working practices are in a position to cope with the change.

Standards that may affect strategic choice

In order for computers and computer equipment to successfully work together there need to be standards. For example, most organisations exchange data with their partners. Your school or college will exchange data with the examination board they use. Exchange of data in this way saves time because the data is in a form that can be used by both ICT systems. This means the school and examination board have to use the same standards so their systems can communicate and exchange data with each other, thus eliminating the need to re-key the data.

Questions and Case study

▶ Questions 1 pp. 52–54

1 All organisations should have an ICT strategy which says in broad terms how ICT will support the business aims of the organisation. There are a number of factors influencing this ICT strategy in an organisation.

 Describe, by giving suitable examples in each case, how each of the following factors influences the ICT strategy:
 (a) Business goals (2 marks)
 (b) Available finance (2 marks)
 (c) Geography of clients. (2 marks)

2 The factors which influence an ICT strategy of an organisation can be divided into internal and external factors.
 (a) Explain the difference between internal and external factors giving one example for each. (4 marks)
 (b) Explain the meaning of the term 'compliance' in the context of the management of an ICT department. (2 marks)

 (c) In many cases new ICT systems must interface with legacy systems and this needs to be reflected in the ICT strategy. Explain what is meant by a legacy system. (2 marks)

3 ICT systems have to manage an increasing amount of data over time.
 Explain why the above statement is true and explain why this needs to be considered by organisations when deciding on their ICT strategy. (4 marks)

4 Technology is constantly changing so organisations have to adapt to this change.
 Explain how an organisation needs to cope with this change and what needs to be in the corporate ICT strategy to document the organisation's philosophy for this change. (5 marks)

5 Standards exist which affect strategic choice.
 Give one example of a standard that affects strategic choice. (2 marks)

▶ Case study 1 pp. 52–54

Managing information assets over time

Many large organisations have lawsuits pending with over £10 million at stake. About 40% of the largest organisations spent upwards of £2.5 million on legal fees for court cases. What this means is that companies must keep comprehensive records for legal reasons as well as for their day-to-day operations.

Many companies now store details of instant messages, e-mails and voicemails. Some companies even routinely store video from their security cameras and this needs a huge amount of storage (e.g., 1 Terabyte per day). What this means is that organisations are storing more and more data and that this data is stored for quite long periods such as up to 10 years.

Because of increased data retention and the fact that this data needs to be easily found if needed, disk storage rather than tape storage is used.

Most organisations also have data that has been stored by legacy systems. They do not know what this data is because it is so old but they are worried about getting rid of it in case they need it.

1 Organisations store huge amounts of data routinely and some of this data has to be kept for many years.
 (a) Give **two** reasons why data might need to be stored for such a long time. (2 marks)
 (b) Give **three** examples of different types of data that will need to be stored over time by an organisation and explain why such data may be needed in the future. (3 marks)
 (c) Companies have to store increasing amounts of data. Explain why this requires careful management. (2 marks)

2 Backups and archives of data used to be stored on magnetic tape but many organisations are now storing this on magnetic disk.
 Suggest **two** reasons for this. (2 marks)

3 Apart from the data used for data processing for an organisation, give three examples of other data that is used that will need to be stored over time. (3 marks)

4 Data is sometimes stored for legacy systems.
 Explain what is meant by a legacy system and suggest a reason why this data may still need to be stored. (4 marks)

Exam support

Worked example 1

1 (a) Give **two** reasons why all organisations should have an ICT strategy. **(2 marks)**
   (b) Outline **two** factors that the organisation will need to take into account when preparing their ICT strategy. **(4 marks)**

Student answer 1

1 (a) So that the organisation knows where they are going with the ICT in their organisation.

The strategy will set out what they will do with ICT. For example, part of the strategy might be for every computer in the organisation to be networked and have high speed access to the Internet.

(b) How much money is available. It is no use specifying the latest technology in the ICT strategy if there is unlikely to be enough money in the budget to pay for it.

They may need to develop systems that can still communicate with some of the older systems which they do not want to replace. This will restrict the type of systems they can produce.

Examiner's comment

1 (a) The first statement in the first sentence is too vague to be given a mark. They would have been better clarifying this answer with an example.

The second statement is really a repetition of the first answer. It is important to always check that when you are asked to give two answers, then one answer is not simply a re-hash of the other answer.

Here the second answer gains marks as no marks were given for the first answer. One mark is given for this part.

(b) These are two factors but it would have been better to have named the factors (i.e., available finance and the need to interface with legacy systems).

Three marks are given here. **(4 marks out of 6)**

Student answer 2

1 (a) The ICT strategy sets out what is required from the ICT resources of the organisation in order to meet the short- and long-term aims of the organisation.

The ICT strategy states in general terms the direction of the ICT developments in the organisation. For example, they may state that in the long term a data warehouse will be set up to which all employees have access.

(b) Business goals, because they determine the overall business aims of the organisation and this in turn determines the ICT which is needed to support them. For example, if an organisation wants to increase the service level to customers by suggesting what other purchases they would like to make based on what they have bought in the past, then the ICT strategy would be to collect and be able to process all customer order details.

Compliance with external legislation. For example, a company might want to sell personal information to other organisations but finds that the Data Protection Act will only allow this to take place with data subjects' permission.

Examiner's comment

1 (a) The two reasons are quite similar but the second reason gives an appropriate example, so this part to the answer is given full marks.

(b) The first part to this answer is good as it shows that the student understands the factor and realises that ICT strategy is written in general rather than detailed terms.

The second part to the answer identifies a correct factor and then goes onto give an example of how it restricts the ICT strategy. Both these answers deserve full marks.
(6 marks out of 6)

Examiner's answer

1   (a)   One mark for each reason which should be different. If the reasons are slightly similar then an example would need to be given in order to get both the marks.
Suitable reasons include:
>   So that the ICT resources in the organisation are properly managed and in a cost-effective way.
>   To ensure that ICT is developed in such a way as to support the general business strategy for the organisation.
>   To ensure that the ICT can meet the business needs of all the users.
>   To ensure that the company remains competitive by ensuring the costs of administration are reduced and productivity is increased.

   (b)   Two factors (two marks each). For two marks there must be further detail or a suitable example. Example factors include:
>   Business goals – the ICT strategy must complement the overall business goals of the organisation (1). ICT is a tool that supports all the core business operations and helps with the management of the business (1).
>   Available finance – the ICT strategy has to be realistic and within the finances of the organisation (1). There is no point in outlining state of the art technology if the budget is unlikely to be sufficient to implement it (1).
>   Legacy systems – sometimes it is necessary to interface new systems with older systems (i.e. legacy systems) and this needs to be stated in the ICT systems strategy (1). Any new systems developed will need to bear this in mind (1).
>   Geography of clients and business fulfilment – if clients are situated all around the world, then communications systems will need to be used (1). The systems developed will need to cope with differences in currencies, time zones, languages, etc. (1).
>   Compliance – organisations that need to exchange data with external organisations need to ensure that their data is compliant with the other organisations' systems (1). They need to ensure that their use of ICT does not breach any of the legislation about ICT such as the Data Protection Act 1998 (1).

Summary mind maps

The factors that influence an ICT system strategy within an organisation

FACTORS AFFECTING ICT SYSTEM STRATEGY

- BUSINESS GOALS
- THE NEED TO INTERFACE WITH LEGACY SYSTEMS
- THE GEOGRAPHY OF CLIENTS AND BUSINESS FULFILMENT
- AVAILABLE FINANCE
- LEGISLATION
- COMPLIANCE

The need for a corporate strategy covering technology for ICT systems in large organisations

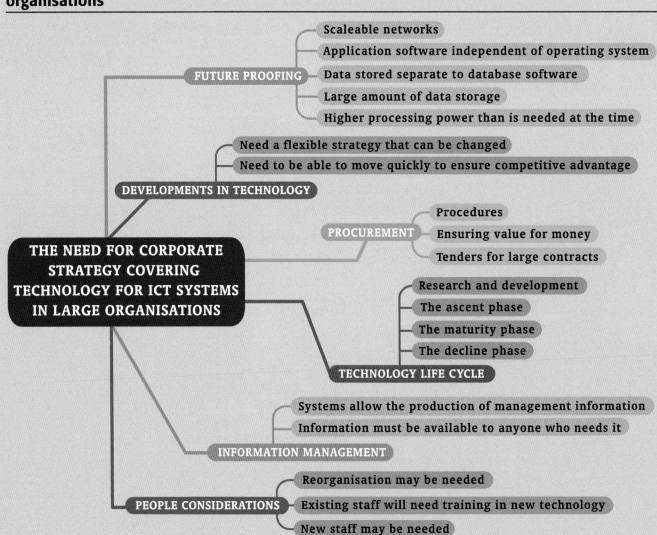

THE NEED FOR CORPORATE STRATEGY COVERING TECHNOLOGY FOR ICT SYSTEMS IN LARGE ORGANISATIONS

- FUTURE PROOFING
  - Scaleable networks
  - Application software independent of operating system
  - Data stored separate to database software
  - Large amount of data storage
  - Higher processing power than is needed at the time
- DEVELOPMENTS IN TECHNOLOGY
  - Need a flexible strategy that can be changed
  - Need to be able to move quickly to ensure competitive advantage
- PROCUREMENT
  - Procedures
  - Ensuring value for money
  - Tenders for large contracts
- TECHNOLOGY LIFE CYCLE
  - Research and development
  - The ascent phase
  - The maturity phase
  - The decline phase
- INFORMATION MANAGEMENT
  - Systems allow the production of management information
  - Information must be available to anyone who needs it
- PEOPLE CONSIDERATIONS
  - Reorganisation may be needed
  - Existing staff will need training in new technology
  - New staff may be needed

TOPIC 5: ICT policies

You briefly looked at ICT policies in Topic 3 on Managing ICT. Having ICT policies in place is essential for all organisations, so in this topic you will be looking at the particular policies and their components in more detail.

▼ The key concepts covered in this topic are:

▶ The reasons why organisations have different policies covering the use of ICT

▶ Security policies

▶ Procurement policies

▶ Training policies

CONTENTS

1 ICT policies **60**
The reasons organisations have different policies covering the use of ICT, security policies, procurement policies and training policies.

2 Questions and Activity **62**

3 Exam support **63**

4 Summary mind maps **65**

Unit 3 Use of ICT in the Digital World

ICT policies

▼ **You will find out**

▶ About the reasons why organisations have different policies covering the use of ICT

▶ About security policies

▶ About procurement policies

▶ About training policies

Introduction

ICT systems need to be developed and used by people. Components of ICT systems such as hardware, software, consumables and services need to be bought from somewhere. ICT policies are put in place by organisations so that staff adopt sensible and legal procedures for the use of ICT within their area of work, and their procurement of goods and services is in the best interests of the organisation.

In this section you will look at the policies that organisations have in order to make the best use of resources and prevent a number of problems that can occur. Policies are only any good if all staff know about them and adhere to them, so training is very important in this area.

The reasons organisations have different policies covering the use of ICT

ICT is such an important resource and lies at the heart of any organisation, so it is necessary to protect this resource and ensure that all staff who use or provide services for it, abide by a set of policies.

Most organisations will have policies covering the following:

- Security – to protect against certain misuses and other threats to ICT systems.
- Procurement – to ensure that the organisation's money is not wasted during the purchase of hardware, software, consumables and services.
- Training – to ensure that all staff use ICT equipment safely, legally, correctly and do not expose ICT systems to threats.

Security policies

ICT systems are vulnerable to all sorts of threats, both internal and external, so security policies are put in place to reduce these threats and ensure that all

staff are able to make the best use of the ICT resources.

Legal issues

The laws applicable to ICT include:

- Data Protection Act 1998
- Copyright, Designs and Patents Act 1988
- Computer Misuse Act 1990.

In all cases involving a breach of the law, legal sanctions may apply.

Passwords and usernames

The granting of access rights to some ICT facilities will be by the provision of username(s) and password(s) giving access to ICT locations, hardware and/or software facilities.

- Passwords must be kept confidential and not disclosed to others.
- Usernames and passwords must not be shared.
- Users having logged in, must not leave ICT facilities unattended and potentially usable by some other person.

Non-institutional use

Only work produced for the organisation can be peformed using the organisation's ICT facilities unless prior senior management permission has been given.

Equipment

- Users are responsible for ensuring they use the ICT facilities safely.
- No equipment should be moved without prior permission.
- No equipment should be connected to the network without permission.
- Facilities may only be borrowed with written permission in the appropriate form from the designated authority or someone with delegated authority.

Use

- Users must not cause damage to the ICT facilities or services.
- Users must adhere to the terms and conditions of all licence agreements relating to ICT facilities which they use including software, equipment, services documentation and other goods.
- Users must not modify any software.
- Users must not load any software onto the ICT facilities without permission from the designated authority.
- Users must not deliberately introduce any virus, worm, Trojan or other harmful or nuisance program or file into any ICT facility.
- Users must not delete or amend the data or data structures of other users without their permission.
- Consumables including stationery must be used for the purpose for which they are supplied and their consumption should be minimised as far as is reasonably possible.
- Users must not interfere with the use by others of the ICT facilities, they must not remove or interfere with output belonging to another user.

Behaviour

- The creation, display, production, downloading or circulation of offensive material in any form or medium is forbidden.
- Users must ensure that the content and tone of their e-mail messages cannot be considered offensive or abusive or of a discriminatory or bullying nature or constituting harassment of any kind.
- Users must take every precaution to avoid damage to equipment caused by eating or drinking in its vicinity.

- Users must respect the rights of others and should conduct themselves in a quiet and orderly manner when using ICT facilities.

Health and safety

- Users must conform with organisational requirements for health and safety.
- Areas must be kept tidy, free from obstruction and fire hazards. Cables should not be allowed to trail over the floor.

Infringement

- Any infringement of these regulations may be subject to penalties under civil or criminal law and such law may be invoked by the institution.
- Any infringement of these regulations constitutes a disciplinary offence under the applicable procedure and may be treated as such regardless of legal proceedings.

Procurement policies

Procurement policies cover the purchasing of ICT hardware, software, consumables and services. Procurement policies are usually divided into the following sections:

- supplier selection
- purchase of hardware
- purchase of software
- purchase of services.

Supplier selection

It is not true that people buy goods or services on price alone. If we did this, we would all drive the same car (i.e., the cheapest model). Suppliers must be chosen so that above a certain value, tenders are used to select the supplier. Tenders for goods or services are sent out to a minimum of three suppliers and the best one is chosen.

Suppliers should be chosen according to the following:

- The financial health, size and stability of the company, e.g. will it still be trading in 18 months? How used is it to dealing in large quantities, etc.?

- The ability/willingness to meet specific delivery requirements. Will they stick to delivery dates?
- The reliability, stability, upgrade-ability, compatibility, maintainability and suitability of the supplier's systems.
- The ability/willingness to provide technical services (e.g., user support, help-desks, maintenance support, response times, warranty, etc.).
- Conformance with all EC and UK health and safety and environmental regulations.

Purchase of hardware

When purchasing hardware it should be shown that:

- The hardware is above a certain minimum specification.
- The hardware has a low total cost of ownership (i.e., the costs of running the equipment should be taken into account and not simply the initial cost of buying the hardware).
- The hardware is capable of running or being used by the current operating system and applications software being used by the organisation at the time.

Purchase of software

When purchasing software it should be shown that:

- There should be an agreement for keeping the software up-to-date and any bugs which are discovered should be corrected.
- The software must be capable of being run by the existing operating system software.
- The software must be a quality product and be thoroughly tested and as far as is possible free from bugs.

Purchase of services

When purchasing services it should be shown that:

- There are penalties on the organisaiton supplying the service if their service falls below a minimum standard.

- A standard contract for the organisation should be used for the supply of services. This means the supplier has to accept our conditions and not the other way around.

Training policies

Well-trained staff are at the heart of any organisation and are the key resource to its success. In order to have a well-trained staff there must be an overall training strategy containing a number of policies that would typically involve the following:

- Every job in the organisation should have a job description – this sets out the key responsibilities and duties and details of the skills and knowledge needed to perform the job. The job description will also stipulate personal attributes for the role. This ensures that people are recruited with a certain minimum competence to carry out the job.
- Staff must be knowledgeable about the existing laws applicable to the use of ICT and, where gaps exist, the staff will attend training appropriate to their role.
- Staff must have an interview with their training manager/department manager to identify training needs at regular intervals (usually yearly).
- Each employee will be given a training plan outlining what further training is needed and any training needed to enhance promotion prospects. Training will be based and booked according to this plan.
- Staff must be trained in all the security policies applicable to their use of the ICT facilities.
- Whenever new ICT systems are introduced staff must receive training that is appropriate to their use of the system. For example, managers would learn more about the management information systems.
- Each member of staff will have a training record that will be kept by the human resources department. Staff will be given an up-to-date copy of this information at regular intervals.

Questions and Activity

▶ Questions 1 | pp. 60–61

1 (a) Give **two** reasons why staff who use ICT facilities in an organisation need to be fully trained. (2 marks)

  (b) Explain **one** way by which the training needs of staff can be identified. (1 mark)

  (c) Describe **two** methods of training which could be used when an organisation introduces new systems. (2 marks)

2 An organisation has an ICT security policy covering issues connected with the secure use of the ICT facilities as well as the security of the data held by them.

  (a) An information security policy will contain procedures needed to protect systems and data. Give **three** such procedures and explain how each helps to protect systems and data. (6 marks)

  (b) Give the names of **two** pieces of legislation that should be mentioned when writing the information security policy. (2 marks)

3 Describe **four** factors that should be considered when writing a training policy. (4 marks)

4 Many organisations have large ICT budgets covering the purchase of hardware, software, consumables and services.

  (a) Give the names of **four** consumables connected with ICT that the organisation is likely to purchase. (2 marks)

  (b) Most organisations have procurement policies. Explain what a procurement policy is and describe **three** procedures it would be likely to contain. (6 marks)

5 Many organisations have an Internet acceptable use policy which outlines those things that employees must not do when using the organisation's computers to access the Internet.
Discuss the reasons for organisations having an Internet acceptable use policy and outline what such a policy is likely to include. (8 marks)

6 Organisations have an overall ICT strategy. They also have many policies applicable to the use of ICT. Explain, by giving a suitable example, the difference between an ICT strategy and ICT policies. (3 marks)

7 Part of the procurement policy for a government department is shown below.
The overall aim of procurement is always to achieve best value for money. That means balancing direct and indirect costs against direct and indirect benefits, not simply appointing the supplier who offers the lowest price. Our aim is to procure the right services or goods:

    to the right quality
    in the right quantity
    at the right price
    for the right time
    for the right place.

  (a) Explain why organisations do not always choose goods and services on price alone. (3 marks)

  (b) Give **two** reasons why organisations have an ICT procurement policy. (2 marks)

▶ Activity Finding out about policies

All organisations should have policies relating to security, training and procurement.

Your task is to investigate the components of each of these policies. You can do research using the Internet or you may choose to find out about the policies for an organisation such as a school, college, or an organisation where you have a part-time job, or where your parents work, etc.

When you have completed your research, you need to outline the main components of each policy and for each one explain the reason why the policy was needed.

Exam support

Worked example 1

1 **Most organisations make use of an ICT security policy.**
   (a) **Give two reasons why organisations need to have an ICT security policy. (2 marks)**
   (b) **Discuss what should be included in an ICT security policy. (8 marks)**

Student answer 1

So that they are protected from all the bad things that can happen to an ICT system.

To ensure all the staff who use the ICT facilities are aware of what they can and cannot do using the facilities and are aware of the sanctions that can apply if they do not obey the instructions.

The following should be included:

- Not to use each other's passwords and usernames.
- Not to leave a terminal logged in when a user is away from the computer.
- To obey with all the laws such as the Data Protection Act, Computer Misuse Act, etc.
- Not to copy company data onto portable media such as flash drives or portable hard drives without permission.
- Not to do your own work using the ICT facilities in the organisation's time.
- To take as much care as possible so that viruses are not introduced into the system.
- Not using copyrighted work for presentations, reports, etc.
- Not disposing of old computers incorrectly.

Examiner's comment

1 (a) The first sentence in this answer is far too general to be awarded a mark.
The second answer is much better as it clearly states a reason and then adds further detail. One mark is given.

(b) The question clearly states discuss and a bulleted list should not have been given here, the answer should have been given as continuous prose.
A 2-mark penalty has been given for this making 6 the maximum available marks for this answer.
This is a good answer notwithstanding the above problem and 8 marks could have been given for the eight points. Only 6 marks are given. **(7 marks out of 10)**

Student answer 2

1 (a) The security policy is needed because staff need to be clear about those policies that will keep the ICT systems secure from unauthorised access.
A security policy will also outline the things users are not allowed to do using the ICT facilties. For example, some organisations forbid the copying of sensitive personal data onto laptops because they tend to be used in public places.

(b) The ICT security policy should outline acceptable use for e-mail, use of the Internet, downloading of material off the Internet, use of computers for an employee's own work and outline steps that need to be taken to protect the ICT facilities.

Users should not use e-mail to send offensive material such as pornographic images or jokes and it should not be used for bullying other employees.

The policy will cover the downloading of material off the Internet as this is one of the ways viruses can enter the organisation's systems.

Downloading copyright material such as programs and music files will be forbidden, as downloading without permission breaches the Copyright, Designs and Patents Act.

There will be policies which cover the use of network facilities and these will detail the need to keep passwords private and will forbid the use of someone else's password.

There will also be a backup and recovery policy which outlines how often backups are taken, how they are taken, where they are kept and the procedures that need to be taken should any of the data be lost.

... Examiner's comment page 64.

Exam support *continued*

Examiner's comment

1 (a) This student has clearly stated two reasons why an ICT security policy is needed. Both marks are given for this answer.

(b) The student has produced some good answers for this part of the question and outlined some of the things that should be included in the policy.

Marks are awared for the statement of a policy. A better structure would have allowed this student to gain more of the eight marks allocated for this part of the question. Students are advised to plan this type of question with headings covering the different areas of the policy as it is hard for students to ensure that they are discussing the issues effectively.

This student has covered the following points:

- e-mail policy
- policies re downloads
- username and password policy
- backup and recovery policy.

These four points give four marks for this part of the answer. **(6 marks out of 10)**

Examiner's answer

1 (a) One mark for each reason, to a maximum of two marks, such as:

To ensure all staff in the organisation are aware of the security issues and to take them seriously (1).

To make sure that the security of hardware, programs and data is not compromised by internal or external threats (1).

To let employees know precisely what they can and cannot do using the organisation's ICT resources (1).

(b) One mark for each separate point with some relevant explanation or futher description up to a maximum of eight marks. The answers should be written in continuous prose and not simply be a bulleted list. If a bulleted list is given then the maximum number of marks for this part of the question should be reduced from 8 marks to 6 marks.

A list of points is given here, but students should give their answer as continuous prose.

E-mail policy – policy towards personal use of e-mail

- monitoring of e-mail for security purposes
- use of e-mail for bullying/harassment.

Password/username – non-disclosure

- forbidding logging on as a different user.

Download policy

- copyright implications
- danger from viruses.

Policy re use of removable storage – not allowing storage onto flash drives/removable hard drives.

Non-institutional use – forbid work being done for outside organisations without permission.

Equipment

- ban movement of equipment without permission
- ban the connection of equipment to the network without permission.

Use – not to cause damage

- obey licensing agreements
- not modify sofware
- not load unauthorised software
- not deliberately introduce viruses
- use consumables wisely
- not interfere with other users' use of the ICT facilities.

Behaviour

- no downloading of or distribution of offensive material
- no bullying or abusive e-mails
- respect the rights of others.

Heath and safety – agree to work according to laws/guidelines.

Summary mind maps

Security policies

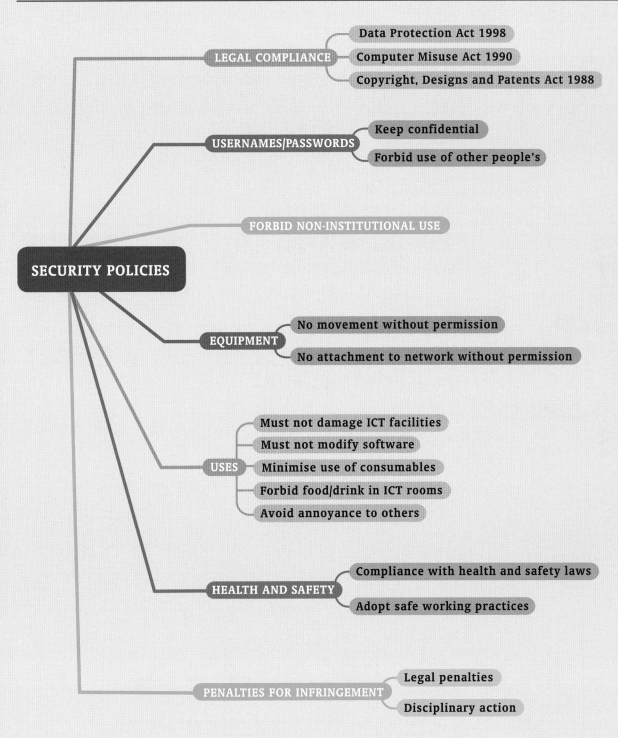

SECURITY POLICIES

LEGAL COMPLIANCE
- Data Protection Act 1998
- Computer Misuse Act 1990
- Copyright, Designs and Patents Act 1988

USERNAMES/PASSWORDS
- Keep confidential
- Forbid use of other people's

FORBID NON-INSTITUTIONAL USE

EQUIPMENT
- No movement without permission
- No attachment to network without permission

USES
- Must not damage ICT facilities
- Must not modify software
- Minimise use of consumables
- Forbid food/drink in ICT rooms
- Avoid annoyance to others

HEALTH AND SAFETY
- Compliance with health and safety laws
- Adopt safe working practices

PENALTIES FOR INFRINGEMENT
- Legal penalties
- Disciplinary action

Procurement policies

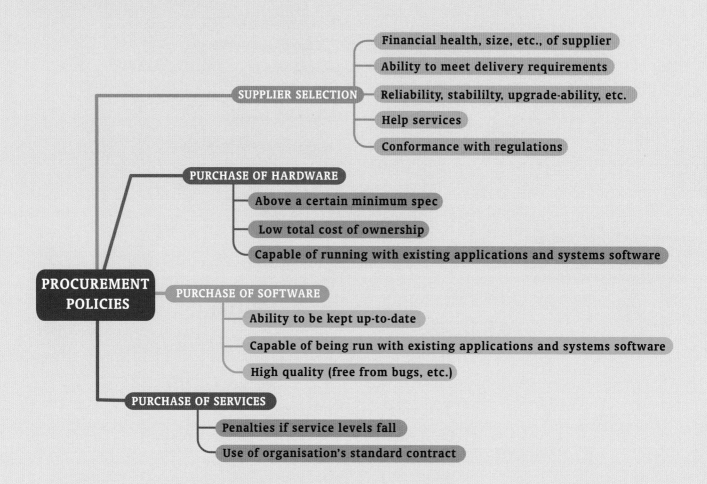

SUPPLIER SELECTION
- Financial health, size, etc., of supplier
- Ability to meet delivery requirements
- Reliability, stabililty, upgrade-ability, etc.
- Help services
- Conformance with regulations

PURCHASE OF HARDWARE
- Above a certain minimum spec
- Low total cost of ownership
- Capable of running with existing applications and systems software

PROCUREMENT POLICIES

PURCHASE OF SOFTWARE
- Ability to be kept up-to-date
- Capable of being run with existing applications and systems software
- High quality (free from bugs, etc.)

PURCHASE OF SERVICES
- Penalties if service levels fall
- Use of organisation's standard contract

Training policies

- JOB DESCRIPTION TO DEFINE SKILLS AND KNOWLEDGE NEEDED
- TRAINING RE LAWS APPLICABLE TO ICT
- INTERVIEW WITH TRAINING MANAGER ANNUALLY

TRAINING POLICIES
- USE OF TRAINING PLAN TO IDENTIFY TRAINING NEEDS
- SECURITY POLICY TRAINING
- TRAINING ON NEWLY INTRODUCED ICT SYSTEMS
- TRAINING RECORDS FOR ALL STAFF

TOPIC 6: Legislation

There is much legislation governing what people can and cannot do using ICT, and organisations must ensure that these laws and regulations are adhered to by their staff. In some cases, organisations can be fined if their staff do things that are against the law even if they did not know about them.

You covered the legislation that applies to ICT as part of your AS studies. In this topic you will learn how organisations must develop ICT policies and procedures to ensure these laws and regulations are not broken.

▼ The key concepts covered in this topic are:

▶ The implications of legislation for ICT policies

▶ How legislation will impact on procedures within an organisation

CONTENTS

1 The implications of legislation for ICT policies and organisational procedures 68
The Copyright Designs and Patents Act 1988, Computer Misuse Act 1990, Data Protection Act 1998, Freedom of Information Act 2000 and Health and Safety at Work Act 1974.

2 Questions and Case study..71

3 Exam support...72

4 Summary mind map..74

Unit 3 Use of ICT in the Digital World

The implications of legislation for ICT policies and organisational procedures

Introduction

Organisations are not free to do what they like using ICT. There are lots of laws which govern what can and cannot be done, and it is important that organisations are aware of all the laws applicable to their particular business and they take suitable steps to ensure that they operate inside these laws.

In this section you will look at the main pieces of legislation and the policies and procedures that need to be put in place to ensure that the organisation is compliant with the legislation.

The implications of legislation for ICT policies

Being compliant with all the pieces of legislation introduced is very difficult for companies. In large organisations someone is appointed to the post of compliance officer to be responsible for this.

ICT policies have to be drawn up to ensure that all proposed developments and all activities involved in day-to-day ICT use are within the law.

The Copyright, Designs and Patents Act 1988

The Copyright, Designs and Patents Act protects intellectual property such as the following from being copied:

- software
- a new innovative human–computer interface
- hardware (e.g., a flexible screen, the design of a power-saving chip, etc.)
- books and manuals
- images on websites.

Organisations are responsible for the acts of their employees, so firms have to be prudent to check there is no unauthorised software on the organisation's computers. They must also check that employees are not illegally downloading music and films and other copyright material.

Organisations must also ensure that they are only running the number of pieces of software as allowed by the licensing agreement. This means that if there is a site licence for 100 users of Microsoft Office, the organisation must ensure that they are not running more than this.

Organisations must ensure their employees are not committing copyright theft.

Policies would need to be laid out to prevent staff from:

- copying images or text without permission
- copying sections of websites without permission
- sharing digital music illegally using peer-to-peer file sharing software
- running more copies of software than is allowed by the site licence
- forcing employees to copy software illegally.

Usually such policies would be laid out in either the ICT code of practice for ICT users or an acceptable use policy.

The Computer Misuse Act 1990

The Computer Misuse Act covers the following:

- deliberately planting or transferring viruses to a computer system to cause damage to programs and data
- using an organisation's computer to carry out unauthorised work
- hacking into someone else's computer system with a view to seeing the information or altering it
- using computers to commit various frauds.

Policies must be in place to help prevent employees from doing such things as well as preventing external risk, and such policies would be included in the ICT code of practice for ICT users or an acceptable use policy. For example, the following preventative measures could be included in the policy:

- A ban on the downloading by staff of any program without the permission in writing of the network manager – this will help prevent the introduction of viruses, Trojans and worms (i.e., mischievous programs).
- A ban on the use of another person's username and password, so that it is always possible to identify the person who has logged on.
- Regular audits to check that money is not going missing into bogus accounts.

The Data Protection Act 1998

The Data Protection Act is used to protect personal data from misuse and in order to comply with the Act, organisations have to adopt a number of policies such as:

- Appointing a senior member of staff to the data controller role. The data controller is the person in the organisation who is responsible for the processing of personal data and who informs the Information Commissioner's Office of details of the data, how it is processed and who it is passed to.
- Notifying the Information Commissioner's Office that the organisation is processing personal data.

- Putting mechanisms in place to enable data subjects (i.e., the people the personal data is about) to be able to see the information held about them and have it corrected if it is wrong. This is called subject access.
- Ensuring data security is not compromised on portable devices such as laptops, PDAs and portable media such as portable hard drives, flash drives, CDs, etc. Usually there will be a policy where all data on portable devices is encrypted.
- Ensuring that all staff understand the data protection principles as laid out in the Data Protection Act 1998. These principles require that data shall be:
  1. fairly and lawfully processed
  2. processed for limited purposes
  3. adequate, relevant and not excessive
  4. accurate
  5. not kept longer than necessary
  6. processed in accordance with the data subjects' rights
  7. secure
  8. not transferred to countries outside the EU without adequate protection.

Several policies will cover the issues raised by the Data Protection Act. For example, the training policy will ensure that all employees who deal with personal data are aware of how they have to deal with personal data.

The security policy will deal with making sure that personal data is kept secure and not compromised by storing on insecure media such as flash memory, or stored on laptops which often get stolen.

The ICT code of practice for ICT users or an acceptable use policy can deal with confidentiality of data and things staff must do when working with personal data.

EXAM TIP

This section of the specification on legislation assumes you have read and thoroughly understood the section on the Safety and Security of ICT systems you covered for AS level. You are advised to look back at this before your examination.

Organisations must have procedures to ensure only authorised access is given to personal data.

> identity matched
> access granted

The implications of legislation for ICT policies and organisational procedures *continued*

The Freedom of Information Act 2000

The Freedom of Information Act covers public authorities such as local councils, hospitals, schools, etc., and using this Act a member of the public can apply for information such as e-mails, research reports, accounts, minutes of meetings, etc. For example, if the planning permission for a new extension was refused, then a person could apply to see all the documents the council used to make their decision.

Public organisations therefore need policies and procedures to provide such information when requested.

The Telecommunications (Lawful Business Practice) (Interception of Communications) Regulations 2000

This Act allows the interception and monitoring of communications in certain circumstances by an organisation without the consent of the sender and the recipient. This is only allowed in certain circumstances which include:

- Keeping transaction logs for the purposes of performance monitoring and quality control. This would include monitoring phone calls to customers for training purposes.
- Access and activity logs maintained to enable investigation or detection of computer misuse or unauthorised use of the systems.
- Monitoring to ensure the effective operation of the systems, for example monitoring for and deleting viruses, checking for and stopping other threats to the system, such as hacking or denial of service attacks and e-mail logs.
- Inspection of file contents to detect misuse.

"Oh, it was just like any other day at work. Except for the part where I sneezed by the paper shredder."

It is therefore possible for organisations to check the e-mails sent by a particular person or the phone calls made by that person. An organisation needs to have policies stating under what circumstances this will happen and they need to make staff aware that such monitoring may take place.

Health and Safety at Work Act 1974

Under the Health and Safety at Work Act 1974, employers have a duty to minimise the risk of injury to employees in the workplace.

The more detailed regulations concerning the use of computers are contained in the Health and Safety (Display Screen Equipment) Regulations 1992.

Health and safety policies must be in place to protect employees and these would include:

- Inspections of chairs, workstations, desks, keyboards and computer screens to ensure they meet the regulations. This must be done on a regular basis.

EXAM TIP

This topic is not simply about the legislation that is applicable to ICT but about the procedures an organisation needs to have in order to comply with the law. You need to read any questions carefully and make sure that you do not simply discuss the laws themselves rather than the policies and procedures.

- Putting in working practices and procedures to allow staff to change tasks in order to reduce repetitive strain injury (RSI).
- Ensuring staff are properly trained to minimise the risk to their health. This training would include ensuring they understand how to adjust their chair and screen, the need for regular breaks, the adjustment of the human–computer interface, etc.
- Paying for eye tests and any glasses needed for those staff that use computer screens.
- Ensuring that any software created is not frustrating or stressful to use.

Questions and Case study

▶ Questions 1   pp. 68–70

1 An organisation stores and processes personal data and transfers this data to other organisations in the UK.
   (a) Give the name of the Act which covers the processing and transfer of personal data. (1 mark)
   (b) A company has a series of policies to make sure they comply with this Act. Describe, by giving suitable examples, policies that the organisation will need to put in place in order to comply with this Act. (6 marks)

2 Describe **two** pieces of legislation applicable to the use of ICT in the workplace and explain how such legislation is likely to impact on the procedures within the organisation. (8 marks)

3 The Computer Misuse Act 1990 is an important piece of legislation that was designed to prevent a number of misuses of ICT systems in the workplace. Describe **two** misuses and explain how an organisation can use procedures and policies to minimise their risk from these misuses. (6 marks)

4 Government departments and local authorities have to comply with requests for information under the Freedom of Information Act 2000. Explain the purpose of this legislation and describe the procedures that would need to be put in place in order to comply with the legislation. (6 marks)

▶ Case study 1   pp. 68–70

The Information Commissioner forces Virgin to encrypt portable devices

A day doesn't seem to go by without an organisation losing a portable device containing personal data on a train, in a café, in a taxi and so on.

Virgin Media, the cable TV, broadband and phone company, was found to be in breach of the Data Protection Act 1998 by the Information Commissioner's Office. This happened because they lost a CD containing the personal details of 3000 of its customers. The data on the CD was not encrypted, which meant anyone finding it could read all the information it contained.

The disk contained the personal details of customers from the Carphone Warehouse who were interested in opening a Virgin Media account and was lost during the transfer between the two.

Virgin Media was ordered by the Information Commissioner's Office to encrypt all portable devices or media used to store personal information. They also ordered any companies processing personal data on behalf of Virgin Media to do the same.

They also stated that this condition must be stated in all contracts.

The Data Protection Act clearly states that information must be kept secure and Virgin Media agreed to take action to ensure that this data loss does not happen again.

1 Give the names of the two Acts that the Information Commissioner oversees. (2 marks)

2 The Data Protection Act 1998 contains eight principles. One of the principles requires that data be kept secure.
   (a) Explain **two** other principles that are part of the Data Protection Act 1998 that organisations need to adhere to. (4 marks)
   (b) It has been argued that organisations will not take the Data Protection Act seriously unless there are actual prosecutions with large fines. Other people argue that the best way forward is to educate organisations and users.
   Give a reasoned argument in favour of the method you think is best. (2 marks)

3 Virgin Media, the firm mentioned in the case study, would need to have new policies in place to ensure that this security breach did not reoccur.
   Outline the policies the firm should put in place. (4 marks)

4 Several policies deal with the issues of the Data Protection Act 1998 in an organisation. Discuss the policies that will deal with the issues and how organisations must put in place procedures to comply with this law. (6 marks)

5 (a) Explain why the growth of portable high capacity storage devices has led to problems with the security of personal data. (3 marks)
   (b) Explain how training will be needed to deal with these problems. (2 marks)

Exam support

Worked example 1

1 ICT policies outline how an ICT strategy would be put into operation.

Part of the ICT strategy for a company states that 'the company will ensure that all its ICT operations comply with all relevant legislation'.

Discuss the policies the company should have in place to ensure compliance with all the relevant legislation applicable to ICT. **(10 marks)**

Student answer 1

1 The policies must ensure that the data is kept safe and that the employees do not disclose it to anyone else.

There must be a purchasing policy which sets out that you should not give orders to your friends.

A security policy will set out what employees can and cannot do with the organisation's data. For example, the employees may not be able to copy this data in case it gets lost and other people find it.

A training policy will set out that all employees will get proper training for their jobs so that they do not make mistakes.

Examiner's comment

1 This answer is poor. For a start the student has failed to understand the question. The answers they have supplied relate to policies but they do not relate to policies that help to ensure compliance with legislation.

When answering this question the student should have thought about the various pieces of legislation that apply to ICT such as the Data Protection Act, the Computer Misuse Act, the Health and Safety at Work Act and the Copyright, Designs and Patents Act and then thought about what organisations have to do to ensure compliance. They could then have put these into the relevant policies such as training, security, procurement, etc.

The answer the student has supplied is worth only the marks for mentioning the names of the three policies. **(3 marks out of 10)**

Student answer 2

1 They should have a training policy that sets out what training is needed in order to comply with the legislation. For example, it would specify the following:

What health and safety training is needed when using computers to ensure that employees understand the dangers and take steps to minimise the risks.

When new systems, hardware or software are introduced into the organisation, the employees are trained in their use. This avoids employee stress.

All employees should have a training plan which will get the best work out of the employees.

They need to make sure they match the employees to the jobs.

The security policy would set out the following:

Rules about the transfer of personal data onto portable media or portable devices such as laptops and PDAs in order to ensure that personal data is not lost or accessed by others.

Keeping personal data private is a requirement under the Data Protection Act.

Rules forbidding the employees from illegally downloading or copying programs and data against the terms of the Copyright, Designs and Patents Act.

Rules forbidding the employees doing work for someone else when they are supposed to be doing company work. This contravenes the Computer Misuse Act.

Examiner's comment

1 The student has produced some good answers but at stages they have drifted off into answers about training or security in general, forgetting that the question wanted to know about policies which helped with compliance with legislation. Luckily the student has produced many other good answers to compensate for this.

It is important to be able to cite the name of the legislation to which the particular policy applies and this student has done this in some of their answers.

The student has mentioned a training policy and a security policy so two marks for these and there are over nine points made here which could be awarded marks so this student gains full marks. **(10 marks out of 10)**

Examiner's answer

1 One mark for the name of each relevant policy such as:

    Training policy
    Security policy
    Internet acceptable use policy
    Privacy policy.

One mark for each point about the policy relevant to compliance with legislation.

One mark for further explanation of the point or a mention of the specific legislation to which it applies. Examples of points for which marks are awarded include:

Check to make sure that the number of allowed users as per the licence for software is not being exceeded (1).

Regular checks to make sure users do not have any unauthorised software loaded on their computers (1)

Training the employees to use ICT equipment safely and forcing them to adopt safe working practices by incorporating it into their code of conduct (1).

Monitoring the Internet sites employees visit to ensure they are not downloading illegal images (1).

Ensuring staff responsible for the procurement of goods or services do not buy fake goods such as illegal copies of software (1).

Ensuring that all information about products and services advertised on the organisation's website is true (1) and thus complies with the Trade Descriptions Act (1).

Ensuring that employees cannot transfer personal data onto portable devices, which compromises the privacy of the data held, through the use of devices to prevent removable media being inserted (1) – for example, you can get devices that do not allow CD/DVD drives or USB ports to be accessed thus preventing unauthorised copying of data (1).

Rules forbidding the employees doing work for someone else when they are supposed to be doing company work (1). This contravenes the Computer Misuse Act (1).

To ensure software includes suitable auditing so that transactions can be tracked and individuals involved in the transactions can be traced in case there are discrepancies (1).

Ensuring that personal data is only ever processed in line with the description of the processing given to the Information Commissioner (1) as a requirement of the Data Protection Act 1998 (1).

To ensure that the subjects of personal data can access the data about them and have it corrected if it is wrong (1). This is a requirement under the Data Protection Act 1998 (1).

To use controls on the network to restrict the number of users of a particular piece of software so that the users are within the licensing allowance (1).

To ensure that information is given to outside people or organisations under the Freedom of Information Act (1).

Summary mind map

The implications of legislation on ICT policies and organisational procedures

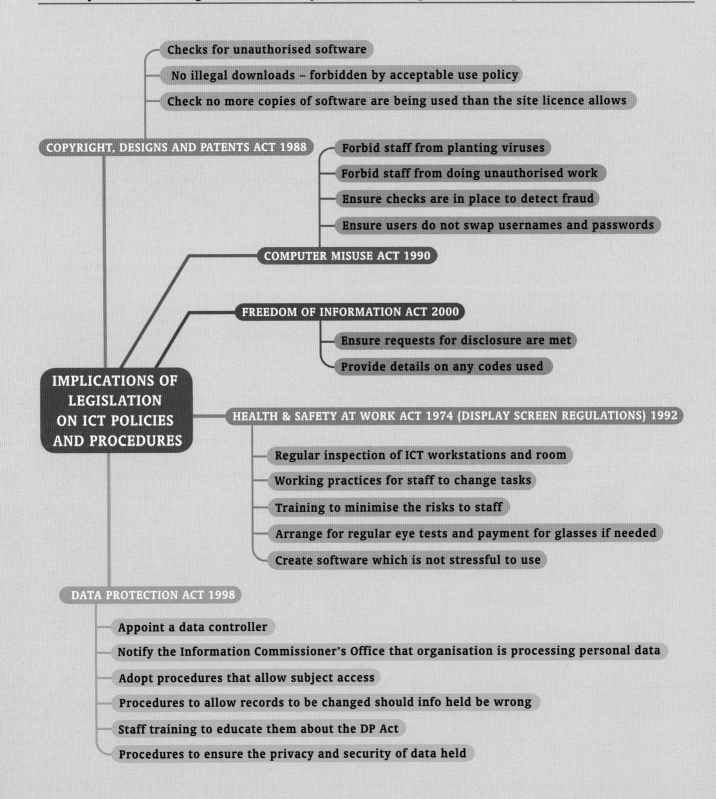

Checks for unauthorised software

No illegal downloads – forbidden by acceptable use policy

Check no more copies of software are being used than the site licence allows

COPYRIGHT, DESIGNS AND PATENTS ACT 1988

Forbid staff from planting viruses

Forbid staff from doing unauthorised work

Ensure checks are in place to detect fraud

Ensure users do not swap usernames and passwords

COMPUTER MISUSE ACT 1990

FREEDOM OF INFORMATION ACT 2000

Ensure requests for disclosure are met

Provide details on any codes used

IMPLICATIONS OF LEGISLATION ON ICT POLICIES AND PROCEDURES

HEALTH & SAFETY AT WORK ACT 1974 (DISPLAY SCREEN REGULATIONS) 1992

Regular inspection of ICT workstations and room

Working practices for staff to change tasks

Training to minimise the risks to staff

Arrange for regular eye tests and payment for glasses if needed

Create software which is not stressful to use

DATA PROTECTION ACT 1998

Appoint a data controller

Notify the Information Commissioner's Office that organisation is processing personal data

Adopt procedures that allow subject access

Procedures to allow records to be changed should info held be wrong

Staff training to educate them about the DP Act

Procedures to ensure the privacy and security of data held

TOPIC 7: Developing ICT solutions

Many ICT systems are not successful in either giving the end-user what they want or producing a working system at all. In some cases, the project goes out of control with the costs escalating and the progress of the project falling behind. Lack of project control can occur for a number of reasons: key personnel can leave; managers do not keep a grip on the schedules and costs and so on. In this topic you will look at what makes ICT projects successful or unsuccessful.

▼ The key concepts covered in this topic are:

▶ Factors that contribute to a successful development process

▶ Factors during the development process that might contribute to the failure of a newly introduced system

CONTENTS

1 Factors that contribute to a successful development process..**76**
Management and end-user involvement at appropriate times and effective teamwork.

2 Factors that might contribute to the failure of a newly introduced system...........................**78**
Factors which can lead to a poor ICT system.

3 Questions, Case study and Activity...**80**

4 Exam support..**82**

5 Summary mind maps..**83**

Unit 3 Use of ICT in the Digital World

Factors that contribute to a successful development process

▼ **You will find out**

▶ About the factors that contribute to a successful development process

Introduction

If they are to be successful, ICT projects require careful management by being produced on-time and within the allocated budget and producing all the hoped for business benefits. Unfortunately, for many reasons, projects can go out of control in a variety of ways. In this section you will be looking at those factors that will contribute to a successful development process.

Management and end-user involvement at appropriate times

ICT projects usually have a project sponsor who will be a senior manager or a group of managers who have asked for a problem to be solved using ICT. The project sponsors are the people the ICT staff, who are developing the project, report to and they will have extensive knowledge of the business area the project affects.

These managers, the project sponsors, will be able to give the ICT staff developing the project information about all aspects of both the existing system (if one exists) and the proposed new system. This information will include what the system must be capable of doing.

In addition to this the project sponsor will need to set up:

- a budget for the project
- a timescale for the project.

Project sponsors must take an active role during the development to ensure that the above two items are not exceeded.

End-users, the people who will be using the ICT system on a day-to-day basis, will also need to be consulted at all stages throughout the project. It is these people who know about their part of the business in depth and they can give useful input to the development team on how things should ideally be done. If there are shortcomings in the system, then the end-users would find the system frustrating to use.

Here are some of the ways management and end-user involvement helps:

- They can be clear about the objectives for the project, the scope of the project and the project requirements before the project is started.
- They can agree a budget and timescale for the project.
- They can agree on milestones and deliverables (see next section for further details).
- They can be consulted during the analysis phase so the development team fully understand the area of the business being analysed.
- They can check that the system will supply management information as well as deal with the day-to-day transactions.
- The project managers and other business managers involved in the areas of the project can be consulted on how things work,

Teamwork is essential for an ICT project's success.

the design of user interfaces, the content of reports from the system and so on.

- The project sponsor can be present at progress meetings to check that the budget and timescales are not likely to be exceeded.
- They can ensure that the development team are producing the system they actually need rather than the system the development team think they need.

Effective ICT teamwork

Many ICT projects are large and cannot be completed by one person in a reasonable time, so instead they are completed by a project team.

Each member of the team is allocated a proportion of the overall task. In many ways, working as a team member is harder than working individually, since you may have to work closely with someone who you do not necessarily get on with. Another problem causing friction between team members is the unequal division of the work. Some team members may have to work much harder than others. Other team members may start to work as individuals and the whole project becomes very difficult to manage. Without careful monitoring and control the project can go wildly out of control and end up having to be abandoned due to spiralling costs and lateness.

For a project team to work together harmoniously, the team needs to reach a consensus on the overall aims and goals of the project. The team members should agree on a certain solution to the problem and stick to it. If the project involves a customer, then consensus should also be obtained from them, and the customer should be involved throughout the whole project. A customer who is kept informed in this way is less likely to be disappointed, and have less cause for complaint if the new system does not match their expectations.

A summary of the reasons for working in a team

The main reasons for adopting a team approach for solving ICT problems are outlined here:

- Many ICT tasks or projects are far too big to be performed by a single person.
- A team brings together people with expertise in different areas.
- Members of the team are able to 'bounce' ideas off each other and this can produce better solutions to ICT problems.
- Effective teams can produce work which is far superior to that which could be produced by individual members of the team.

There are some other factors that lead to the development and subsequent implementation of a successful information system and these are as follows.

Clear timescales

Projects will tend to take any amount of time given to them, so it is important at the outset to agree on the time allocated to the parts or tasks that make up the whole project. Once these small tasks have a timescale it is easy to work out manually or by using project management software, how long the overall task will take.

Milestones can be used whereby parts of the project must be completed by certain dates. The project manager will review the project from time to time and if the timescales of some of the tasks start to drift then remedial action can be taken to put the project back on course again.

Deliverables

Deliverables are those smaller tasks that together make up the project. Deliverables are agreed by the project team in advance and when they are completed, the team will meet with the users or the project sponsor to sign off these deliverables. This means that that particular task had been completed successfully.

Before the project is started, the team will need to agree between themselves and with the users or project sponsor what these deliverables are.

"Before I begin, I'd just like to make it known that I didn't volunteer to do this presentation."

> **KEY WORDS**
>
> **Milestones** – points in a project that mark the ends of logical stages in the project where the project is reviewed or part of the project is delivered
>
> **Deliverables** – parts of the project that are completed and signed off as being acceptable by the client/ project sponsor

Factors that might contribute to the failure of a newly introduced system

▼ **You will find out**

▶ About factors during the development process that might contribute to the failure of a newly introduced system

Introduction

Unfortunately many projects do not deliver what they are supposed to or they are late or wildly over budget. There are many examples of projects which were started but abandoned because they went out of control and the costs escalated thus wasting money.

Factors which can lead to a poor ICT system

Factors which can lead to a poor ICT system include the following.

Formal methods are important for development of a system.

Complexity of the system

Systems need to be complex enough to be able to deal with the detail some managers will require from the system but not too complex from a usability point of view. MIS need to be simple to use so that all managers are capable of using them in their day-to-day work.

Some ICT systems are very complex.

Lack of formal methods

There are many different ways in which a system can be developed and each method is called a methodology. What all these methodologies have in common is that the system is developed in a formal way. This avoids systems analysts taking short cuts and ending up developing a less than perfect system. Proper systems analysis does take time and effort but the resulting MIS is much better than MIS developed using less formal methods.

Inadequate initial analysis

If the initial analysis is done by someone inexperienced, they might not appreciate the need to fully analyse the information requirements of management. Such an analysis will be based on incomplete information and will never produce a flexible and fully functional ICT system. Inadequate analysis usually manifests itself when the system is unable to perform a key task or the system does not behave in a manner that is consistent with the original objectives.

Lack of management/user involvement in the design

ICT specialists usually take charge of the development of the information system, since they have the knowledge about how to perform a rigorous systems analysis, although their actual business knowledge about the areas they are looking at may be much weaker than the managers who are in charge of these areas. It is therefore important that these managers should be part of the development team and that there is constant consultation between them and the developers of the system. The result of this involvement should be a technically good system solving the managers' needs.

Inappropriate hardware and software

Hardware issues such as the speed of the file server, the speed of data transfer all affect the speed at which information can be extracted from all the data held. If the system is too slow then managers will only use the system when absolutely necessary.

The software should make it easy for managers to construct conditions for the extraction of the information they need and they should be able to choose how the information is presented.

Lack of management knowledge about ICT systems and their capabilities

Management may not be aware of the latest developments in ICT and they usually place their trust in ICT specialists, who they assume will have the latest knowledge. However, the ICT specialists cannot possibly be experts in all parts of the business, so management will also be expected to keep up-to-date with the latest developments in their particular area of management. For example, the personnel manager will probably subscribe to professional magazines and in these there will occasionally be articles on the latest developments in this area and many of these will involve the use of ICT. Management should go on training courses to equip them with the skills in extracting management information and teach them the value of having this information.

Poor communications between professionals

Managers and ICT professionals should work together to produce a management information system that meets the demands of the managers who will be using the system. Poor communication between managers and ICT staff may result in a system that does not meet the needs of the managers. Such systems may not extract the information needed, or may be cumbersome to use, which discourages managers from using them.

Lack of professional standards

The British Computer Society (BCS) sets minimum standards of practice to be observed by all its members. Many ICT professionals are members of the society and membership shows the employer or the person paying for their services, that the job will be performed in a professional manner. Not all computer

"This is a major project of utmost importance, but it has no budget, no guidelines, no support staff, and it's due in 15 minutes. At last, here's your chance to really impress everyone!"

professionals are members of the society and so do not have to conform to their standards. Some computer professionals are motivated by their own career progression and everything they do has this aim in the background. For example, if they need experience in a certain new area of computing, such as in the use of intranets, they may then try to persuade their organisation to get one regardless of whether one is needed, simply so that they can put that they have had experience of using one on their CV. Some 'computer professionals', especially those engaged in contract work, may take on jobs for which they have little experience in the hope that they will 'get the hang of it' once they start work.

Losing control of the project plan

Before a project is started there will be a project plan which will set out the following:

- a budget (i.e. an amount of money set aside for the project)
- the staff who will work on the project
- which parts of the project they will work on
- deliverables (what needs to be produced by certain dates)
- dates for completion of the deliverables (called milestones)
- a date for completion of the overall project.

It is very easy to lose control of one or more of these and in most cases losing control of one of these causes the loss of control of other factors. For example, if key staff leave half-way through the project, then it may be difficult to recruit new staff and this takes time, which will cause a delay in the project. The organisation may be forced to take on expensive contract workers, which could cause the project to go over budget.

"It took us five days to figure out how to finish our project two days early. That's why we're three days late."

Questions, Case study and Activity

▶ Questions 1 | pp. 76–79

1 Explain why it is important that the end-user of a new ICT system is consulted at various stages during its development. (4 marks)

2 Many IT projects are started and never completed.
   (a) What are the main reasons why this happens? (3 marks)
   (b) Explain what is meant by the following:
      Deliverables (2 marks)
      Milestones. (2 marks)

3 Explain why effective ICT teamwork is essential to the development of a successful project. (6 marks)

4 State **two** factors that contribute to a successful ICT development project.
   Explain, by giving suitable examples, why each factor is important. (6 marks)

5 There are many examples of unsuccessful ICT projects and many of them waste huge amounts of money or do not work properly when introduced.
   Explain **two** factors during the development process that might contribute to the failure of a newly introduced system. (4 marks)

▶ Case study 1 | pp. 76–79

A project out of control

This true scenario, outlining the problems with a huge IT project, highlights many of the things which can go wrong and it also looks at what could have been done to put them right.

   The project was a new air traffic control system. Even on starting the system, it was four years late! The system made use of large computers that had been used for an air traffic control system in the United States. The software for the new system was being developed from scratch and is currently running at two million lines of code even though the American system, which copes with a similar volume of air traffic, uses only one million lines of code. At one time the programs contained an estimated 21,000 bugs and there were also scalability issues. These scalability issues meant that although the software worked when it was being used with a relatively small number of terminals (about 30), as soon as the number was increased, the system started to fail. The operational air traffic controllers who eventually had to use the system on a day-to-day basis were shown the system at a very late stage (i.e., almost when the project was complete). These important end-users

should have been consulted at a much earlier stage and this would have meant fewer changes needing to be made to the system that increased costs and further delayed the project.

   The whole system showed the early signs of a project out of control. These signs included:

- Delays in the delivery of the system means that the hardware and software is now seven years out-of-date and there is the danger of replacing one out-of-date system with another.
- Consulting the end-users at such a late stage means that software had to be changed to take account of their views.
- Deadlines previously set were not met and new revised deadlines were agreed. These revised deadlines have also been missed.
- The people who were eventually going to use the system had no confidence in it.
- There was strong resistance by the project team to an independent audit to determine whether the project was being properly and adequately controlled.

Case study 1 (continued) pp. 76–79

1 Explain what is meant by the terms 'milestones' and 'deliverables' in the context of ICT project management and explain why it is important to have them. (3 marks)

2 End-users should be consulted about the new system at all stages of the ICT project. Explain, by giving a suitable example, why this is so. (3 marks)

3 Poorly managed projects can go wildly out of control and cause a project to be unsuccessful. Discuss the factors by which the development of a project can be deemed a success. (6 marks)

4 In the case study it mentioned that 'the people who were eventually going to use the system had no confidence in it'. Describe what could have been done to make sure that the end-users had confidence in the new system. (8 marks)

5 Describe **three** factors during the development process that might contribute to the failure of a newly introduced system. (6 marks)

▶ Activity Produce an essay entitled 'ICT projects out of control'

Projects that go drastically wrong are always of interest to computing professionals as they are able to learn by the mistakes of others. Occasionally, the projects are so disastrous that they are even newsworthy enough to reach the national newspapers.

By using the websites of the main national newspapers and the computer press such as Computing or Computer Weekly, identify some interesting stories where projects went seriously out of control. Using at least **three** of these stories, produce an essay explaining the facts surrounding each case. You need to identify the reasons the projects went wrong and also explain where you got the information from in the form of a bibliography at the end of the essay.

This essay is a substantial piece of work and should go through several versions before the final version is produced. Your essay should be word-processed, spell checked and grammar checked. It should also contain headers and footers on each page containing your name, your group, the date, the title of the essay and the page numbers on each page.

Exam support

Worked example 1

1 A new ICT system can fail because of a lack of teamwork during its development.
  Describe **three** other factors that might cause the ICT system to be unsuccessful. **(6 marks)**

Student answer 1

1 People not working properly together – people refusing to work with each other cause communication problems which means important information about the project is not passed on.
  The developers not keeping users and managers involved in the project – this means that the solution does not completely do what it was supposed to do.
  Losing control of the project plan – not keeping an eye on the costs has meant that the whole project has gone well over budget.

Examiner's comment

1 The student has not read the question carefully because the question wants factors other than teamwork. No marks for this first answer.
  The second factor is correct and further amplification is included so this is worth two marks.
  The final answer is good and worth two marks. **(4 marks out of 6)**

Student answer 2

1 There may be situations that happen unexpectedly, such as staff involved in the project being ill, staff leaving and staff getting promoted to other jobs, etc.
  There may have been insufficient analysis during the analysis stage and this will mean that the developed solution does not meet all of the needs of the users.
  Staff leaving might mean that contract staff or staff from a company outside need to be brought in, resulting in the costs increasing beyond what was originally thought.

Examiner's comment

1 For the first point the student should have mentioned how this would affect the project or in what way it would make the project unsuccessful. Only one mark is given here.
  The second point identifies the factor (i.e., insufficient analysis) and explains further how this results in an unsuccessful project. This is worth two marks.
  The third point has to some extent been covered in the first answer. Students often do this and they need to ensure that their answers are distinctly different.
  One mark is given for the part about the rising costs. **(4 marks out of 6)**

Examiner's answers

1 One mark for one factor and one mark for an example or further description of the factor × 3.
  Lack of management/end-user involvement at the appropriate time (1), resulting in a system that is incapable of performing what users/managers require (1).
  Inadequate analysis (1) because there was not enough consultation, involvement and approval during this stage (1).
  Lack of management knowledge of ICT and what it can do (1) resulting in managers having unrealistic expectations of the new system (1).
  Loss of control of the project plan (1) which means the project costs rise and the project is late or has to be abandoned (1).
  Lack of communication between the developers and the users/managers (1) meaning that the system has been built with little consultation and cannot do what users or managers hoped (1).
  Lack of professional standards (1) meaning the system is hard to maintain or update in the future (1).

Summary mind maps

Factors that contribute to a successful development process

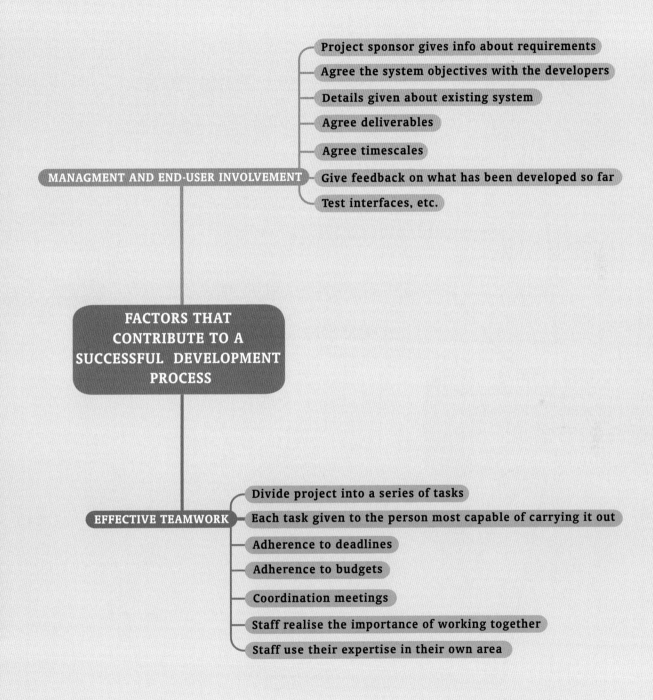

MANAGMENT AND END-USER INVOLVEMENT

- Project sponsor gives info about requirements
- Agree the system objectives with the developers
- Details given about existing system
- Agree deliverables
- Agree timescales
- Give feedback on what has been developed so far
- Test interfaces, etc.

FACTORS THAT CONTRIBUTE TO A SUCCESSFUL DEVELOPMENT PROCESS

EFFECTIVE TEAMWORK

- Divide project into a series of tasks
- Each task given to the person most capable of carrying it out
- Adherence to deadlines
- Adherence to budgets
- Coordination meetings
- Staff realise the importance of working together
- Staff use their expertise in their own area

Factors that might contribute to the failure of a newly introduced system

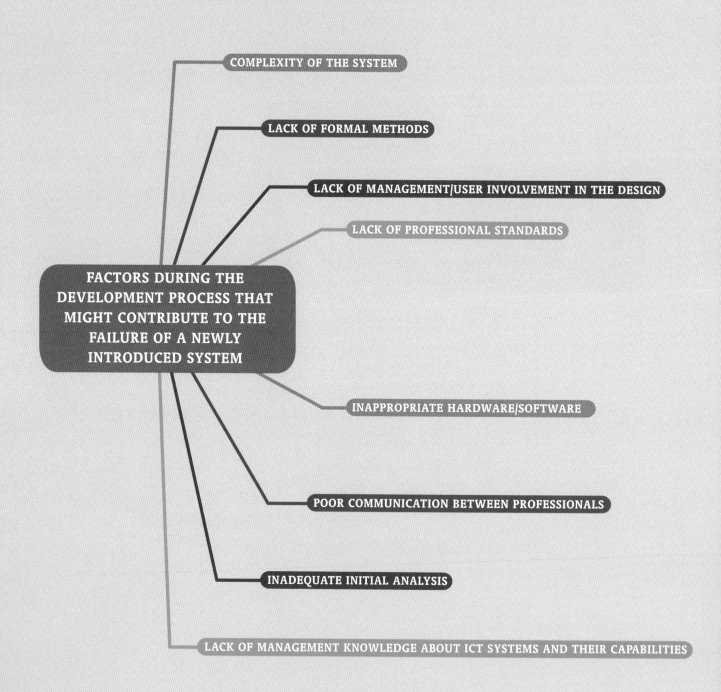

COMPLEXITY OF THE SYSTEM

LACK OF FORMAL METHODS

LACK OF MANAGEMENT/USER INVOLVEMENT IN THE DESIGN

LACK OF PROFESSIONAL STANDARDS

FACTORS DURING THE DEVELOPMENT PROCESS THAT MIGHT CONTRIBUTE TO THE FAILURE OF A NEWLY INTRODUCED SYSTEM

INAPPROPRIATE HARDWARE/SOFTWARE

POOR COMMUNICATION BETWEEN PROFESSIONALS

INADEQUATE INITIAL ANALYSIS

LACK OF MANAGEMENT KNOWLEDGE ABOUT ICT SYSTEMS AND THEIR CAPABILITIES

TOPIC 8: Development methods

If systems are to live up to expectations, they need to be developed in a formal manner. The systems development life cycle is a series of steps that are taken when developing a new system or altering an existing system.

In this topic you will learn about the steps involved in the systems development life cycle and how they are applied to the development of a new computerised system.

▼ The key concepts covered in this topic are:

▶ Systems development life cycle

▶ The stages of development

▶ The need for systematic, formal methods

▶ Development methodologies

CONTENTS

1 The systems development life cycle 86
System investigation/feasibility, analysis of the problem and proposed solution, design and specification of the solution, build/constructing the solution, testing, installation and conversion, and review and maintenance.

2 The need for systematic, formal methods 90
Reasons why systematic, formal methods are needed, project management and the steps involved in project management.

3 Development methodologies 92
The waterfall method – a linear method and iterative methodologies.

4 Questions, Activity and Case studies 94

5 Exam support 96

6 Summary mind map 98

Unit 3 Use of ICT in the Digital World

The systems development life cycle

▼ You will find out

▶ About the systems development life cycle (SDLC)

▶ About system investigation/feasibility

▶ About analysis of the problem and proposed solution

▶ About design and specification of the solution

▶ About build/constructing the solution

▶ About testing

▶ About installation and conversion

▶ About review and maintenance

Introduction

The systems development life cycle (SDLC) is a sequence of activities which are performed when a system is analysed, designed and implemented. Look at the following diagram and you will notice that it is cyclic. This is because once the system has been completed and is working, it is usual to periodically look at what improvements can be made to the system. This results in the activities shown in the diagram being repeated.

System investigation/ feasibility

System investigation starts with identifying the problem that needs to be solved using ICT and then stating what the problem is in clear terms by writing a project definition. Projects are normally started at a strategic level in an organisation because of the high level of expense and risk associated with many projects. Included in the project definition will be the stated aims and objectives of the new system.

Aims and objectives for new ICT systems might include the following:

- automating much of the ordering process thus allowing staff involved in this to work on more customer service oriented roles thereby increasing sales
- being able to accurately predict delivery dates for customer orders
- reducing the number of input errors
- reducing the number of part deliveries by having a much more efficient and accurate stock control system
- improving management information, enabling department managers to make more accurate and timely decisions.

Feasibility is an initial investigation to look at the likelihood of being able to create a new system with stated aims and objectives at reasonable cost. The results of this exercise are summarised in a document called a feasibility report and it is this document that is used by senior managers/directors to assess a project's feasibility. Once the feasibility has been assessed, the project can either go ahead or be abandoned.

Feasibility is an important activity because it makes sure that new systems are not developed that have little chance of success. There are many examples of new systems being abandoned after a significant amount

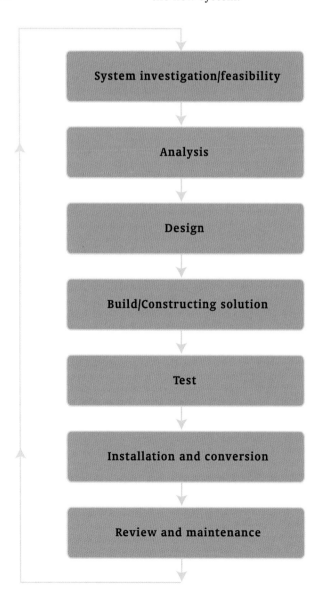

Systems development life cycle.

> **KEY WORDS**

User testing – a series of methods for testing an ICT system by collecting data from people who are actually using the system

of work has been done on them and you will read about some of them later on in the case studies.

Feasibility will normally involve the following:

- an initial fact find which will give information on what is required from the project
- an investigation into the technical, legal, economic, operational and schedule implications
- identifying the costs and benefits for the new system and weighing them against each other
- making recommendations as to the feasibility of the project
- a draft plan for the implementation of the project.

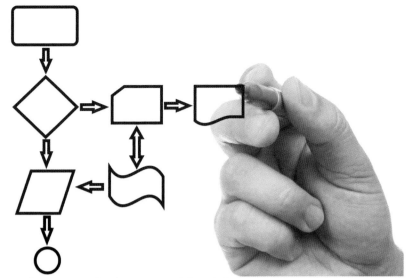

Systems diagrams can be drawn to explain existing systems.

Previous system documentation can be a useful source of information.

Feasibility weighs up the cost of the new system against the benefits it brings.

Analysis of the problem and proposed solution

Analysis looks in detail at the current system or the requirements for a task that has never been performed before. The person performing the analysis, called a systems analyst (or just analyst for short), investigates the requirements for the new system.

Analysis will normally involve the following:

- understanding the existing system
- understanding the proposed system if there is no existing system
- gathering and analysing different user requirements
- setting out the solution in a logical way using tools and techniques such as data flow diagrams, data models, process specifications and systems diagrams (this is called logical design)
- producing a logical specification.

Design and specification of the solution

To complete the design stage, the systems analyst will start to produce a design and specification that will enable the system to actually be built in the next phase.

Design and specification will normally involve the following:

- designing the system in line with the user requirements
- creating the design specification for hardware, software, telecommunications, databases, personnel and procedures that will enable the useable system to be built.

Topic 8 Development methods

Build/constructing the solution

This is the stage where the system is actually built according to the design produced in the previous stage. All the different staff in the project team will bring their particular expertise to the project and work together to produce the working system.

Build will normally involve the following:

- staff using the physical design produced in the previous stage to produce a working system
- programmers writing any programming code needed for the working solution
- customising a software package to tailor it to the needs of the organisation
- producing the framework needed for databases
- using software tools to produce the working version
- modifying existing software
- producing the working system according to the user requirements.

Testing

Most ICT projects involve lots of different people working on different aspects of the system. Each person in the team will be responsible for their own part of the project and they will have to test what they have done to make sure it works.

Testing will normally involve the following:

- testing at very detailed levels (i.e., individuals will thoroughly test their part)
- testing at a higher level (i.e., when the various parts of the system are joined together)
- testing at a systems level (where all the parts are tested as a whole system)
- testing each field using correct, erroneous and extreme data
- testing the system with real-life data.

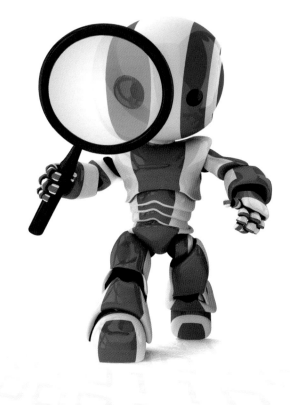

Testing is performed at a number of different levels.

There are a number of different parts to the testing process and they are as follows:

- **Functional testing** – checks that the system being developed meets both the system and business requirements. It involves checking the validity of formulas and calculations as well as testing that the user interface works as it should.
- **System testing** – once any software used by the system has been tested, the whole system can then be tested. System testing is testing using certain hardware, users and environment which match the system being used in the real-life situation.
- **Operational testing** – is testing performed by the end-user on software which is being used in its normal operating environment. It is sometimes hard to test a system in the environment where it is normally used. For example, it is quite hard to

operationally test a website where lots of users are using the website during a particularly busy period such as during a sale. You would normally want to find out beforehand whether the site might fail, so action can be taken to prevent it happening.
- **User testing** – allows teams of users to test the software or system. Websites should always be tested by users who will look for such things as ease of use, consistency of design, links that do not work, use of language, choice of graphics and so on. Other systems can be tested by observing people using the system to see how easy or not they find it to complete a task. It is useful to ask the them to give a running commentary and their thoughts as they are using the system. Another way would be to design a questionnaire for the users to answer.

Installation and conversion

This is the stage where the completed and fully tested system is installed on operational equipment for real-life use. Implementation will normally involve the following:

- installing hardware
- installing software on operational hardware (NB systems are often developed on equipment not used for operations on a day-to-day basis for security reasons)
- conversion of previous data that can be used
- training of all users of the system
- production of documentation and training guides to help people understand the system.

The help-desk is an important aspect of review and maintenance.

Installation of hardware can be very complex for large networks.

Review and maintenance

The review and maintenance stage normally takes place a few weeks after the installation and conversion stage as it is only then that users and others involved in the development of the system will find out about any problems or shortcomings.

Review and maintenance will normally involve the following:

- checking that the original user requirements and performance criteria have been fully met by the new system
- assessment of how happy the clients are with the development of the new system
- setting up a review cycle so that the system is checked periodically to make sure that it is still meeting requirements
- setting up help-desk facilities to help users who experience problems with the new system.

Once developed, systems cannot be left until a new system is developed to replace them. Changes in the way the business or organisation operates will need alterations in the system. Programs may need to be written or altered. For example, the rate of VAT could change, or changes in income tax could trigger the need for changes.

Maintenance will normally involve the following:

- extra functions which need to be added to the existing system are identified at the review meetings
- maintenance teams will alter existing programs or create additional ones
- any operational issues such as poor performance or software bugs will be identified at the review meetings and corrected by the appropriate staff
- any system crashes to be investigated to find out the reasons for their occurrence
- managing interfaces with other systems, such as Internet, e-mail and intranets.

One task when implementing a solution is the installation of software.

The need for systematic, formal methods

▼ **You will find out**

▶ About project management

▶ About agreed deliverables

▶ About milestones

▶ About sign-off and approval to proceed

Introduction

You could just sit down and create a system without any proper analysis and design, but unless the system was very simple it would not be very good. Experience has taught us that systems are complex and need to be developed in a systematic and formal manner. This is why the systems development life cycle is used.

In this section you will learn about project management and the methods used to try to ensure that projects are completed on time.

Reasons why systematic, formal methods are needed

Once thorough analysis has taken place the developer (or systems analyst) will need to draw up a systems specification in consultation with the managers and users. In this the managers outline details of their needs from the new ICT system.

There may be a tendency to develop an information system informally without using the various steps as outlined in the systems development life cycle, but this should be resisted as the use of formal methods always leads to a much better system.

Project management

When a project is undertaken there will be a person with overall responsibility for the project who is called the project manager. The project manager is the person who is in charge of the development teams and they are ultimately responsible if things go wrong with the project.

The project manager will have some tools and techniques which will ensure that the project stays on track and runs smoothly. The project manager will first start off with a project plan which clearly shows what will be delivered

and when. They will also be given a budget for the project that will have to be adhered to. The project sponsor, the person usually at director level who has asked for the development of the project, will regard the project as a success if it:

- matches all the user requirements exactly
- is completed on-time
- does not go over budget.

There are some other factors that lead to the development and subsequent implementation of an ICT system and these are as follows.

Clear timescale

Projects will tend to take any amount of time given to them, so it is important at the outset to agree on the time allocated to the parts or tasks that make up the whole project. Once these small tasks have a timescale it is easy to work out manually or by using project management software how long the overall project will take.

Milestones

Milestones can be used whereby parts of the project must be completed by certain dates. The project manager will review the project from time to time and if the timescale of some of the tasks start to drift then remedial action can be taken to put the project back on course again.

Agreed deliverables

Deliverables are those smaller tasks that together make up the project. Deliverables are agreed in advance by the project team and when they are completed, the team will meet with the users or the project sponsor to sign off these deliverables. This means that that particular task had been completed successfully. Before the project is started, the team will need

to agree between themselves and with the users or project sponsor what these deliverables are.

Approval to proceed

Most projects have a project sponsor who is a senior manager or director of the organisation and who will be in charge of the project. To get approval to proceed, the project team will prepare a feasibility study to look at the costs of the system and the benefits to be obtained from it. The feasibility report is a formal document outlining the results and conclusions of the study and it will be presented to the personnel who have the necessary authority to give the go ahead for the development of the system.

The steps involved in project management

Creation of the specification of the project with the project sponsor

A specification is the definition of your project: a statement of the problem, not the solution, and everyone concerned must be in agreement with this specification. The specification will detail:

- the context of the new system – how it fits in with the other systems used in the organisation
- how the system needs to interface with other systems – what data needs to flow between other systems
- timescales – an accurate assessment of the times for completion of each part of the project and the overall project
- resources – the materials, equipment and manpower which are needed for the project. This is important as the senior managers need to know how much money is needed to fund the project.

Breaking down the work

This involves breaking down the project into a series of simpler tasks and this means that a complex project can be more easily understood. Each task should be clearly defined so that a member of a project team could take it away and work on it.

Allocating tasks

Once the tasks have been identified the next step is to allocate the tasks to different people in the team and, at the same time, order these tasks so that they are performed in a sensible sequence. The tasks need to be given to the project team members with the most appropriate skills to carry them out.

Estimating the time involved to complete the tasks and hence the whole project

A fairly accurate estimate of the time to complete the tasks is needed in order for the more senior managers (i.e., the project sponsors) to allocate the resources for the project (i.e., human resources, money, etc.). This is often 'guesstimation' but it is still possible for an experienced project manager to derive a schedule for the entire project based on their experience of other projects.

GLASBERGEN

"Before we begin our Time Management Seminar, did everyone get one of these 36-hour wrist watches?"

Establishing controls

Once the project is underway the project manager will need to establish control of the project by constantly monitoring its progress and checking the costs of the project do not exceed the budget allocated. There must be efficient communication between the project groups and the project manager. Regular progress reports and meetings are used to monitor progress and to put in place remedial action should it be needed.

Planning for errors

A good project manager will realise that few projects go completely smoothly, so they will sometimes change the project plan to take account of these problems. Project managers will usually build some time into schedules for problems such as staff leaving, sickness, technical problems, etc.

> **KEY WORDS**
>
> **Deliverables** – tasks that make up part of the project when completed
>
> **Milestone** – point at which the progress of an ICT project is assessed. A milestone is a point in time by which certain parts of the project should be completed so that remedial action can be taken if needed

GLASBERGEN

"The key to time management is strict and disciplined adherence to a rigid schedule, while remaining flexible enough to let anything happen at any time."

Topic 8 Development methods

Development methodologies

Introduction

There are many different methodologies for developing new ICT systems and two of the main methods are linear and iterative.

The waterfall method – a linear method

In the waterfall methodology one stage of the system is perfected and completed before the next stage is started. This means that the waterfall method is a linear method. If you look at the diagram below you will see that each task is separate and leads on to the next task. There is no looping back to a previous stage. The problem with this is that it can be too rigid a method because it is hard to achieve in practice. For example, you may find later that you had not thought of something in an earlier stage and you need to go back to that stage and change it. This methodology assumes that you can perfect one stage before moving to the next stage.

Advantages of the waterfall methodology include:

- it offers a simple, disciplined approach to systems development
- each task is completed fully, so any problems are dealt with at the time so you do not need to go back to them later
- bugs found early on in software development will cost less to correct than if they are discovered later on

- it places more emphasis on documentation, which means that if a member of the project team leaves, it is easier for a new member of staff to take over.

Disadvantages of the waterfall methodology include:

- real projects do not lend themselves to the sequential approach as you often have to go back to a previous stage and make changes
- in some projects the client will want to see a rough working version in order to make comments on it and this method does not allow for this
- a working version is not produced until late on in the project development.

Iterative methodologies

With iterative methodologies the project is broken down into stages and each stage undergoes a cyclic development process. As each stage is completed it is evaluated and if the stage is unsatisfactory, the system developed is improved and only when the developer and the user are happy with the progress will the next stage be started. Testing, and evaluation after feedback from the user, may result in dissatisfaction with the system so far, so this is corrected and taken into account when completing the other stages making up the whole project. This means that successive steps in the project benefit

from what has been learnt from previous steps so the system is successively improved upon until the whole system is produced.

Advantages of an iterative methodology include:

- it highlights the value of project learning – this means that the project improves each time a step is completed
- it allows for more user involvement as the customer can see what is being produced at each stage – this makes for a better solution as users have given their input throughout the development
- it places higher emphasis on prototyping and user interface in the early stages – this means that there is less documentation and more deliverables.

Disadvantages of an iterative methodology include:

- greater user involvement may cause problems as users are taken away from their day-to-day activities
- increased user involvement may mean that the user will want increased functionality from the system and this can involve greater cost and could cause delays in project completion.

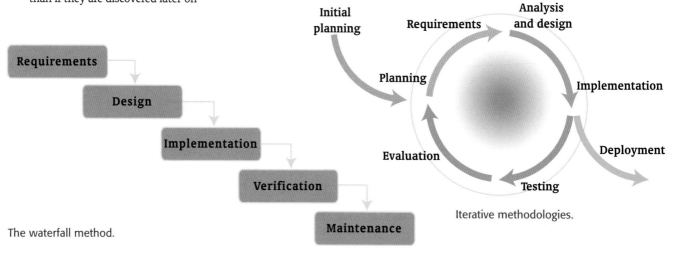

The waterfall method.

Iterative methodologies.

Other development methodologies

There are a number of other development methodologies used which combine the best features of both the linear method and the iterative method.

The spiral methodology

The waterfall methodology is a linear methodology and it offers an orderly structure for the development of systems; however, if a system is needed quickly, its rigid series of steps makes its use inappropriate. A better methodology would be where the various steps are staged for multiple deliveries. One methodology which does this is called the spiral methodology, which takes advantage of the fact that development projects work best when both linear and iterative methods are used. Having a method which is a combination allows the development team to start small and benefit from enlightened trial and error through the development.

The advantages of the spiral methodology include:

- rapid prototyping means development time is less
- developers can work in parallel on different parts of the project
- designing and building can be performed at the same time
- tasks and deliverables are identified for each step in the spiral.

Choosing a development methodology

There are many different methodologies available to the systems developer and which one is chosen depends on a number of factors. Here is a summary of the situations and systems which suit particular methodologies:

Linear method

A linear method, such as the waterfall methodology, is an appropriate methodology in the following situations:

- Where the project is large, complicated and expensive – as this methodology is more rigorous so there is less risk.
- Where pressure does not exist for immediate implementation – allows time to perfect each stage before the next stage is started.
- Where the project has clear objectives and solutions – need clarity before starting, as the methodology relies on not re-visiting previous stages.
- Where the project requirements can be stated unambiguously and comprehensively – so that each stage can be identified and then completed.
- Where the project team are inexperienced – so they are able to be guided by the more rigid project development structure.

Iterative method

An iterative method, such as prototyping, is an appropriate methodology in the following situations:

- Where the project is for an on-line system such as a website, e-commerce site, etc., where there is extensive user/client dialogue – so users/clients can constantly give feedback, which is then acted upon.
- Where the project objectives are unclear – so that the project objectives are flexible and can be altered as the project progresses.
- Where there is pressure for the immediate implementation of something – so that the user can see and use part of the project early on.
- Where project team members are experienced – so that they can use their experience and expertise to cut out steps which take time.

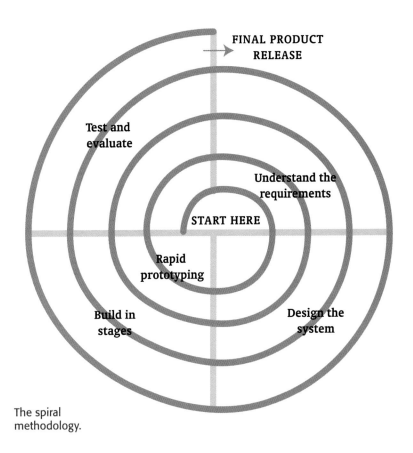

FINAL PRODUCT RELEASE

Test and evaluate

Understand the requirements

START HERE

Rapid prototyping

Build in stages

Design the system

The spiral methodology.

Questions, Activity and Case studies

▶ Questions 1 pp. 86–93

1 (a) Name **three** steps in the systems development life cycle. (3 marks)

(b) For each of the steps named in part (a) describe the steps involved. (6 marks)

2 (a) Explain why formal methods are used for the development of systems. (4 marks)

(b) There are two main development methodologies. Describe the features of each of the following methodologies:

(i) linear methods

(ii) iterative methods. (6 marks)

3 When ICT systems are developed it is important that the project is managed properly. Describe how each of the following is used to help with the management of a project:

(a) agreed deliverables (2 marks)

(b) clear timescales (2 marks)

(c) approval to proceed. (2 marks)

4 Two systems analysts are talking about different methodologies used to develop new ICT systems.

One analyst says that the waterfall method is the best system development methodology but the other analyst says that the iterative method is better. Discuss the two methodologies, highlighting their relative advantages and disadvantages. (10 marks)

5 Give **two** reasons why projects are often broken down into tasks with each task being given to a project team. (2 marks)

6 Explain the purpose of feasibility in the systems development life cycle. (2 marks)

7 (a) ICT projects consist of agreed deliverables. Explain what is meant by an agreed deliverable. (2 marks)

(b) For each of the following stages of the systems development life cycle, identify a deliverable:

(i) Analysis (1 mark)

(ii) Design (1 mark)

(iii) Implementation. (1 mark)

8 Explain **three** steps involved in the management of a project. (3 marks)

▶ Activity Researching methodologies

The development of many ICT systems can go wrong for a number of reasons but one main reason is the lack of formal methods. This means that the development of the system has not followed rigorously the steps in one of the many methodologies that are available.

For this activity you have to research three different methodologies of which two must be the following:

- A linear method
- An iterative method

You are free to pick a methodology of your choice for the third one.

In your research you need cover the following:

- The name of the methodology and a brief description of the steps it involves.
- The relative advantages and disadvantages of each methodology.
- The types of systems being developed for which the methodology is most appropriate.

Once your research is complete you need to produce an essay on the three methodologies. Your essay should be written in continuous prose and not simply in note form. Remember to spellcheck, grammar check and proof read your essay before submitting it to your tutor for marking.

▶ Case study 1 | pp. 86–93

User testing websites

The following case study looks at advice given by a website designer on how users should be used to test websites.

One of the problems you have with websites is that once you have lost a customer you have lost them for good. For example, if your site does not load in a reasonable time or appears cluttered and unprofessional, then users will click straight onto the next site. Website designers refer to this as churn. Churn normally happens because people are unhappy with the design of the site.

How do you stop churn? This is easy – you simply ask people. You get people to actually use the site and see what they think. If it is an e-commerce site, for example, you could get people to make mock orders and ask them about how easy it was to find the products and how easy it was to complete the order. It is a good idea to watch them at work in order to understand the difficulties they have. Ask them to explain what they are doing, what they expect to happen next, what they find frustrating, etc. Get them to get into the habit of saying what they are thinking.

It is very important that your user testing is done by typical users. For example, if you are testing a website for senior citizens, then there is not much point allowing teenagers to test use the site.

You must make sure that your users are critical enough because the general public will be.

1. (a) Explain what is meant by the term 'user testing' and explain how user testing is important to the success of an e-commerce website. (4 marks)
   (b) Describe, by giving suitable examples, how an e-commerce website can be tested by users. (6 marks)
2. A person who is designing websites says 'it is essential, when user testing websites, that the testing is performed by typical users'.
   Give two reasons why this is important. (4 marks)
3. Discuss the implications of not properly user testing a website. (4 marks)

▶ Case study 2 | pp. 86–93

Abandoned computer projects wasting billions of pounds

Since the year 2000 the government is estimated to have wasted £2bn on abandoned computer projects. One instance involved an upgrade of a system for the Child Support Agency (CSA), which cost £486m and resulted in a £1bn claims write off. The CSA system that was developed could not deal with the existing 1.2m claims and plunged the department into chaos.

Other systems which were abandoned include a benefit card system which was based on outdated technology.

A website which was developed in order for members of the public to report crimes or suspected crimes was supposed to have allowed them to provide photographic and video evidence using the Internet. The idea was that this information would then be sent to the relevant police force and prioritised. Initially it was being used to report around 30,000 crimes per year but started to fail when a new company was brought in to build a replacement system a few years later. Costs then started to spiral out of control and the new system was deemed to be unfit for purpose and the whole project was then abandoned.

The government has a huge annual spend on ICT projects each year amounting to around £14bn and it is estimated that only about 30% of the projects and programs are successful.

A government spokesperson said about these abandoned projects: 'It is not sustainable for us as a government to continue to spend at these levels. We need to up the quality of what we do at a reduced cost of doing so.'

1. One reason why some ICT projects fail is the lack of formal methods.
   Explain why formal methods are important during the development of new ICT systems. (3 marks)
2. Lack of proper project management is often cited as being a reason why some projects go wildly out of control.
   Explain how the following aspects of project management are essential components of a successful project:
   (a) Establishing controls (2 marks)
   (b) Planning for errors. (2 marks)
3. Discuss the ways that the development of an ICT system can go wrong, causing the abandonment of the project. In your answer you should refer to examples you have come across. (8 marks)
4. Explain the contribution of the following to the successful development of a new ICT system:
   (a) Agreed deliverables (2 marks)
   (b) Clear timescales (2 marks)
   (c) Milestones. (2 marks)

Exam support

Worked example 1

1 The system development process consists of a number of stages.
Give the names of **two** of these stages and for each one, describe the tasks that would normally take place during the stage. **(6 marks)**

Student answer 1

1 Maintenance – this means getting rid of the bugs in the software. Adding extra functionality of the software, which means getting the software to do more things.
Testing – at unit, module and system level to ensure that sections of code, large sections of code that work together and entire systems operate as expected.
Each pathway through a program is checked either manually or making use of automated software routines.

Examiner's comment

1 One mark given for correctly naming the stage (i.e., maintenance).
The first point is true to some extent but more detail is needed for the mark to be awarded as a maintenance issue.
The second point needs a bit more detail for the mark but as the mark for the first point was not given and the answer was half-way there, the examiner has decided to award a mark here.
Testing is correct for one mark. This is a very good description of the testing process and two points are made so full marks are awarded for this part. **(5 marks out of 6)**

Student answer 2

1 Feasibility – producing an initial investigation of the requirements for the new system in order to find out what the aims and objectives for the new system should be. The estimated costs for the new system are determined and these are weighed against the likely benefits. A decision as to whether to go ahead with the development is then made.
Constructing the solution – a ready-made package is customised to the organisation's requirements. This could be done using a database package where structure of the database is created by specifying tables, fields, relationships, etc.
Some programming may need to be done in Visual Basic, if the program does not allow you to do certain things. Once the structure has been created, you can design forms for the input of data and reports for the output of information.

Examiner's comment

1 One mark for the correct development stage (i.e., feasibility) and one mark for the answer in the first sentence. A mark is not given for the last two sentences as the student needs to make it clear that the analyst/developer can only give recommendations to the directors/leaders of the organisation as to whether to proceed with the development.
One mark for the correct development stage (i.e., constructing the solution).
This is a good answer as the student has related this stage to what they did in their project work. Full marks are given for this part. **(5 marks out of 6)**

Examiner's answer

1 One mark for the correct name of the stage and one mark each to a maximum of two marks for two correct points that further describe the stage.

System investigation/feasibility (1)
An investigation of a problem that needs to be solved (1) along with an assessment of achieving the stated aims and objectives for the project in a reasonable timescale and at reasonable cost (1). Recommendations are given to the senior managers who make the decision as to whether or not to proceed with the system (1).

Analysis (1)
Taking steps to understand the current system (1) and gathering user requirements for the new system (1) and setting out the solution in a logical way using tools and techniques that will aid the design of the new system (1). The result is a logical specification that can be used in the next stage (1).

Design (1)
Taking the logical design from the analysis stage (1) and the user requirements and turning it into a physical design that is capable of being built and implemented (1).

Build/constructing solution (1)
Teams of developers/programmers write programs or customise packages using tools and techniques (1) according to the physical design (1) to produce a working version of the solution (1).

Testing (1)
Testing at very detailed levels (i.e., individuals will thoroughly test their part) (1). Testing is at a higher level (i.e., when the various parts of the system are joined together) (1). Testing is at a systems level where all the parts are tested as a whole system (1). Testing each field using correct, erroneous and extreme data (1). Testing the system with real-life data (1).

Implementation (1)
The completed system is installed on operational computers (1). Users are trained in the use of the new system (1). Files and data from previous systems are converted if necessary and stored on the new system (1). User and technical documentation are produced (1).

Evaluation and review (1)
Checking that the original user requirements and performance criteria have been fully met by the new system (1). Assessment of how happy the clients are with the development of the new system (1). Setting up a review cycle so that the system is checked periodically to make sure that it is still meeting requirements (1). Setting up help-desk facilities to help users who experience problems with the new system (1).

Maintenance (1)
The review meetings might identify new functionality to be added (1). Maintenance staff who have knowledge about the developed system will add this additional functionality (1). The maintenance team may fix bugs which come to light after large numbers of users use the new system (1).

Summary mind map

The systems development life cycle

SYSTEMS DEVELOPMENT LIFE CYCLE

1 SYSTEM INVESTIGATION/FEASIBILITY
- Project definition
- Aims and objectives of new system
- Initial fact find
- Investigation into the technical, legal, economic, operational and schedule implications
- Cost/benefit analysis
- Recommendations as to feasibility

2 ANALYSIS
- Understanding the existing system
- Gathering/analysing user requirements
- Using tools and techniques such as data flow diagrams, data models, process specifications and systems diagrams
- Producing a logical specification

3 DESIGN
- Designing the system in line with the user requirements
- Creating the design specification for hardware, software, telecommunications, databases, personnel and procedures

4 BUILD/CONSTRUCTING SOLUTION
- Use the physical design to produce a working system
- Write programming code/customise package
- Use software tools to produce working version
- Producing working system to user requirements

5 TEST
- Testing at very detailed levels
- Testing at a higher level
- Testing at a systems level
- Testing each field using correct, erroneous and extreme data
- Testing with real-life data

6 INSTALLATION AND CONVERSION
- Installing hardware
- Installing software
- Conversion of previous data
- Training of all users
- Production of documentation and training guides

7 REVIEW AND MAINTENANCE
- Checking solution meets user requirements
- Setting up review cycle
- Setting up help-desk
- Adding extra functions
- Fixing bugs
- Managing interfaces with other systems

TOPIC 9 Techniques and tools for systems development

In this topic you will look at a variety of techniques and tools used for the development of ICT systems. You will look at the investigating and recording techniques used during the investigations of systems and how business processes can be modelled using a variety of diagrams and tools.

Also covered in this topic are the construction of diagrams used to model data flows in an organisation and the techniques used to produce models which can be used to explain existing systems or describe new systems. The variety of techniques used for testing a solution will also be looked at.

▼ The key concepts covered in this topic are:

▶ Investigating and recording techniques

▶ Business process modelling tools

▶ Data modelling tools

▶ Techniques for testing

CONTENTS

1 **Investigating and recording techniques** 100
Interviews, observations, inspection of records and questionnaires.

2 **Business process modelling tools**..102
Decision tables, flowcharts and systems diagrams.

3 **Data modelling tools** 106
Data flow diagrams (DFDs), entity relationship models (ERMs) and entity relationship diagrams (ERDs).

4 **Techniques for testing**..112
What does testing involve? The techniques used for testing and use of simulated environments.

5 **Questions** 114

6 **Activities** 115

7 **Exam support**..117

8 **Summary mind maps**..119

Investigating and recording techniques

Introduction

In this section you will be looking at the investigating and recording techniques used to investigate an existing system or the user requirements for a new system.

Investigating and recording techniques

Before work can start on analysing the system, it is necessary to find out many facts about the organisation and the tasks they want the new system to do. You therefore need to investigate the existing system and also the requirements for the new system so that the analysis can be performed.

In order to improve an existing system it is essential to understand how it works. The process of finding out is called investigation or fact finding. There are a number of different ways information about the existing system can be found out and these are:

- interviews
- observation
- inspection of records
- questionnaires.

Interviews – interviews with managers will normally reveal how their particular department works and any problems they are having with the existing system. They will be able to offer information about how they would like the new system to work and they will be able to tell you about information that they would like the new system to provide.

Operational staff are those members of staff who perform the majority of the day-to-day work of the organisation and their knowledge of the organisation is usually restricted to their own area of work. They will be able to supply the fine detail about particular ways that jobs are done.

Collection of information using interviewing is time consuming.

Fact finding – initial investigation of a system before a feasibility study is carried out

Observation – if you wanted to take someone else's job over then the best way to learn what you have to do is to either sit for a few days with the person whose job you are taking over or sit with someone else who does a similar job. Observation involves sitting with a person and observing what they do in order to understand the information flows and processes they perform.

Inspection of records – many organisations still use and generate paper-based documents which are used in their business. By examining these documents you can understand what information is held and the way it is communicated between different departments or between the organisation and suppliers and customers.

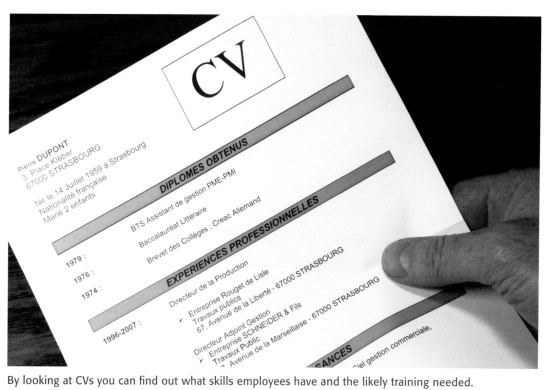

By looking at CVs you can find out what skills employees have and the likely training needed.

Documents giving general information would include:

- organisation charts (this is a chart showing the hierarchy in the organisation and can be used to find out who reports to whom)
- staff CVs – useful to assess the skills or training needs of employees
- job descriptions – give details of the tasks undertaken by different people
- policy/procedure manuals – useful to understand the way the organisation works
- previous systems documentation – paper documents when previous systems have been produced.

Documents giving specific information would include:

- product catalogues
- order forms
- invoices
- despatch notes
- picking lists (for warehouse staff).

Questionnaires – at first sight, questionnaires seem an ideal way of collecting information about a company. You do not have to spend time interviewing people and a questionnaire sticks to the important points without digressing, which can occur in an interview.

Organisation charts help you understand the structure of the business.

Questionnaires can be used to collect information about organisations.

However, questionnaires have drawbacks. Many people forget to fill them in, which can result in an incomplete picture of a system. Respondents may misunderstand some of the questions, if the forms are simply posted to them and no personal help is offered.

Nevertheless, questionnaires are useful when information needs to be collected from a large number of individuals, as they consume a lot less staff time than interviews.

When compiling questionnaires, the following should be borne in mind:

- Make sure that the questions are precisely worded so that the users do not have to interpret the questions.
- It is best for respondents not to have to put their name on their questionnaire, as otherwise you may not get honest answers.
- Structure the questionnaire so that general questions are asked first, followed by more specific ones. It is also worth dividing the questionnaire into functional areas, so for example, one part could deal with sales order processing, another with stock control. Obviously this approach will vary depending on the type of organisation.
- Avoid leading questions (questions which suggest a preferred answer).
- At the end of the questionnaire, always add the question: 'Is there anything I have missed that you think I ought to know about?'.

Business process modelling tools

▼ **You will find out**

▶ About decision tables

▶ About flowcharts

▶ About systems diagrams

Introduction

There are a number of business processing modelling tools used to help understand and show the processes which are carried out on the inputs to a system. These process modelling tools include decision tables and information flow diagrams and flowcharts.

Decision tables

A decision table provides a simple way of displaying the actions to be taken when certain conditions occur.

Looking at the diagram (above right) you will see the following sections:

- Conditions stub: these are the situations or events which need testing. They are the cause of the actions which need to be taken in the actions stub section. A typical condition might be 'is person's age over 18?'.
- Actions stub: these are the actions which are taken depending on the combination of general conditions in the conditions stub that apply. For instance, 'may be served alcoholic drink' could be an action.
- Conditions entries: these give an indication of which of the conditions apply. This is done by placing Y or N next to each condition depending on whether the condition applies or not.
- Action entries: these give the action to be taken depending on the conditions which apply. A cross is marked in the decision table to show which action or actions should be taken.

This all sounds complicated! However, they are much more difficult to describe than to do, so we will now look at a simple example with which you should be familiar.

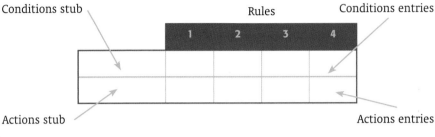

The standard way of laying out a decision table is shown here.

Example: A decision table for a set of traffic lights

In order to understand how decision tables can be created, it is best to look at a non-ICT example (e.g., that of showing the operation of a set of traffic lights).

The general conditions are obviously the colours of the lights and the general actions are whether to stop, carry on, etc.

The first step is to write in simple English the general conditions which here will be the colours of the three lights. We similarly write the general actions to be taken.

For the conditions in the conditions stub we have:

RED
AMBER
GREEN

and for the actions in the action stub we have:

STOP
GO
CALL POLICE (since lights aren't working properly)

We now need to set out the table, so we need to know how many rules there will be. Theoretically, we can work this out by putting two to the power of the number of conditions in the conditions stub, which will be 3 in this case. Hence there will be 2^3 = 8 rules. For the sake of simplicity we will assume that all these rules are possible (there are in fact fail-safe systems in use in actual traffic light systems, so some of these rules will be impossible).

The rules for a traffic light can be set out in a decision table.

	Rules							
	1	2	3	4	5	6	7	8
RED	Y	Y	Y	N	N	N	Y	N
AMBER	Y	Y	N	Y	N	Y	N	N
GREEN	Y	N	Y	Y	Y	N	N	N
STOP	X	X	X	X		X	X	X
GO					X			
CALL POLICE	X		X	X				X

Traffic light decision table.

We can now draw the grid and fill in the conditions stub, actions stub and the combinations of Ys and Ns which make up the condition entries. When putting the Ys and Ns in, it is best to adopt a system so you could put all the Ys in first then the three combinations with two Ys and one N, then one Y and two Ns and finally all three Ns.

To fill in the action entries we look at the combinations to see what particular action or actions should be taken. We mark a cross in the relevant places to show the action or actions which should be taken.

Advantages of decision tables

The main advantages of decision tables are:

- You can make sure that all the combinations of conditions have been considered.
- They are easy to understand, since all the information needed is held in one table.
- There is a standard layout so everyone uses the same format.
- Programmers may use them to write programs and they are useful for working out logic conditions in spreadsheets and databases.
- They show cause and effect and are therefore understood by most people.

Creating a carriage costs decision table

In some situations, there is no point in writing down and considering all the rules, since some of them may be impossible. Take the following example:

Suppose the carriage to be paid when ordering CDs from a club is as follows:

    1–3 CDs carriage is £2.50
    4–6 CDs carriage is £3.00
    7+ CDs carriage is £4.00

Since there are 3 general conditions there are 8 rules. If we look at some of these rules we find that some of them are impossible. For instance, YYY would be impossible since the number of CDs ordered can only have one Y. We get impossible rules when the questions in the decision table are related to each other.

To take account of these impossible rules, we leave them out of the decision table.

By eliminating the impossible rules, the following decision table is obtained:

Carriage costs decision table.

	Rules		
	1	2	3
1 – 3 CDs ordered	Y	N	N
4 – 6 CDs ordered	N	Y	N
over 7 CDs ordered	N	N	Y
Carriage of £2.50	X		
Carriage of £3.00		X	
Carriage of £4.00			X

Flowcharts

Flowcharts are used to show the order in which a series of processes should be performed. There are three main constructs used when drawing flowcharts and their purpose is to alter the order in which the processing steps are performed. These three constructs are as follows.

Sequence

This is simply a list of processes in which each process is always carried out after another, and always takes the same path. The various processes are placed in the correct order and are obeyed in sequence. A flow chart for three processes in the order X, Y and then Z is shown here:

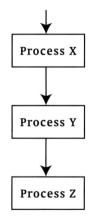

Flowchart showing three processes carried out in sequence.

Selection

Sometimes it is necessary, within a program, to decide whether to take one particular path or another, depending on a certain condition. If this condition or factor is 'true' then one path will be taken, and if 'not true' then the other will be put into effect. In other words, depending upon conditions, the computer is able to decide which path to take through the program. If several selections are included, the number of possible paths through a program increases.

Take the following English description of a selection: 'If condition X is true then do process B'. The flowchart for this is shown here:

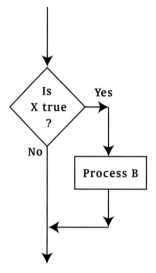

Flowchart section showing a conditional selection construct.

Another form of selection can be represented by the following English statement: 'If condition X is true then do process B otherwise do process A'. This is shown in the following diagram:

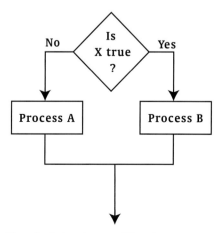

Flowchart showing conditional process selection construct.

Business process modelling tools *continued*

Iteration (repetition)

An iteration is a section of a program which is repeated a number of times. The following English statement represents a typical iteration statement: 'While condition X is true, repeatedly do process A'. The diagram to the right shows the flow chart for this construct.

Iteration of a set of program instructions can take place in one of three ways:

1 a condition is tested for after the first run of the sequence
2 a condition is tested at the start of a sequence
3 an instruction is given for the sequence to be carried out a certain number of times.

Flowchart section showing an iteration construct.

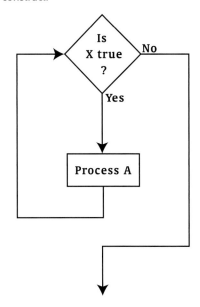

Systems diagrams

Systems diagrams/flowcharts provide a pictorial representation of how an ICT system works by showing inputs to a particular part of the system, what actions are taken to process the data, and what moves out of this part to somewhere else. They also make clear the broad flow of the operations in a system and the hardware and media that are involved in these operations. The system flowchart also shows where the inputs originate and the mode (manual or computer-based) of processing is also made clear.

Symbols used in systems flowcharts.

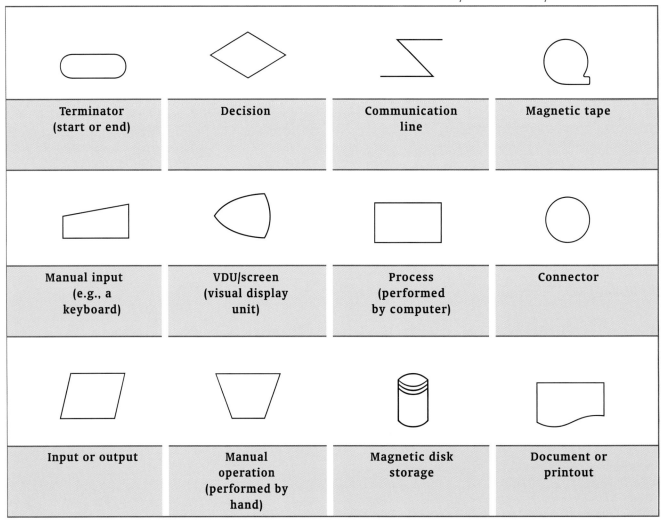

Terminator (start or end)	Decision	Communication line	Magnetic tape
Manual input (e.g., a keyboard)	VDU/screen (visual display unit)	Process (performed by computer)	Connector
Input or output	Manual operation (performed by hand)	Magnetic disk storage	Document or printout

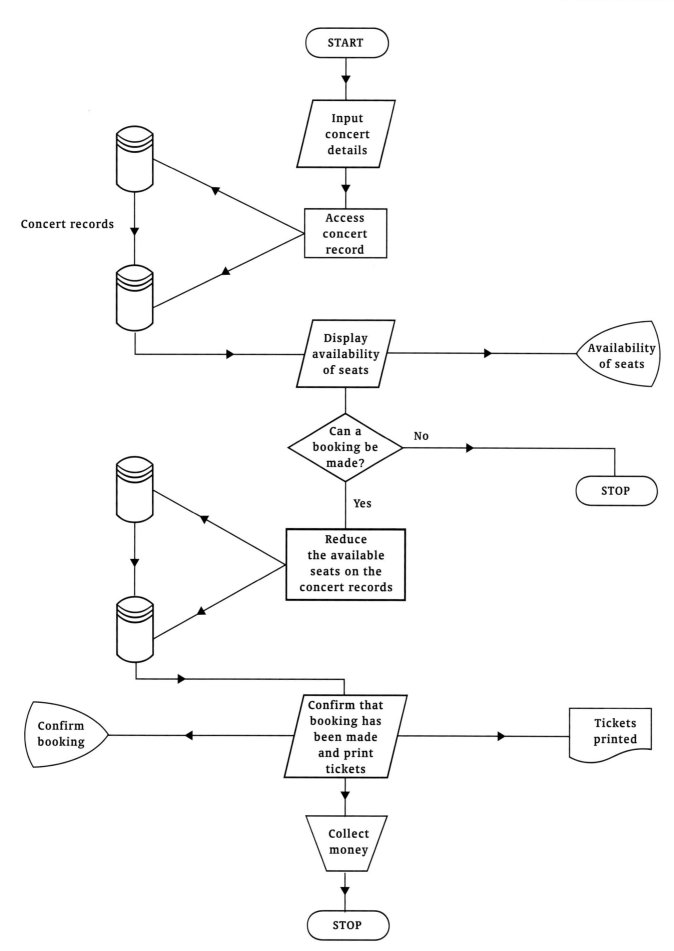

The system flowchart for a concert booking system.

Data modelling tools

Introduction

There are a number of tools and techniques used to help understand and analyse systems but in this section we are looking at the tools and techniques that can be used to help in understanding the data flows.

Data flow diagrams (DFDs)

It is important, when explaining an existing system, to look at the data/information flows within an organisation. This is often done diagrammatically using DFDs. These are used as a first step in describing a system and they look at inputs, what processes are performed on the inputs and the outputs produced.

Unfortunately there are many different ways of drawing DFDs and it can all get very confusing. The method shown here is the method used with SSADM (Structured Systems Analysis and Design Methodology).

An initial investigation of the system is performed in the feasibility study. This looks at the inputs to the system, what processes are performed on them and the outputs from the system. The scope of the system is also specified in this phase. To help further analysis, DFDs are drawn. DFDs are used to consider the data, while ignoring the equipment used to store it. They are used as a first step in describing a system.

A series of symbols is used in these diagrams; unfortunately different authors use different-shaped symbols, which can be very confusing.

A process or action – is a rectangular box and it represents a process that does something with the data (it could manipulate it in some way or perform calculations on it, for example). The box is divided into three parts, the top left box having a number in it which identifies the box. The main body of the box is used to record a description of the process and the top right of the box is used to record the person or area responsible for the process.

1	Wages clerk
	Calculate wages

A process.

External source of data (where it comes from) or an external sink of data (where it goes to)

This is an oval box which is used to describe where, outside the system, the data comes from and goes to. We are not concerned with what happens to the data before it reaches the box (if it is a source) or what happens to it when it goes past a sink.

Customer

External object.

Data flow

Data flow is shown by an arrow pointing in the direction of the flow. Usually it is advisable to put a description of the data flow on the arrow to aid understanding. By convention, we never use a verb on a data flow.

Credit card details

Data flow.

A store of data

The symbol for this is shown in the diagram. A data store can be anywhere data is stored; it could be a drawer where you keep letters, file boxes, folders, books, a filing cabinet (or a certain drawer of a filing cabinet), magnetic disk, CD, etc. Again, the symbol bears a number which is used to reference the store when describing it, but there is also a letter placed in front of the number. M is used for a manual store and C for a computer store.

C1	Customer accounts

This data store contains customer account details and is on a computer.

Levels of DFDs

When analysing systems it is usual to draw DFDs at different levels. The level used reflects the depth in which the DFD looks at the system being investigated.

The context diagram

The first DFD drawn is called the context diagram, because it puts the system being investigated into context. It is a high-level DFD showing the entire system under investigation as a single box and the information flows between external entities such as suppliers and customers. The diagram might show the flow of orders from the customers (an external entity) to the sales department and goods being despatched from the warehouse to the customers.

The aim of the context diagram is to show the scope of the system.

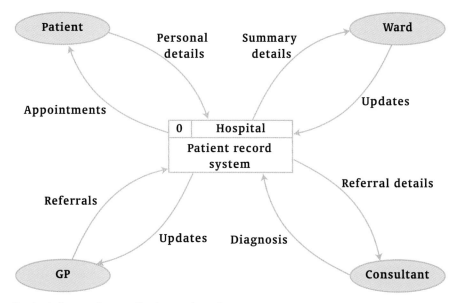

Context diagram for a patient records system.

Level 1 DFD

The level 1 DFD shows the main processes in the system and presents a more detailed view of the data flows in the system. You should aim for no more than about six process boxes in this diagram.

Level 2 DFD

A level 2 DFD breaks down the process boxes in the level 1 DFD and thus presents an even more detailed view of the processes. To do this, one of the process boxes (i.e., the rectangular

ones) from the level 1 DFD is taken, and the process it represents is, if possible, broken down into a series of more detailed sub-processes.

The advantage of this 'zooming in' approach is that by looking at each level starting with the outline DFD, we can gradually build up a complete picture of the information flows through the system. Instead of having a single DFD with a large number of processes shown, we end up with a whole family of DFDs showing different levels of detail. High-level DFDs can be broken down into further diagrams showing greater levels of detail.

Using DFDs

DFDs can be used:

- during system investigation to record findings
- during system design to illustrate how a proposed system will work
- when outlining the specifications of new systems.

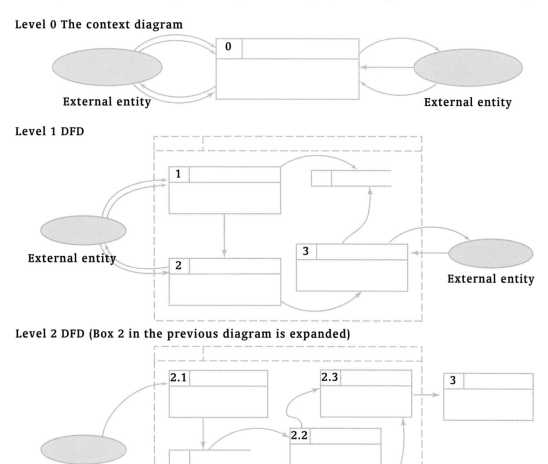

The decomposition (i.e., the levelling) of the DFDs.

Topic 9 Techniques and tools for systems development

Data modelling tools *continued*

Entity relationship models (ERMs)

Entity relationship modelling is a technique for defining the information needs of an organisation to provide a firm foundation on which an appropriate system can be built. Putting it simply, entity relationship modelling identifies the most important factors in the organisation being looked at. These factors are called **entities**.

Also looked at are the properties which these factors possess (called **attributes**) and how they are related to one another (called **relationships**). Entity models are logical, which means that they do not depend on the method of implementation. If two departments in an organisation perform identical tasks but in different ways their entity models would nevertheless be identical, since they would be using the same entities and relationships. But their DFDs could be different, since their information flows may well differ. Entity models are particularly useful because they are independent of any storage or ways of accessing the data. They are thus not reliant on any hardware or software at this stage.

An entity model is an abstract representation of the data in an organisation and the aim of entity relationship modelling is to produce an accurate model of the information needs of an organisation which will aid either the development of a new system or the enhancement of an existing one.

An entity relationship model (ERM) describes a system as a set of data entities with relationships between them (one-to-one, one-to-many, many-to-many).

Entity relationship diagrams (ERDs)

Entity relationship diagrams look at any components important to the system and the relationships between them.

So what is an **entity**? An entity can be anything about which data is recorded. It could include people, places, objects, customers, sales, payments or employees. Each entity has some associated **attributes**. An attribute is detail about an entity. Let us look at an example. In the following table the attribute for the entity 'customer' contains further details.

Entity	Attributes
CUSTOMER	Customer number
	Company name
	Postcode
	Telephone number
	Credit limit
	Amount owing

Each entity is represented in an entity diagram by a rectangle with the name of the entity written inside. The relationship between the entities is shown as lines between these boxes. The entity is always written inside the rectangle in capital letters and always in the singular because the use of plural would imply a certain type of relationship. So instead of CUSTOMERS we would need to use CUSTOMER.

The entity STUDENT could have the following attributes: student number, student address, telephone number, date of birth, tutor, course number. It is important, when developing databases, to check each attribute to decide whether it is possible to break it down further into more attributes. The attribute student address could be further broken down into the attributes; street, town and postcode. When attributes need not be broken down any further, they are said to be atomic. Hence street, town and postcode are atomic.

Breaking down attributes to produce atomic attributes allows the flexibility to manipulate the data. For example, we could search for students who have a certain postcode or sort students according to the town they are from.

Relationships

A relationship is the way in which entities in a system are related to one another. A relationship may be one-to-one (1:1), one-to-many (1:m), or many-to-many (m:n).

These three possible kinds of relationship between two entities A and B are shown here:

A one-to-one relationship, a one-to-many relationship and a many-to-many relationship.

Entity relationship modelling for a CD e-commerce store

Here is how an entity relationship model can be constructed for a CD store that sells CDs by mail order using the Internet. The first thing to do is to identify those entities that are essential for this system. Four entities are used here:

CUSTOMER
CD
ORDER
DELIVERY

You now need to think about how these entities are related. It is a good idea to write these as a list like this:

- a customer places an order
- an order consists of one or more CDs
- delivery consists of the CDs in the order
- delivery is made to the customer.

It is now possible to draw the relationships between the entities like this:

A simple relationship model for the system but the orders (one-to-one, one-to-many, etc.) have not been added.

Entity – an object of the real world that is relevant to an ICT system, e.g. a place, object, person, customer, invoice, product, course, etc.

Attribute – a single item of data which represents a fact about an entity. An attribute can be thought of as something which adds further detail/information to the entity

The diagram is far from perfect. If an order consists of several CDs this is not indicated. In addition, if the club runs out of a popular CD, the part of the order that is in stock will be sent, with any out-of-stock CDs to follow.

Let us now look at the relationship between two of the entities: ORDER and CD. We need to examine the relationship from both ends. Looking in the direction from ORDER to CD we can see that one order can be for many CDs. Looking in the reverse direction we can see that a particular CD (that is a particular title) can be in many different orders. In other words, the relationship between ORDER and CD is many-to-many.

The diagram above shows the many-to-many relationship between ORDER and CD.

We can see from the diagram that many members order many CDs. This would imply that an order is for many CDs but it is impossible to say which CD the order is for. There needs to be a way of linking the CDs to each order so that they can be cross-referenced. We do this by creating a new entity called ORDER LINE. This entity indicates the CD which is on a particular line in a particular order.

The ORDER LINE entity avoids having a many-to-many relationship.

When you come to create your own entity relationship models, you will have to produce a new entity each time you come across a many-to-many relationship.

Once the new entity ORDER LINE has been created it is necessary to look at the relationships between ORDER and ORDER LINE. This relationship is one-to-many because one order may consist of many order lines. Looking at the relationship between CD and ORDER LINE we can see that this is also a one-to-many relationship because a particular CD can be in many different order lines.

Here is the entity relationship model for the system:

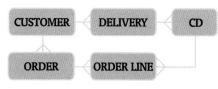

The complete entity relationship model for the system.

Deciding on the type of relationship

In entity relationship modelling it is necessary to decide on the type of relationship between entities. This is best done by looking at the entity from both ends. Take the relationship between students and courses in a college. Looking at the relationship from the student end first we can see that a student could take more than one course. Looking at the relationship from the college end, we see that a single course can be taken by many students. So the relationship between COURSE and STUDENT is many-to-many.

Notice the use of words on the relationships.

The entity relationship diagram tells us:

- one course contains many students
- one student can be enrolled on one or more courses.

As we have already seen, many-to-many relationships cannot be implemented, so in this case we need to create a new entity that would link a student to a course. In a college this is called an ENROLMENT. If a student takes several courses, there will be an enrolment for each course and the attributes of the enrolment record will include the student number (to identify the student) and the course number (to identify the course) as the primary keys.

The entities are now shown here.

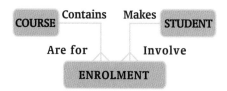

The final entity relationship diagram showing the relationships between the entities: COURSE, STUDENT and ENROLMENT.

Using keys

You have already seen that each entity can be described by a number of attributes. Keys are attributes that have special significance. There are two main types of key: primary keys and foreign keys.

Primary key

A primary key is usually one or occasionally several attributes that can uniquely define a particular entity. For example, the CUSTOMER entity could be uniquely defined by a unique attribute such as customer number. The PAYROLL entity could be uniquely defined by the entity employee number.

Data modelling tools *continued*

Foreign key

When one of the attributes that is a primary key in one entity also appears in another entity, it means that there is a relationship between the entities. In the other entity the attribute is not a primary key because it may no longer be unique. Instead it is known as a foreign key.

Suppose you supplied goods to other companies and you wanted to set up a system to keep the details of these contacts. There are two entities; the COMPANY and CONTACT. Here are the attributes for each of these entities:

CONTACT	COMPANY
Contact_ID	Company_ID
FirstName	Name
LastName	Address
Company_ID	TelephoneNumber

Each contact will be allocated a unique number so Contact_ID is the primary key for the CONTACT entity. In the COMPANY entity, the attribute Company_ID is unique and therefore the primary key. Notice that the attribute Company_ID appears in both the entities and that in the COMPANY entity it is the primary key. In the CONTACT entity Company_ID is a foreign key and since the attributes appear in both entities, we can link them. Hence the entity CONTACT has a relationship to the entity COMPANY.

You may be wondering why we have two entities rather than combine them and just have the one containing the contacts and the company they work for. If there was only a single contact for each company then it would be appropriate to put the company and contact details together. However, in reality there will be more than one contact in each company; if we store contact details, the name of the company and its address will appear in many different contacts' details. Hence the name and address of the company would be a repeating group of attributes. The main problem with this is that if the company changes address then it would be necessary to change the address for each contact working for that company. If two entities are used then if the address of the company changes, it will only need to be changed once in the company entity.

Making sure that attributes are atomic

As well as making sure that repeating attributes are removed and placed in their own entity, you also have to make sure that all the attributes are atomic. Atomic attributes are attributes that do not need to be broken down any further.

For example, a beginner new to systems analysis and database design might use an attribute called Name to hold the following data items:

Mr Stephen Doyle

The trouble with this is that if a sort is now performed it will be done in order of title so names starting with Miss will appear before names starting with Mr. Additionally, if you want to search for the surname Doyle, then this can only be done if you know the title and forename. Using a single attribute called Name causes problems because the attribute is not atomic. Instead it needs to be broken down into three attributes which can be called Title, Forename and Surname.

Creating the database structure

Once the problem of many-to-many relationships has been solved, you can start thinking about the tables used to store the data. Each table can be given the same name as the entities and the field names can be the same as the names given to the attributes. We then have to plan out the structure of each table separately.

Important note

In a many-to-many relationship decomposed to a one-to-many and a many-to-one using a link table, the link table should have a compound key (e.g., in a rental table you might need a compound key of Cust_ID, Tool_ID, and Dateout).

Always make sure that the keys used uniquely define a row in the table.

Data dictionaries

A data dictionary system is a tool used during systems analysis and particularly during database design. The purpose of a data dictionary is to provide information about the database, its uses and participants in the system. A data dictionary could be said to provide 'data about data'.

The contents of the data dictionary

Data dictionaries usually contain some or all of the following features:

Entity names

Each entity needs to be given a name and these names need to be recorded and described in the data dictionary.

Relationships between the entities

The relationships between the entities can be described and then shown in an entity relationship diagram (ERD).

Attribute names

Each attribute should be given a name, and these names should be chosen so that they describe the data as fully as possible without being too long. It is best to avoid leaving spaces in field names, using - or _ to separate the words instead.

Synonyms

Synonyms are alternative names for the same thing. In many large organisations, a database is at the centre of the computer system and is used by different departments for various activities. It is therefore common to find users in different departments employing a different name for the same concept; this can be very confusing for systems analysts trying to design and build a new system. To prevent confusion, users should list any alternative names in the synonyms section of the data dictionary.

Data type

A data type needs to be specified for each attribute. It is very important that once an attribute's data type is set, it has the same data type wherever it occurs. In most cases, relationships can be made only between attributes with exactly the same attribute names and data types.

Format

Details of formats should be included in the data dictionary for those attributes which have formats set by the user. For instance, a numeric field can be a short integer, long integer, currency, etc., and dates can be given as 12 June 2001, 12/06/01, etc.

Description of the attribute

Each attribute should have a description, and these descriptions can be transferred to this section of the data dictionary.

Attribute length

Here we specify the length of the attribute for those attributes that can have their lengths set.

The names of other entities in which the attribute appears

An attribute may appear in more than one entity. For example the attribute Order_Number could appear in the entities ORDER and ORDER_LINE. If we wanted to change the name of an attribute then it is useful to know the entities where it is repeated.

Here is a data dictionary entry for an attribute called REORDER_QUANTITY:

Attribute name	REORDER_QUANTITY
Synonyms	None
Data type	Numeric
Format	0 decimal places (i.e. an integer)
Description of the attribute	The number of units of a stock item which can be ordered at any one time
Attribute length	4 digits
Entity names	STOCK_LIST
	STOCK_LIST_EXCEPTION
	REORDER

Data dictionaries are always created when large commercial databases are being built, especially if the databases are to be used in many different applications. The purpose of the data dictionary is to make sure that data across the whole system is consistent. Large systems are built by large project teams, with each team working on a part of the whole system; in this situation, consistent terminology is vital, and the data dictionary is invaluable. The data contained in data dictionaries is often referred to as metadata.

Data dictionaries can be built as a manual system but there are clear advantages in maintaining a computerised data dictionary. Most relational database management systems have software which creates and maintains a data dictionary. It is kept as a separate database and is automatically updated as changes are made to the structure of the main database.

Optional features of the data dictionary

In addition to the essential features listed above, some data dictionaries provide the following additional information:

- validation checks
- details of the validation checks performed on data entered for each attribute
- a key
- the type of key specified.

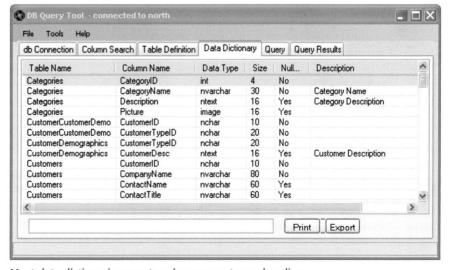

Most data dictionaries are stored on computer and on-line.

Techniques for testing

▼ **You will find out**

▶ About the range of techniques available such as test harnesses, volume testing, scalability testing, prototyping, multi-platform testing and the use of simulated environments

Introduction

Testing needs to capture as many bugs as possible before the system becomes operational. Although testing in a linear methodology, such as the waterfall method, comes near the end of the development process, it is better if testing takes place right the way through the design and build stages as well as in its own stage.

In this section you will look at the techniques for testing and how these techniques are used to test for different elements.

What does testing involve?

Most ICT projects involve lots of different people working on different aspects of the system. Each person in the team will be responsible for their own part of the project and they will have to test what they have done to make sure it works.

Testing will normally involve the following:

- testing at very detailed levels (i.e., individuals will thoroughly test their part)
- testing at a higher level (i.e., when the various parts of the system are joined together)
- testing at a systems level where all the parts are tested as a whole system
- testing each field using correct, erroneous and extreme data
- testing the system with real-life data.

The techniques used for testing

There are a number of techniques used for testing and these techniques are outlined here.

Test harnesses

Test harnesses are used in software testing for automating the testing process. Test harnesses consist of software and test data which will run the developed programming code under different conditions and monitor its output against the output that should have been produced. How well the program behaved and produced accurate results is summarised in a report which the tester can use to help make any necessary adjustments to the program code. The main advantage in using test harnesses is that they automate some of the testing and this means testing takes less time and the quality of the final software is better.

Performance testing

Performance testing is testing that is performed to determine how fast some aspect of a system performs under a particular workload. Performance testing can demonstrate that the system meets performance criteria, it can compare two systems to find which performs better or it can measure what parts of the system or workload cause the system to perform badly.

Scalability testing

Scalability testing is a type of performance testing focused on ensuring the application under test is able to cope with increases in workload.

Volume testing

Volume testing confirms that any values that may become large over time (such as accumulated counts, logs and data files) can be accommodated by the program and will not cause the program to stop working or cause poor performance.

Usability testing

Usability testing is a means for measuring how well people can use an ICT system or part of an ICT system (such as a webpage, a computer interface, a document, or a device) for its intended purpose, i.e. usability

Testing is much more than just removing program bugs.

testing measures the usability of the object. If usability testing uncovers difficulties, such as people having difficulty understanding instructions, knowing what to do next, or interpreting feedback, then developers should improve the design and test it again.

Multi-platform testing/portability testing

Multi-platform testing/portability testing is aimed at demonstrating the software can be ported (i.e., transferred across) to specified hardware or software platforms.

Prototyping

Prototyping involves producing working versions of the ICT system at different stages during its development. The user is given each version to test and evaluate and any problems can be ironed out before the next improved version is produced.

Prototyping is a quick way to incorporate feedback from real users into a design. You involve the users of the product in the design right from the start, so you end up with a product that matches the user's needs and expectations. This is a much better way to test user opinion than to leave it to the end, when their comments are difficult to react to because it would take too much time and effort to make the changes.

Paper prototyping

There is a method which can be used for mocking up a user interface for users to test before it is finally produced using the software. This method also involves using paper and it is called paper prototyping. Paper prototyping uses the following:

- paper
- scissors
- Post-It notes or similar stickies.

The idea is that you sit with a user as they accomplish a task using your paper pages. If you see them struggling with your design then you may need to help them by adding new buttons, hints, etc. It is easy to add these to the design – you simply write them on a piece of paper. You can immediately observe the user to see how they now accomplish the task.

After several runs of testing and design with different users, putting together a website or other multimedia product will not take as much time and you will have saved lots of time by making design changes early on.

The easiest way to see how a paper prototype could be produced is to look at an example you are familiar with.

Suppose you wanted to produce a paper prototype for the software Microsoft Word. The first page would contain a brief sketch of what you would see when you opened the package (i.e., the blue part with Document 1 – Microsoft Word and the menu bar, etc.). If the user was to touch the word 'File' on the menu bar, we would produce a page containing the file menu (with New, Open, Close, Save, etc.). If the user was then to select 'Open', we would give them the Open window, etc. We need to prepare all the slips of paper beforehand and then we act as the computer handing the user the relevant piece of paper depending on what they do.

If they select something we do not have a piece of paper for, then we can quickly create the piece of paper. If they want to do something we had not thought of, this can also be included. While watching users work with your paper prototype you can jot down notes which you should include as evidence for your design and testing.

Using paper prototypes for testing

As well as using paper prototypes for interface design, they can also be used for testing purposes. You can put the paper prototypes in front of users and watch how they work with them. You can watch them get frustrated when things do not work exactly as expected. You can then correct them by altering items on the paper.

Use of simulated environments

Sometimes it is difficult to see how a large system will behave when used with hundreds of terminals until you actually run it with that number of terminals. The use of simulated environments gets around this problem by behaving as though it were being used with a large number of terminals. This allows the developer to test the system before the system goes live.

Simulated environments can also be used to see how the system behaves when it is subjected to a series of controlled inputs. Any errors the system throws up can be dealt with by the developers.

The behaviour of networks can be assessed using simulated environments.

Questions

▶ Questions 1 | pp. 101–112

1 A systems analyst has been brought in to investigate the current manual system used by a college library. The systems analyst has no detailed knowledge of how a library works. Describe the methods they could use to find out about the existing system. **(8 marks)**

2 Discuss the relative advantages and disadvantages in using the following techniques for the investigation of an existing system before creating a new system: **(8 marks)**

   Observation
   Interviews
   Questionnaires
   Inspection of documents/records.

3 (a) Explain the meaning of the following terms giving a suitable example for each:
   (i) Entity **(2 marks)**
   (ii) Attribute **(2 marks)**
   (b) Attributes should be atomic. Explain what this means. **(2 marks)**

4 A college library uses a relational database management system to operate a membership and loans system. Staff and students can borrow as many books as they wish at any given time.
   (a) Name **three** entities that you would expect to find in this system and for each entity you have named, give a list of the attributes for each table, identifying in each case the primary and foreign keys. **(9 marks)**
   (b) Draw an entity relationship diagram to show the links between the database tables named in part (a). **(3 marks)**

5 Your lecturer/teacher has said to you that 'many-to-many relationships between two entities should be avoided'.
   In a college enrolment system you have identified two entities: STUDENT and COURSE. It is possible for the one student to be enrolled on more than one course and the one course can contain many students. The relationship between the two entities is a many-to-many relationship.
   Explain how to resolve the above problem and draw an entity diagram representing the final system. **(5 marks)**

6 Data modelling is a useful technique used during systems analysis. What is data modelling and in what ways does it help the analyst? **(3 marks)**

7 A database is to be set up to hold details about crimes, offenders and officers. Before setting up the database, an initial investigation was conducted and some analysis performed. The investigation revealed the following list of entities:

   OFFICER
   CRIME
   OFFENDER
   VICTIM

   (a) Explain what is meant by the term 'entity'. **(2 marks)**
   (b) The analyst drew the following relationship between the two entities VICTIM and CRIME.

   Give the name of this type of relationship and describe why it causes a problem when creating the ICT system that uses these two entities. **(3 marks)**
   (c) To solve the problem a new entity is created called VICTIM_HISTORY and the relationship between this and the previous entities is shown here:

   Explain how the creation of this new entity solves the problem of the many-to-many relationship. **(3 marks)**
   (d) On investigating the other entities, the following entity relationship model (ERM) was constructed.

   Label the entity relationship by placing an appropriate label on each link. **(4 marks)**

Activities

▶ Activity 1: Creating a decision table

To pass a course in computer studies at college a student must satisfy the following conditions:

They must pass all the Computing units.

They must pass English and Maths.

They must have at least 80% attendance (unless they satisfy this attendance rule they will fail, even though they might have passed all the units).

The actions that can happen are:

Pass course

Re-do English or Maths or both

Re-do failed Computing modules

Fail course

Draw a decision table to show these rules.

▶ Activity 2: Which of these are atomic?

Which of the following attributes could be considered to be atomic?

Video details

Date of birth

Membership number

Member name

Enrolment

Quantity in stock

Product number

For each of the above attributes that are not atomic suggest suitable attributes which are atomic that can replace them.

▶ Activity 3: Entity relationship diagrams

Draw entity diagrams to show each of the following relationships:

1 Classes consist of many students.
2 One customer has many orders.
3 One tutor lectures on many courses.
4 Each module is taught by one tutor.
5 Many students enrol on many courses.
6 Many customers order many products.

▶ Activity 4: Creating an entity relationship model for an ICT system

A market research company takes on staff on a per job basis, although as one job finishes another one starts. It has asked a consultant to build a database system to store details about staff, jobs, rates and the hours they work. Initial analysis reveals the following entities:

EMPLOYEE

DATE

HOUR

JOB

RATE

Further investigation revealed the following:

At a given moment one employee can work on only one job with that job having only one rate. The one job can have many hours and can be done over many dates. The one rate can also be paid over many hours and worked over many dates. Finally, one employee can work many hours over many dates.

Produce an entity relationship model to show this system.

▶ Activity 5: Deciding on attributes for entities

A college library borrowing system has been looked at and was found to have the following entities:

MEMBER (a person who is a member of the library and eligible to borrow books)

BOOK (a book which may be borrowed)

LOAN (a link between a particular book and the person borrowing it)

RESERVATION (books may be reserved by members, so that when brought back they are kept aside for another person).

The above system is only part of the whole library system.

For this activity you have to identify and list the attributes for each of the above entities. You will need some attributes which uniquely define the entities MEMBER and BOOK. Although the ISBN (International Standard Book Number) is used by bookshops to identify book titles, a library might have many copies of the same title, in which case the ISBN could not be used to distinguish each copy.

Produce your list and show it to your tutor.

Activities *continued*

▶ Activity 6: Listing the attributes of entities

Here is a list of some entities and your task is to write down five attributes that could go with each entity. Further information contained in brackets will provide you with a context for the entity.

GOAL (scored in a football match)
CD (in a music catalogue)
EMPLOYEE (in a personnel system)
STUDENT (for a college administration system)

▶ Activity 7: The removal of many-to-many relationships

The following many-to-many relationship may be encountered in a hospital or GP system.

DOCTOR — PATIENT

This entity relationship shows that one doctor deals with many patients and that one patient sees one or more doctors. There is therefore a many-to-many relationship.

(a) Explain the reason why many-to-many relationships cannot be implemented on a database.

(b) Re-draw the diagram by including a suitable intersection entity and give this new entity a suitable name.

▶ Activity 8: Creating entity descriptions for a data dictionary

Produce a brief, clear description for each of the following entities. The context in which the entity appears is outlined in brackets after the entity.

PATIENT (as applicable to a GP)
DVD (in a DVD hire system)
RESERVATION (in a seat reservation system for an airline)
STOCK (in a warehouse system)

▶ Activity 9: Describing the relationships between entities

Look at the following entity relationship diagrams from both ends and write down the two descriptions for each diagram.

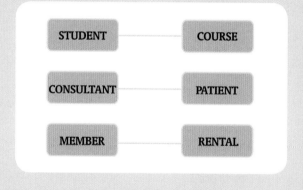

▶ Activity 10: Drawing an entity relationship diagram for an order processing system

The order processing system is responsible for receiving orders, verifying inventory quantities, arranging delivery, sending invoices to customers, and processing customer payments. Salespeople call on customers for orders and complete an order form, which is a 3-part form. The form is sent to Wendy, who does the following:

For a new customer, Wendy fills out a customer card with the person's name and address, and files it in the customer card file.

For existing customers, she looks up their account balance in the customer card file. If money is owing, the order is rejected and is returned to the customer.

If the order is accepted, Wendy checks the quantities ordered against those on hand as recorded in the inventory file.

If the order can be filled, Wendy adjusts the quantities by hand on the inventory file, and enters the quantity shipped into the appropriate column on the order form.

Finally, Wendy sends one copy of the form to the warehouse, and a second copy to Cindy; she retains the third copy for her files. Cindy is 'Accounts Receivable', and is responsible for calculating prices, entering the amount on the customer's card, sending invoices, and recording the payment amounts received in the customer file.

Tasks

1   Draw a context diagram for the order processing system.
2   Draw a level 1 DFD for one of your processes.

Exam support

Worked example 1

1 A hotel has two halls which are used for weddings, parties, conferences, etc., called the Derby Suite and the Sefton Suite. There is also equipment that can be booked with the halls such as plasma TV, data projector, music system, etc. Each suite has its own set of equipment.

When one of the suites is booked, at the time of booking, the equipment is also booked.

When the systems analyst investigated the data requirements of a new ICT system for the booking, the following rules were found to apply:

When a booking is made, it is for one suite only (i.e., Derby Suite or Sefton Suite).

A member of the public or group, called the customer, can make one or more bookings.

Each piece of equipment belongs to only one suite.

A booking may require many pieces of equipment.

Complete the following entity relationship diagram by showing the relationships between the entities. Label all the relationships. **(8 marks)**

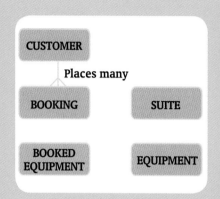

Student answer 1

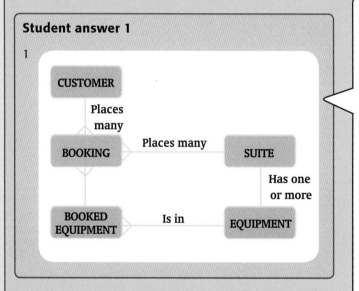

Examiner's comment

1 This student has drawn two out of the four relationships correctly.

The relationship between Suite and Equipment is one to one. This would imply that there is only ever one piece of equipment associated with one of the suites, which is incorrect. If this were the case then the entities Equipment and Suite could be combined as the equipment could be considered an attribute of Suite rather than a separate entity. The relationship between Booking and Booked Equipment is the wrong way around. A Booking is the entity which links a Customer to the Booked Equipment and it was created by the analyst to remove the many-to-many relationship that previously existed between Customer and Equipment. One booking is only ever for one piece of equipment but the one piece of equipment can appear in many bookings.

The labelling of the relationships is incomplete as only three out of the four are given. The student should really at least have guessed. What probably happened is that they forgot to put this in. Remember to check your work as this one mark lost could have been on the grade boundary that divides one grade from another.

The student should have been guided by the label given. If they had done this they would have seen that the type of relationship should be included in the label.

This means the 'Is in' label is insufficient so only two of the labels are correct so two marks are awarded for this. **(4 marks out of 8)**

Exam support *continued*

Student answer 2

1

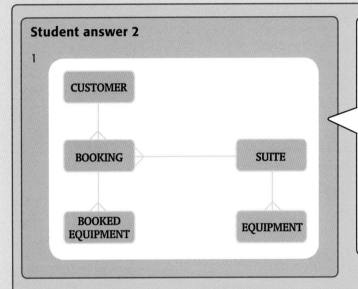

Examiner's comment

1 The student has identified three correct relationships, so three marks here. They have missed the relationship between Booked Equipment and Equipment. Students need to be aware that the Booked Equipment entity has been included in order to remove the many-to-many relationship that would have existed between Booking and Equipment.

This student has not labelled any of the relationships. This is probably due to not reading the question properly and they have thrown away four relatively easy marks here. **(3 marks out of 8)**

Examiner's answer

One mark for a correct relationship (not to include the relationship shown in the question) to a maximum of four marks.

One mark for a word or short series of words that describes the type of relationship.

A typical solution would be:

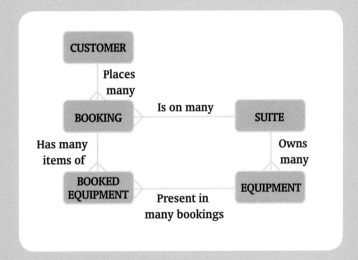

Summary mind maps

Investigating and recording techniques

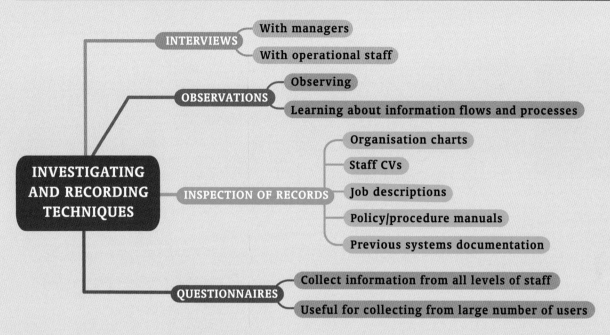

Business process modelling tools

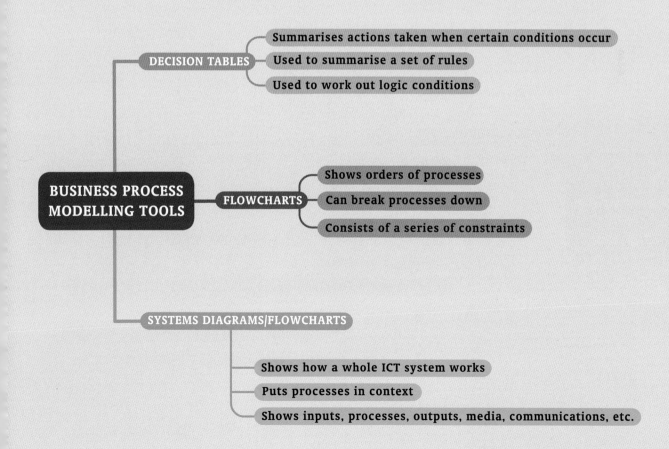

Summary mind maps *continued*

Data modelling tools

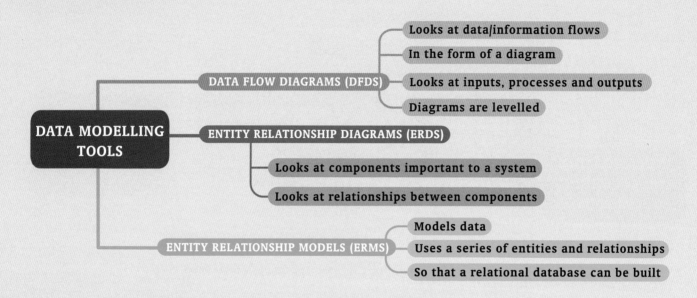

Techniques for testing

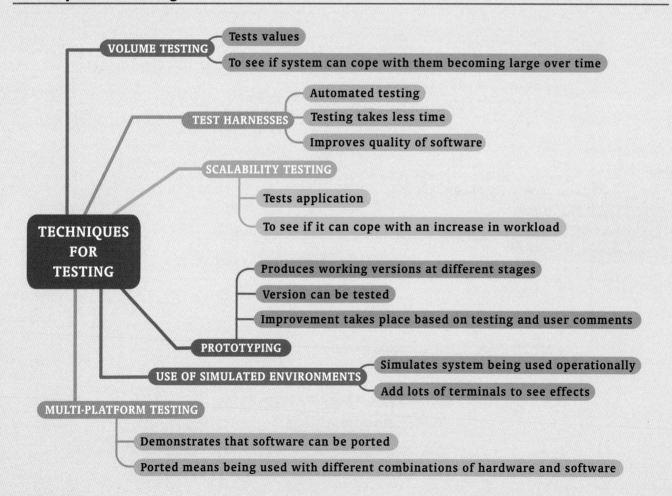

TOPIC 10: Introducing large ICT systems into organisations

In this topic you will learn about how large ICT systems are introduced into organisations.

In some cases the organisation may choose to purchase a software package that can be customised to their particular business with the customisation being performed by their own ICT staff or outside consultants.

In many cases the organisation will have their own ICT development staff and will choose to develop some or all of the ICT system in-house.

▼ The key concepts covered in this topic are:

▶ Scale

▶ Reliability and testing

▶ Installation

▶ Backup and recovery

▶ Maintenance

CONTENTS

1 Scale, reliability and testing 122

Scale, NHS systems locally and nationally, reliability and testing, ensuring that large ICT systems always operate as expected, designing testing to ensure reliable operation – techniques and the people involved, alpha and beta testing, the specialist skills and facilities required for the testing of network-based systems and testing networks using network tools.

2 Installation 126

Methods of introducing systems, hardware installation and testing, software installation and testing, documentation and resources.

3 Backup and recovery 128

Strategies for backup of large-scale systems, risk analysis, scale of backup, procedures for recovery of large-scale systems, disaster recovery/contingency planning, options for recovery and training.

4 Maintenance 132

Maintenance releases of software, the three types of system maintenance on large systems: perfective, adaptive and corrective, maintenance teams and user support.

5 Questions and Case study 134

6 Exam support 136

7 Summary mind maps 139

Unit 3 Use of ICT in the Digital World

Scale, reliability and testing

▼ You will find out

▶ About scale

▶ About reliability and testing

Introduction

You will already have some understanding of introducing small ICT systems into organisations with the project work you did for the AS Level. Here you will be looking at the introduction of new ICT systems into very large organisations.

In this section you will be looking at the problems that the scale of the organisation presents and also some of the issues involved in the testing of large ICT systems.

Scale

There is a huge range in the sizes of organisations and their corresponding ICT systems, and this affects the way that new ICT systems are introduced. In some cases large ICT systems are used entirely within a large organisation and in other cases the large ICT system is used across multiple small organisations.

Many large organisations will have ICT development staff who will build ICT systems from scratch but others will choose to purchase a software package that can be tailored by the developers.

Take a newsagent as an example. Many of the smaller newsagents are family concerns and are very small organisations. They still have the same information needs as the much larger newsagent chains such as WH Smith, Menzies, etc. They still need to order newspapers, magazines, cards, sweets, tobacco, etc., keep stock and make payments to suppliers. This means that although these small newsagents are separate organisations, they still have the same administrative needs and so a system has been developed that enables them to deal with their supplier using a common ICT system.

The advantages of the Connect2U system for small newsagents are that:

- it allows them to compete with the much larger multiple newsagents
- it gives them management

information such as which magazines and newspapers are selling well – this can vary from week-to-week depending on promotions/TV advertising

- it connects with their EPoS system, which means there is automatic exchange of information
- they can manage their orders on-line by making amendments to orders, viewing sales history, dealing with returns and so on.

Overall it allows small newsagents to have access to all the ordering systems similar to those used by the large multiple newsagents thus allowing them to remain competitive.

Connect2U is a system that enables newsagents to order newspapers and magazines from the supplier WH Smith.

EXAM TIP

You will get asked in the examination to give examples of large ICT systems used within a single organisation or used across multiple organisations. You can give the newsagents system and the NHS care system as examples.

NHS systems locally and nationally

Some of the NHS ICT systems are used nationally, whilst others are used locally. The NHS Care Records Service is an example of such a system. Basically, detailed patient information is kept locally while a less detailed summary of the information is kept nationally.

The detailed patient information is collected and compiled locally and can be transferred between GP surgeries and local hospitals. The summary care record is held nationally and can be used in an emergency. For example, if the patient was ill or involved in an accident in another part of the country, then the summary care record can be accessed. All the patient information is transferred using a secure link thus ensuring the privacy and security of the patient data.

Your GP or consultant already uses a computer system to keep notes of appointments they have with you, plus medicines prescribed, test results and details of any referrals to other health professionals. X-rays and scans are also increasingly held on computers rather than sheets of film. This information is often needed by two health care professionals simultaneously and this is easily supplied using ICT systems. In the past X-rays had to be transferred physically from one department to another and this was wasteful and often resulted in delays.

Connect2U is an ICT system that allows small independent newsagents to compete with the large newsagent chains by offering them similar ordering methods and important management information.

NHS Care Records Service is an example of a system which can be used nationally and locally but with differing degrees of detail.

Reliability and testing

Large systems are developed by large numbers of specialist staff, often in different locations, so they need rigorous testing to ensure they operate correctly. Testing large systems is much more complicated than testing a small system that has been created by a single person. Each person involved in the testing of a large system will have worked on their own part of the project and then all the parts will be put together to form the complete system. Often development teams can run into hundreds of people and there can be huge amounts of money allocated to the development.

The main objectives of any testing are to:

- make sure the software is compatible with other ICT systems with which it should communicate
- eradicate faults in the software by looking at how it will be used, predicting what errors are likely to occur and then designing tests to expose these errors
- test portability – this means checking that the software can be ported to specified hardware and software platforms

- review the software, which is done by presenting the software to project personnel, managers and other interested parties for their comments.

In this section you will be looking at the issues involved in the testing of large ICT systems which are as follows:

- ensuring that large ICT systems always operate as expected
- designing testing to ensure reliable operation – techniques and the people involved.

Ensuring that large ICT systems always operate as expected

When programmers create new programs they create programs in units with each unit performing a certain task. Unit testing is done to verify that the programming code for a particular unit is working correctly.

The next stage of testing is called integration testing and this is where the individual units or program modules are combined and tested as a group. Integration takes modules that have been unit tested and combines then together and applies a series of tests to the group as defined in a test plan.

System testing follows integration testing and covers both hardware and software. This type of testing tests the system as a whole and is a type of black box testing which means that this testing does not look at the logical design of the programs or the programming code itself.

Designing testing to ensure reliable operation – techniques and the people involved

Software testing can be either white box or black box testing. White box testing involves testing of the program by people who are familiar with programming and the program code itself. The testers need to build tests that will allow errors to be identified so that they can be corrected. The white box testing therefore ensures that the programming code is written correctly.

Black box testing is used by people who never look at the programming code. Instead they look at the output produced and they also check to see if the requirements and specifications have been met.

Both black and white box testing are used to ensure as far as is possible that the programming code does what it is supposed to do correctly and does not contain errors (i.e., bugs).

Tests can be manual or automated. Automated tests are ideal for repetitive tests that need to be conducted on a regular basis. For example, a change may have been made that is likely to slow down the performance of the software. Automated tests can pick this up so that a solution can be found.

Many organisations have a test bed computer installed, which is different from the one being used operationally. For security purposes some organisations do not like development staff having access to the computers being used for the day-to-day running of the business.

Scale, reliability and testing *continued*

Alpha and beta testing

Testing can also be classified according to who does the testing. This type of testing is referred to as alpha or beta testing.

Alpha testing is the first stage in the testing of computer products such as software, before they are released for public use. Alpha tests are usually coordinated by the hardware manufacturer or software producer. The alpha tests are usually performed at an in-house site that is not normally involved with the software developers. Alpha testing uses data that is selected by the software producer. When bespoke (i.e., tailor-made) software is tested, the alpha test would normally test the implementation against the design specification to check that it does what it is supposed to do. Larger tests, called beta tests are conducted by users selected by the software producer.

Beta software is the name given to the preliminary version of the program that is widely distributed before commercial release to users. These people test the program by operating it under realistic conditions. Often, heavy duty demanding users are chosen so that any bugs or shortcomings are exposed before final release. With bespoke software this will be the first time that the software is tested off-site using real 'live' data. The purpose of beta testing is to identify any errors not picked out during the alpha testing. It is hard for the software developer to test the software in all the environments it will be used, so this is a very important stage.

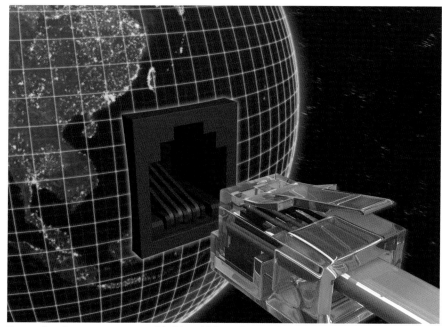
Networks often are set up worldwide which makes testing much more difficult.

The specialist skills and facilities required for the testing of network-based systems

Networks are complex systems and need to be set up (i.e., configured) in order to give their best performance. Testing network systems is complex because networked computers are usually located in hundreds of different places (often around the world) so there needs to be a different way of monitoring performance other than testing the performance of each terminal.

The people who test networks are very highly skilled people with technical skills such as:

- a good understanding of hardware and how it functions together
- an in-depth knowledge of network protocols such as TCP/IP over Ethernet
- selecting benchmarks for network performance.

With black box testing, the programming code is not looked at during testing.

> ### KEY WORDS
>
> **Network testing** – the actual measurement and recording of a network's state of operation over a period of time. It involves recording the current state of network operations to serve as a basis for comparison or control

Testing network-based systems would typically include:

- checking the security of any wireless links (i.e., ensuring that the encryption is working correctly and hackers cannot intercept signals)
- checking the capacity of the network to carry high volumes of traffic at certain times
- testing wireless signal strength by positioning of antenna, checking error rates, etc.
- testing to find network bottlenecks.

Testing networks using network tools

Network testing is a complicated process but luckily there are network tools that will help with this. Network tools are software that will help diagnose problems and come up with solutions. They can be used to help optimise the speed of a network by configuring it in a different way.

Most network tests are scheduled just like virus scans and they collect information about the performance of the network which can be presented to the network engineer in the form of graphs and charts.

The most important thing with networks is to be able to provide measurements of a network's current performance. When network tests are undertaken they can be compared against previous network configurations to see whether the performance has improved or deteriorated. It is also possible to make changes to the network and then see if they have actually improved the performance.

Network testing tools would typically give the following information:

- Station level statistics – this gives the network information about the traffic generated by particular terminals on the network and the type of data being transferred (e.g., multimedia, text, etc.). The network manager/engineer can configure the network for those users who need the greatest speed.

- Segment level statistics – this looks at the network traffic over certain parts of the network which can be used to determine network capacity or troubleshoot a problem that causes the network to run slowly for certain users.
- Filtering – allows only certain samples of data to be collected such as data from certain IP addresses.
- Intelligent monitoring and event logging – this testing tool monitors the network and looks for current problems or for problems that are likely to develop in the future.
- Events that happen on the network that cause changes to the performance are logged so that the network engineer/manager can sort out any problems.

Testing is needed to see how the network is able to cope with different amounts of traffic.

Testing is needed to check signal strength in wireless networks.

Installation

Introduction

Once a system has been developed and the software fully tested, the next stage of introducing the system into a large organisation is to install the hardware and software. Large systems present difficulties due to their size and complexity and there are large risks in installing such systems. In this section you will look at the methods of introducing large systems and what is involved in the installation, testing and documentation of these systems.

Methods of introducing systems

In order to change from one system to another it is necessary to have a changeover method. There are several methods used and these are outlined below.

Changeover methods

Direct changeover

With direct changeover you simply stop using the old system one day and start using the new system the next day. The disadvantage of this method is that there is an element of risk, particularly if the hardware and software are cutting edge. It the system fails then it can be disastrous to the business. The advantage of this method is that it requires fewer resources (people, money, equipment) and is simple provided nothing goes wrong.

Parallel changeover

This method is used to minimise the risk in introducing a new ICT system. Basically, the old ICT system is run alongside the new ICT system for a period of time until all the people involved with the new system are happy it is working correctly. The old system is then abandoned and all the work is done entirely on the new system. The disadvantages of this method are that it involves a lot of

unnecessary work (as the work is being done twice) and is therefore expensive in people's time. It also adds to the amount of planning needed for the implementation.

Phased conversion

One module at a time can be converted to the new system in phases until the whole system is transferred. The advantage of this is that IT staff can deal with problems caused by a module before moving on to new modules. The disadvantage is that it is only suitable for systems consisting of separate modules.

Pilot conversion

This method is ideal for large organisations that have lots of locations or branches where the new system can be used by one branch and then transferred to other branches over time. The advantage of this method is that the implementation is on a much smaller and manageable scale. The disadvantage is that is takes longer to implement the system in all the branches.

▼ You will find out

▶ About the methods of introducing systems

▶ About hardware installation and testing

▶ About software installation and testing

▶ About documentation

▶ About resources

Hardware installation and testing

Hardware needs to be installed and tested before the software is installed. Large systems are bound to be networked, so a large part of the time is spent wiring up the network or setting up wireless networks and then testing them. Most new buildings will have special spaces where network cables and power cables can be hidden thus avoiding the need for trailing wires.

Software installation and testing

Large systems often contain different servers located in different places so all the required software will need to be installed on each server. Software then needs to be configured so that it works

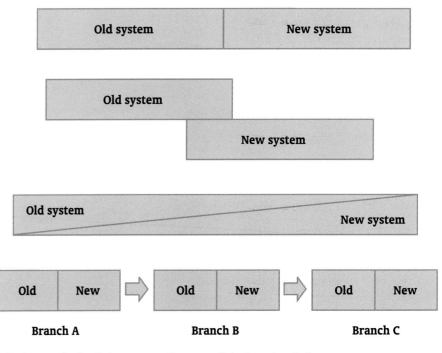

The four methods of changeover: direct, parallel, phased and pilot.

with the network and can be accessed by the computers on the network.

Once the software has been installed, the data needs to be added to the database or data warehouse. Special software called file conversion utilities may be needed to enable the new software to be able to use the old set of data which may have been created using different software.

Once the software and data is in place the whole system needs to be tested for functionality. This means that testers needs to test all the various functions of the system and then correct any problems that may arise with the help of other development staff such as programmers and analysts.

Documentation

There are two types of documentation: user documentation and technical documentation.

User documentation (or user guide) for the system

A user guide or manual is documentation that the user can turn to for learning a new procedure or for dealing with a problem that has cropped up. The guide should cover:

- minimum hardware and software requirements
- how to load the software
- how to perform certain functions
- how to save
- how to print
- frequently asked questions (FAQ)
- how to deal with error messages and troubleshooting
- how to back up data.

It is a good idea to include examples and exercises to help the user understand the system. Since users are usually non-technical, any specialist, technical language should be avoided.

The guide should detail what to do in exceptional circumstances. For instance, if the system fails to read a disk, or data is sent to the printer without it being switched on and the machine is locked, a user will need to know what they have to do. You should also include backing up and closing down instructions.

As always, users have the best view of a system and so should be asked to evaluate any proposed user guide. Their comments should be incorporated into the guide. You have probably tried to find advice in manuals so you will realise just how important they are.

Technical documentation

It is important that systems are fully documented because the person who designed and implemented the system may no longer be around to help with problems. Someone else who may not be as familiar with the system may have to maintain it. In order to do this they will need to understand how the system was designed and implemented. Technical documentation is produced to help systems analysts and programmers understand the technical workings of the system.

You would expect to find the following included in the technical documentation:

- a copy of the system design specification
- all the diagrams used to represent the system (flowcharts, system flowcharts, data flow diagrams, entity relationship diagrams, etc.)
- the data dictionary
- macro designs, spreadsheet formulae or program listings
- screen layout designs
- user interface designs
- test plan.

Resources

Installation takes up different resources but the main cost is in terms of the human resource costs for training the staff that will be using the new system. This often means taking the staff away from their normal operational work and training them to use the new system. Training will be looked at in detail in the next topic.

Staff must be fully trained to use a new system, which takes time and can be expensive.

Backup and recovery

Introduction

When new systems are introduced there needs to be a backup and recovery strategy put in place to cope with all the threats to which ICT systems are subjected.

In this section you will be looking at what a backup and recovery strategy is as well as risk analysis and how companies can recover data should the worst happen.

Backup strategies for large-scale systems

Large-scale systems need to be capable of access 24/7 so any backup strategy needs to take this into account. Downtime needs to be reduced so methods need to be in place so that should computing power be lost then another spare system starts up automatically to take over. Many large systems which need 24/7 availability use distributed computers where processes and storage are replicated across different computers connected to a network.

The storage capacity of the software and data needed by large systems is very large and this means that taking backups on portable media would take too long. Instead computers and storage are used in tandem with the original system so mirroring occurs, which is each system doing exactly the same thing. These systems are in different locations and the data is passed between them using high-speed links.

Disaster planning (backup and restoration)

Sooner or later most companies will have to cope with a situation that will cause the loss of hardware, software, data or communications services or a combination of these. This loss could be caused by:

- hardware failure
- software bugs
- natural disasters (e.g., floods, fire, earthquakes, hurricanes, etc.)
- deliberate damage (malicious damage by staff, viruses, hacking, vandalism, terrorist bombs, etc.)
- accidental damage (e.g., accidental deletion of files, damage to equipment, etc.).

Disaster planning is needed:

- to minimise the disruption caused
- to get the systems working again in the shortest time possible
- to ensure that all staff know what to do to recover data, programs, etc.

"**We back up our data on sticky notes because sticky notes never crash.**"

▼ You will find out

- About strategies for backup of large-scale systems
- About risk analysis
- About scale of backup
- About procedures for recovery of large-scale systems
- About disaster recovery/contingency planning
- About options for recovery
- About training

Establish a disaster recovery programme

All organisations should consider what they would do if they lost their entire ICT facility (hardware and software). Organisations would still have the data, as most data is transferred off-site, should a disaster happen. This is extreme as not many organisations will experience this, although most organisations will experience loss of some part of their ICT facilities.

The disaster recovery programme is a series of steps that would be taken should an organisation lose some or all of its facilities. The idea of the disaster recovery program is to minimise the loss of business and get things back on track as soon as possible.

Backup

Loss of programs and hardware loss are not too much of a problem as these can be replaced. However, if there is no backup, data cannot easily be replaced and such a loss can cause companies such financial loss that many of them go out of business.

Backups should be:

- taken on a regular and routine basis or even taken automatically
- kept away from the computer in a locked fireproof safe or preferably kept off-site
- taken using the grandfather, father and son principle in the case of batch processing systems
- used with a RAID (random array of inexpensive disks) system.

This is a mass storage system used to hold backups.

to identify those systems crucial to the organisation and to look at the possible short- or long-term loss of such systems.

Here are just some of the many consequences of system loss:

- cash flow problems as invoices are sent out late
- bad business decisions through lack of management information
- loss of goodwill of customers and suppliers
- production delays caused by not having the correct stock available
- late delivery of orders causing customers to go elsewhere
- stock shortage or overstocking caused by lack of suitable stock control.

Restoration

It is no use taking backup copies of files and not checking that the original files can be recovered using the backup. It is important that staff understand what they need to do to recover the lost or damaged data. Occasionally, organisations should do a mock disaster recovery to check it actually works.

Identifying risks

There are lots of threats to ICT systems, so organisations need to work out what the risks are, how likely they are to occur, the likely consequences should they occur, what can be done to minimise the risk and whether this can be done at reasonable cost.

Risk analysis is an important part of running ICT systems in organisations, as many of them rely completely on their ICT system. In this section you will learn about risk analysis and how an organisation is able to assess how much money should be spent on the minimisation of risk.

Risk analysis

The main purpose of risk analysis is to make everyone in the organisation aware of the security threats to the hardware, software and data held. They need to be made aware of the

consequences of any loss for a short or sustained period such as the immediate financial loss and the long-term loss caused by lack of customer confidence, the bad publicity in the press and the inability to provide customer service.

In order to perform a risk analysis, it will be necessary to consider the following:

1 Placing a value on each of the components of a successful information system which would include:
   - hardware
   - software
   - documentation
   - people
   - communications channels
   - data.
2 Identifying the risks to the above and the likelihood of their occurrence.

Most organisations have a corporate information technology security review, which looks at the computer processed information with a view to identifying the risks of unavailability, errors and omissions, abuse, unauthorised disclosure and to determining their potential implications. Each risk will need to be examined from the point of view of the security and the loss assessed and its likely occurrence. The aim is

Identify potential risks

If ICT systems are to be protected, then the risks need to be identified. Here is a list of the risks to most ICT systems:

- viruses
- fire
- natural damage (floods, earthquakes, lightning, volcanoes, etc.)
- hacking (tapping into communication lines)
- systems failure owing to machine malfunction
- fraud
- power failure
- sabotage
- theft (hardware, software and data)
- blackmail
- espionage
- terrorist bomb attacks
- chemical spillage
- gas leaks
- vandalism
- spilling a drink over the computer equipment
- failure of the telecommunication links
- problems with data cables in networks
- malfunctioning hubs and routers, etc.
- software failure
- systems software containing bugs causing the computer to crash
- hard drive damage/loss
- strikes.

Backup and recovery *continued*

Risk assessment works out the likelihood of a risk occurring.

Organisations should have a contingency plan to deal with the unexpected.

Likelihood of risk occurring

Some things, such as a power cut, are almost certain to happen sooner or later but others, such as an explosion, are much less likely, but all the threats need to be taken into account. Senior management have to decide the likelihood of the risk occurring and how the risk can be minimised at reasonable cost and what levels of risks are acceptable to the organisation.

Short- and long-term consequences of threat

Threats have short- and long-term consequences. For example, a virus attack could result in data being lost and it would take time and tie up resources to determine what data has been lost and to recover it from the backups. Resources would also be tied

up removing the virus from the system and ensuring that the attack did not happen again.

Short-term consequences include:

- loss of the network for a short period means productivity is lost
- customers needing goods quickly may choose to go elsewhere
- resources are tied up dealing with getting the system working properly again
- cash flow is disrupted requiring emergency funding from banks.

Long-term consequences include:

- lost customers may never return to do business again
- bad publicity means new customers are less likely to want to do business with the organisation
- prosecutions may occur resulting in fines or imprisonment for staff.

How well equipped the company is to deal with threat

Organisations need to continually ask how well they could deal with a threat should it occur. Threats and organisations change over the years so this needs to be reviewed periodically.

The disaster recovery/ contingency plan

The purpose of the disaster recovery programme is to ensure the availability of essential resources (staff, buildings, power, etc.) and computer equipment should a disaster occur. The plan will usually cover the following:

- the total or partial loss of computing equipment
- the loss of essential services such as electricity, heating or air conditioning
- the loss of certain key employees (e.g., losing all the qualified network staff in one go due to them choosing to form their own facilities organisation)
- the loss of maintenance or support services
- the loss of data or software
- the complete or partial loss of telecommunication equipment or services
- the complete or partial loss of the premises housing the ICT equipment.

Options for recovery

Recovering data can be almost instant if distributed computing is used, as the other processors and storage devices can take over if there is a loss of data from another processing device on the network.

For most other ICT systems the data will need to be recovered from the backups. Once a disaster happens, the organisation should implement its disaster recovery plan, which sets out what is needed to recover any lost data and to get the main business functions

Training is essential so that all staff understand how to recover data.

all working again. This can be done without the use of premises or files in order to determine:

- Whether the expected timescales for recovering the key business applications are realistic.
- How well trained and prepared staff are for putting the plan into action.
- Whether any third parties or service providers who are integral to the plan can respond in the expected timescale.

Rules for backing up

- Never keep the backup disks near the computer. If the computer is stolen, then unless the thieves are ignorant about computers, they will probably take the disks as well. Never keep the disks in the drawer of the desk since this is the first place thieves will look.
- If you hold a lot of data then you should invest in a fireproof safe to protect your backups against theft and fire.
- Keep at least one set of backup disks in a different place (i.e., at a different site).

performing again in the least possible time. Equipment will need to be made available and suitable staff brought in to aid the recovery process.

Methods of recovery might include:

- carrying out activities manually until ICT services are resumed
- staff at an affected building moving to another location
- agreeing with another business to use each other's premises in the event of a disaster
- arranging to use ICT services and accommodation provided by a specialist third-party standby site.

Training

Organisations should fake loss of data to ensure that their recovery plans work and all the staff understand their role in the recovery process. This training process is essential as everyone needs to work together to get the system up and running in the least possible time.

Testing the contingency plan

Testing the contingency plan can be time consuming and expensive as it disrupts the day-to-day activities of the organisation. It will test whether the organisation has covered all the angles

and whether the plan is achievable. Testing also makes staff more aware of the plan and also trains them so that they know what to do in different situations.

Organisations can test the contingency plan by carrying out a real restore of data using data that has been backed up to get the systems

If data is kept on the premises it should be secured in a fireproof safe.

Maintenance

Introduction

Once the system has been implemented it will need to be maintained. It is important to note that the people involved in the original project may leave the organisation, so new staff will need to familiarise themselves with and understand the new system. They will need documentation in order to do this, so the first stage of the system maintenance process is the production of both user and technical documentation.

In this section you will learn about the on-going system maintenance needed to satisfy the change in business needs and user requirements. Eventually there will come a point when the system no longer meets the business needs and so a new system will need to be created and all the tasks

Programmers often have to close loopholes in programs to prevent hackers gaining access to data.

Bugs in programs may only reveal themselves once many people use the software.

involved in the systems development life cycle will need to be repeated.

The reasons why maintenance is needed

There are various reasons why maintenance of systems is needed including:

- Bugs in the software may cause the software to crash. It is impossible to test the software so that it is used with every combination of hardware and software. When new hardware or software is added, the original program may behave in an unexpected way.
- User dissatisfaction with aspects of the program may mean that the program may need to be altered.
- A new operating system may be installed and changes may be needed for the software to work with the new operating system.
- There may be changes in legislation. For example, there may be changes in the rate of income tax or VAT, which mean certain programs have to be altered.
- Security updates or patches are needed. Sometimes weaknesses are found in software that cause a security breach and these need to be eliminated by the writing of some new programming code.
- To improve performance. When the number of users of the software on a network increases then it may be possible to improve the speed of the program by altering the program code.

Maintenance releases of software

Maintenance releases of software provide additional functionality and improvement of quality of the original package. It is also an opportunity for software manufacturers to provide patches of code that will enable the software to work with new hardware

or peripheral devices, which were not around when the software was originally developed. Sometimes maintenance releases improve the security of the software.

Maintenance releases may also be sent direct to the customer from the software supplier and this is why it is important to register the software on-line. Usually the maintenance releases are sent with a link to the software producer's website, which means the software can be added automatically.

Maintenance releases are usually to address the following:

- They are used to perfect the software in some way by, for example, improving performance such as the speed with which certain operations are performed, which may improve the use of main memory.
- They may also be corrective. That means that they are used to correct the bugs that come to light after the software has been released.

The three types of system maintenance on large systems

Maintenance of an ICT system (i.e., hardware, software and communications) can be classed as perfective, adaptive or corrective.

Perfective

Perfective maintenance will improve the performance of the ICT system. Usually this will involve adding features not originally present to the software to make it produce the information from a database faster or improve the speed of a network.

Adaptive

The ways of doing things change in an organisation. For example, there may be new laws, which mean that the

Changes in legislation give rise to adaptive maintenance of systems.

system needs changing. Changes in the way the organisation operates may require a change in the system.

Corrective

This is correcting faults or bugs that did not reveal themselves during testing. Sometimes the combination of new software and hardware causes the older software to crash. Software manufacturers often produce updates to deal with these issues and these have to be installed.

Think about what these words mean:

- perfect – to make as good as is possible
- adapt – to make necessary changes
- correct – to ensure that faults or problems are eliminated.

Maintenance teams

When new software is installed there will usually be problems for the first few months, which will necessitate changes being made to the software. Maintenance teams consisting of technical staff and programmers will be made available to deal with these problems as they arise. In most cases these staff will have been involved in the original development of the project and will have a detailed understanding of the system and the programming code.

With the passage of time, problems with the system will diminish and these maintenance teams will move away from performing corrective maintenance and be more involved in adaptive and perfective maintenance.

EXAM TIP

You can remember the three types of maintenance (perfective, adaptive and corrective) in the following way: perfect, adapt and correct (PAC) and then add the ending 'ive'.

User support

Most organisations will make use of a help-desk to support users of the organisation's systems. If a problem causes many user calls to the help-desk then the maintenance teams may consider making adjustments to the system in order to correct the problem. User support will be a good place for the developers to find out about the usability of the system and the difficulties users experience. They can either solve the problem by focusing training on these areas or by improving the user interface or functionality of the software.

Bugs in software necessitate corrective maintenance.

User support includes the help-desk.

Questions and Case study

▶ Questions 1 pp. 122–133

1 (a) An ICT system has just been developed for an organisation.
Compare and contrast the different methods they could use for conversion over to the new system. **(6 marks)**

(b) Once conversion has taken place the system will need to be maintained.

(i) Explain what is meant by system maintenance and give **two** examples of tasks that would normally be completed as part of this maintenance. **(4 marks)**

(ii) Describe **two** different methods of system maintenance, giving an example in each case to illustrate your answer. **(4 marks)**

2 When one ICT system is being replaced by another there are a number of different methods of conversion.

(a) Give the names of **three** different methods of conversion from one ICT system to another and discuss the relative merits of each method. **(6 marks)**

(b) Once the system has been implemented, technical and user documentation will need to be provided. Explain the difference between these two types of documentation and give **three** examples of items which would be included for each of the two types. **(8 marks)**

3 An ICT professional who specialises in software testing makes this comment, 'It is almost impossible for software to be tested in a way that would eliminate all the bugs.'

(a) Explain why in reality it is hard, if not impossible, to produce software without any bugs. **(2 marks)**

(b) Two ways by which software can be tested are the following:

(i) alpha testing
(ii) beta testing.

Explain the essential features of each of these testing methods. **(4 marks)**

4 Before releasing a new package, the software company carries out alpha and beta testing.

(a) What are these two types of testing and why are they both needed? **(6 marks)**

(b) Explain why, once the package has been released, there may be a need for maintenance releases and how these might be dealt with. **(6 marks)**

5 A school is in the process of implementing a new schools information management system, which is to be used throughout the school. Part of this process will be the implementation of a backup strategy and recovery procedures.

(a) Describe the issues that the school would need to consider when deciding on a suitable backup strategy. **(6 marks)**

(b) Describe what the school must consider when deciding on recovery procedures for this new system. **(3 marks)**

6 Explain what is meant by the term 'risk analysis' and explain the processes an organisation must undergo to assess the risks to their ICT system. **(5 marks)**

7 There are three types of system maintenance: adaptive, corrective and perfective.
Describe the main features of these **three** types of maintenance, giving suitable examples where appropriate. **(6 marks)**

8 Discuss the essential features of a successful installation plan for a large-scale ICT system. **(8 marks)**

9 Part of ICT security concerns backup and recovery procedures.

(a) Discuss the methods used by organisations to back up their programs and data. **(6 marks)**

(b) Explain how an organisation can ensure that the original data can be recovered should loss of hardware, software and data occur. **(4 marks)**

A terrorist attack

On a Saturday in June 1996 the police received a coded warning that a bomb had been planted at the Arndale Centre, which is Manchester's premier shopping area. Just over an hour after a speedy evacuation of the Centre and the surrounding area, the bomb exploded, injuring over two hundred people and destroying a large part of the Centre and ripping apart many of the business premises surrounding it. The bomb, which was the largest bomb explosion in peacetime Britain, caused extensive damage to the offices of the Royal and Sun Alliance insurance company where some staff were injured.

As these offices housed the company's mainframe computer it was initially feared that the day-to-day operations of the company would be severely affected. The staff in the Liverpool office, which contained terminals that were networked to the mainframe, found that there was still some life in the system, even though there was extensive damage to the building the computer was housed in. There was some optimism that the system could be recovered, but to prevent the likelihood of gas explosions from the ruptured gas mains, the fire brigade cut off the electrical power. Effectively most of the hardware had been irreparably damaged during the explosion. However, like most sensible companies, this one had a contingency plan and it involved having a contract with a specialist data recovery company who had similar hardware and copies of software being used by Royal and Sun Alliance. Because they needed staff to operate the computer who understood the Insurance business, the Royal's staff were transported to the offices of the recovery company and they set to work recovering the data from the backup media which was kept off-site. By Monday morning all the data had been recovered and a temporary switchboard had been set up and not a single day's trading was lost.

1   The Royal and Sun Alliance insurance company has an ICT security policy. As part of this policy they performed a risk analysis and also established a disaster recovery programme.
   (a) Explain what is involved in risk analysis. (2 marks)
   (b) Describe the techniques used in the disaster recovery programme to recover the data used by the ICT systems. (6 marks)

2   Backup and recovery procedures are an essential part in ensuring the security of ICT systems.
   (a) Explain the difference between backup procedures and recovery procedures. (2 marks)
   (b) Give **three** things that must be considered when choosing a backup procedure. (3 marks)
   (c) Explain why recovery procedures are essential if an organisation such as this insurance company wants to ensure the security of its data. (2 marks)

Exam support

Worked example 1

1 No matter how well software is tested, it still needs to be maintained. Explain the types of maintenance that might be needed and why this maintenance is needed, illustrating your answer with suitable examples. **(8 marks)**

Student answer 1

1 Software may need to be upgraded, which will iron out any bugs or problems that were not discovered during the testing.

Software will need to be changed as the needs of the business change. The software may need to be able to supply files to another piece of software that has recently been bought. This will enable the data from the software to be sent to and used by another piece of software.

There may be new laws which will mean that the software will need to be changed. For example, new data protection laws may mean that the software works in a way that would be illegal under the new laws.

Examiner's comment

1 This answer has made some valid points but it would have been better to have identified the three types of maintenance: perfective, adaptive and corrective and then structure the answers accordingly.

There are five points made in this answer worthy of marks. **(5 marks out of 8)**

Student answer 2

1 Perfective maintenance means that the performance of the software or whole system is improved. An example would be where a new version is produced that runs faster than the previous version, such as where management information is produced in a lot less time than before.

Corrective maintenance is where there are problems with the software that cause crashes, incorrect results, layout problems, etc. The software is corrected by the programmers or program manufacturers.

Adaptive maintenance may be required if the needs of the organisation have changed since the software was developed. The managers may decide that the software should work in a different way and produce more management information. Organisations merge so sometimes systems need to be changed so that they all produce output in a similar way.

Examiner's comment

1 This is a much better answer than the previous one. The student has structured their answer and this has led to them being able to supply good explanations and examples.

This is an excellent answer and there are many more points made than the eight needed for full marks. **(8 marks out of 8)**

Examiner's answer

1 One mark for each point to a maximum of eight. Students can only get a maximum of six marks if they have not given any examples.

Perfective maintenance (1) – improving the performance of the software (1).

Examples: Configuring the network management network (1) to improve the performance of a network such as improving access times to data, speed at which reports are produced, etc. (1).

Software may need to be modified to improve the user interface (1) upon feedback from users who are finding it more difficult to use than it needs to be (1).

Developing on-line tutorials and more help screens (1) to help new staff learn the software (1).

The software provider provides upgrades (1) which will improve the performance of the software (1).

Corrective maintenance (1) – bugs in the software which were not discovered during testing may need correcting (1).

Example: A piece of software may crash (1) when being used with another piece of software (1).

A piece of software may crash (1) when used with a particular item of hardware (1).

Software may present a security risk which needs correcting (1).

Problems with reports not being printed out properly (1).

Adaptive maintenance (1) – software may need to be changed owing to the changing needs of the business or organisation (1).

Example: Software may need altering so that it is more flexible in supplying the managers with information (1) which was not envisaged at the time of development (1).
Changes to values such as the percentage rate of VAT or changes to income tax rates will result in changes to the software (1).

The organisation expands (1) so the software needs to be altered so it is able to cope with an increased number of users (1).
Adapting the software to work with newly developed operating systems software or new hardware (1).
A virus threat/hacker threat (1) means that the software will need to be adapted to protect against this (1).

Worked example 2

2 Once a system has been investigated and analysed, resulting in the implementation of a new system, consideration needs to be given to the changeover strategy.
  (a) Compare and contrast two alternative strategies for the changeover from an old ICT system to a new ICT system. (6 marks)
  (b) Discuss the reasons why users may become increasingly dissatisfied with an implemented ICT solution over time. (4 marks)

Student answer 1

2 (a) You can run the two systems in parallel with each other until users are happy with the performance of the new system. They can make sure that there are no errors produced and then they can start using the new system.
Another way is just to start using the new system. This way is easy because you do not have to waste any time.
  (b) The new system may not be as easy to use as they thought and the training might not be enough, so they are constantly being held up waiting for someone to help them.
They may not like the speed of the network as it may take too long to get jobs done.
They may find that the new system does not do all it was supposed to do, so is a waste of money.

Examiner's comment

2 (a) Although the student has mentioned parallel conversion they have not explained its relative advantages clearly enough. They need to say that it increases the workload on the staff because everything is done twice for the parallel period.
The second part of the answer is superficial. It is always best to mention the name of the method of conversion (i.e., direct conversion/ changeover) in this case. Much more detail is needed here and a comparison should have been made. Two out of the six marks have been given to part (a).
  (b) This answer is good but only worth two of the four marks.
They should have made reference to more things that change over time such as a change in the nature of the business. **(4 marks out of 10)**

Student answer 2

2 (a) Parallel conversion where the new system runs alongside the old system for a few days or weeks until the users are sure that the new system can be trusted to work as expected. This method increases the amount of work the user has to do, as for a period they are doing the work twice. The advantage is that you only have to give up the old system when you are completely happy with the new system, so this method is low risk compared to the next method.
The next method is called direct changeover, which means that the old system is stopped and immediately the new system is used. There is a lot of risk compared to parallel conversion as there is no old system to fall back on.
There is less work though and it is much cheaper in terms of the resources needed.
  (b) There may be dissatisfaction due to the ICT system not fully meeting the user requirements, meaning users find that there are things that cannot be done using the new system.
The business may expand and the new system may no longer be able to cope with the performance demands placed on it. For example, there may be more users, so the whole system runs very slowly.
Maintaining the system may cost too much.

Examiner's comment

2 (a) Both methods of conversion have been well described with their relative advantages and disadvantages mentioned and full marks are given for this excellent answer.
  (b) Only three points have been adequately explained. The last point in the final sentence is not given a mark because it needs further explanation as it fails to mention any examples of maintenance. **(9 marks out of 10)**

Examiner's answer

2 (a) One mark for the correct name and correct brief explanation for each strategy × 2
One mark for the advantage or disadvantage of the method × 2
One mark for a comparison of the method × 2
Direct changeover – stop using the old system one day and start using the new system the next day (1). Element of risk particularly if the hardware and software are cutting edge (1). It the system fails then it can be disastrous to the business (1). Requires fewer resources (people, money, equipment) and is simple provided nothing goes wrong (1).
Parallel changeover – used to minimise the risk in introducing a new ICT system (1). The old ICT system is run alongside the new ICT system for a period of time until all the people involved with the new system are happy it is working correctly (1). The old system is then abandoned and all the work is done entirely on the new system (1). Disadvantages: lots of unnecessary work (as the work is being done twice) and is therefore expensive in people's time (1). It also adds to the amount of planning needed for the implementation (1).
Phased conversion – a module at a time can be converted to the new system in phases until the whole system is transferred (1). Advantage that IT staff can deal with problems caused by a module before moving on to new modules (1). Disadvantage: is only suitable for systems consisting of separate modules (1).

Pilot conversion – this method is ideal for large organisations that have lots of locations or branches where the new system can be used by one branch and then transferred to other branches over time (1). Advantage: implementation is on a much smaller and manageable scale (1). Disadvantage is that is takes longer to implement the system in all the branches (1).

(b) One mark for each point up to a maximum of three. Final mark for a point which applies to increasing dissatisfaction over time with the system.
Example answers include:
The full range of user requirements has not been met, so the system does not live up to user expectations.
Change in business needs means system cannot deal with new demands placed on it.
Failure to supply users with the information they require.
User interface causes many user problems with increased help-desk use.
Problems with the software or system crashing due to lack of rigorous testing.
Network performance or speed of access to stored data becomes unacceptable as more users are added to the system.
Modifications to the system are needed regularly and the system needs replacement with a new one.
Too much time is spent updating the new system.
The cost of user support is too high.
There are security breaches which were not envisaged when the system was first developed.

Summary mind maps

Backup and recovery

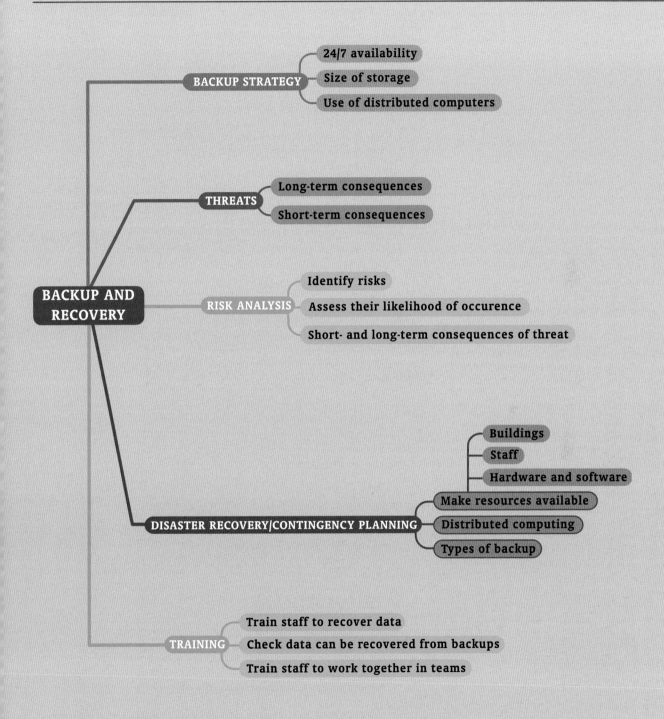

Installation

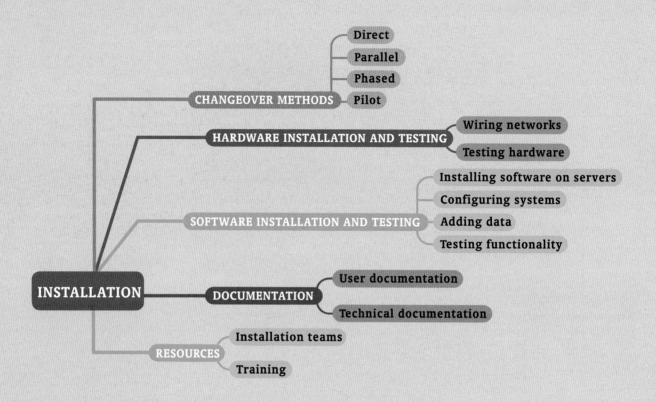

- CHANGEOVER METHODS
  - Direct
  - Parallel
  - Phased
  - Pilot
- HARDWARE INSTALLATION AND TESTING
  - Wiring networks
  - Testing hardware
- SOFTWARE INSTALLATION AND TESTING
  - Installing software on servers
  - Configuring systems
  - Adding data
  - Testing functionality
- INSTALLATION
- DOCUMENTATION
  - User documentation
  - Technical documentation
- RESOURCES
  - Installation teams
  - Training

Maintenance

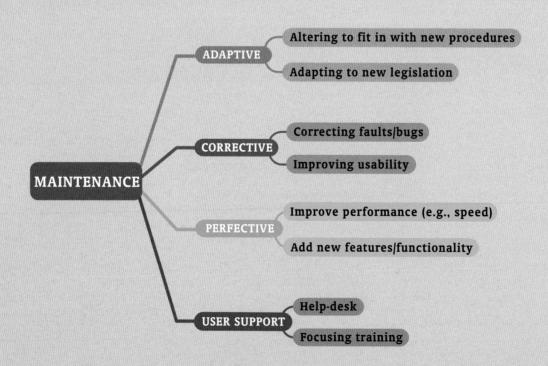

- ADAPTIVE
  - Altering to fit in with new procedures
  - Adapting to new legislation
- CORRECTIVE
  - Correcting faults/bugs
  - Improving usability
- MAINTENANCE
- PERFECTIVE
  - Improve performance (e.g., speed)
  - Add new features/functionality
- USER SUPPORT
  - Help-desk
  - Focusing training

TOPIC 11: Training and supporting users

When a new system is introduced, the people who will be using the system will need to be trained and supported throughout the life of the system. Any training needs to be appropriate to the task being performed and also to the level of the staff using the system. In large organisations staff generally have clearly defined roles and any training will need to help them use the system to perform these roles.

Training will also need to be accompanied by user support, where the user can get help on job-related tasks using the new system. In many organisations this will be provided by a help-desk internal to the organisation. This is not the only way that support can be provided, so in this topic you will also be looking at other methods of supporting users.

▼ The key concepts covered in this topic are:

▶ How users of ICT systems can be both internal and external to the organisation and how the training and support requirements may be different

▶ Training and training methods

▶ Support

▶ Training and supporting customers

CONTENTS

1 Internal and external users and their training requirements..142
How different levels of staff need to learn different functionality of systems to match job and role requirements and how external users may require training.

2 Training and training methods..144
The relative merits of the different methods of training and training methods available.

3 Support..146
Support options available.

4 Training and supporting customers..149
The interfaces available for customers, and managing the interface between the organisation and its customers.

5 Questions..152

6 Activities and Case study..153

7 Exam support..155

8 Summary mind maps..157

Unit 3 Use of ICT in the Digital World

Internal and external users and their training requirements

Introduction

Users of ICT are not always members of the organisation that owns the ICT system. For example, e-commerce sites need to be used by members of the public for placing orders. Bank and building society mortgage application systems need to be used by independent financial advisors who use the system for quotations, etc.

Training users who work within the organisation is easy because you can arrange training appropriate to their existing skills and needs, but providing training and support to users who are external to the organisation is more difficult.

In this section you will be looking at the different training and support needs of different people and how to provide training and support for users who are external to the organisation.

How different levels of staff need to learn different functionality of systems to match job and role requirements

Staff in large organisations perform clearly defined roles such as dealing with accounts, processing customer orders, purchasing supplies, managing a department and so on. Staff using ICT systems will need to be trained and some of this training will relate to their specific role, while other training will be of a more general nature.

Software, especially enterprise software, is capable of being used by all levels of staff but lower down, the software would be used for more day-to-day routine tasks such as dealing with orders, making payments, dealing with customer queries and

so on. Higher up in the organisation managers can use the management information the system supplies to make decisions about the organisation of work in their department or other day-to-day activities.

At the top of the organisation the senior managers, executives and directors will use the system to drill down amongst the huge amount of data to extract information to enable them to make decisions about the general direction of the business (e.g., whether to expand certain areas of the business, whether to relocate the business, etc.).

In order to perform the above tasks, the different levels of staff will need different levels of information from the same system, and to be able to extract this information, they will need appropriate training. Training therefore needs to be specific to particular jobs and at different levels.

How external users may require training

People who do not belong to the organisation may still need to use an organisation's ICT systems. Here are some examples:

- Independent financial advisors using bank and building society systems for mortgage quotations and comparisons between products.
- Franchisees who run their own business under the umbrella of a large organisation (e.g., Subway, Kumon, Coffee Republic, Wimpy, etc.).
- Car dealerships that have an arrangement with car manufacturers to sell their cars but are able to use the car manufacturers' systems to place

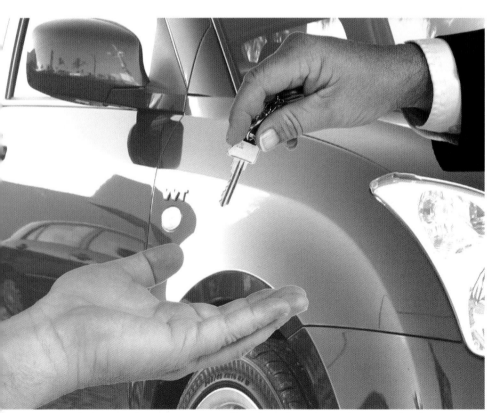

Car dealers need to order new cars direct from the car manufacturer using the car manufacturer's system.

orders, obtain up-to-date prices, view sales targets and information on previous customer satisfaction.

- General practitioners (GPs) using the NHS systems to book hospital appointments for patients or to claim money for their practice.
- Travel agents using holiday companies and airline booking systems for their clients.

The training of customers is more difficult than training employees working within the organisations because they are located in many different places and need to be brought together for training.

There are a number of difficulties in training external users and these are outlined below:

- External users can be scattered all over the country or even the world.
- It is hard to assess the amount of training needed by these users as they have wide-ranging skills and knowledge and there may be no records of their training.
- It is hard to justify time out for training when they are not your employees.
- It is difficult to find a time for training that fits in with all users.

These problems can be overcome in the following ways:

- Use methods such as CBT (computer-based training) for users who find it difficult to find the time for training or who are in remote locations.
- Use questionnaires (on-line or paper-based) to assess the skills and knowledge of users prior to training.
- Collect information from the users about their function and role in their organisation so that you know what part of the ICT to concentrate on for training.

Training of external users can be achieved by:

- sending staff on training courses in hotels, at the organisation's headquarters, etc.
- sending staff from the organisation to the customer's premises for hands-on training using the customer's own equipment
- training using videoconferencing equipment
- training using distance learning materials such as material on DVD/ CD-ROM, instruction manuals, or on-line courses.

Training on procedures

ICT training is not just restricted to showing users how to use new hardware and software. Users also need to be trained on policies and procedures. For example, changes may need to be made to the ICT security policy following an event such as a virus attack or employees spending too much time visiting social networking sites such as Facebook. Social networking sites are a relatively new development, so a policy for this would not have been needed in the past.

Changes in legislation to deal with the abuses of ICT systems will result in the need for training, as will changes in legislation resulting in changes to procedures. For example, it is possible to submit tax returns (details about income and expenditure for businesses) on-line and also on paper and there are different procedures for each method.

> ### ▶ KEY WORDS
>
> **External users** – people who use an organisation's ICT system but who are not actually employed by the organisation
>
> **Internal users** – users of the ICT system belonging to an organisation who are employees of the organisation

Hands-on computer training can be performed in specially equipped rooms.

Many organisations make use of computer-based training.

Staff can be trained on changes in procedures.

Training can be performed using videoconferencing.

Training and training methods

▼ **You will find out**

▶ About the relative merits of the different methods of training for the organisation

▶ About the relative merits of the different methods of training for the individual

Introduction

There are many different ways of training users in the use of new ICT systems. Which method is chosen depends on the ability and motivation of the individual and the amount of money set aside for training.

In this section you will look at the methods of training in terms of the relative merits for the organisation and the individual being trained.

The relative merits of the different methods of training

There are a number of situations which will create a need for ICT training and these include:

- the adoption of a new ICT system
- changes to the existing ICT system (e.g., increased functionality, upgraded software, introduction of new modules, etc.)
- the adoption of a new operating system
- induction training for new employees
- training to make employees aware of security issues (e.g., virus attacks, hackers, etc.)
- training to ensure employees who use ICT equipment adopt safe working practices
- training to make employees aware of relevant existing and new legislation

Users need to be trained to adopt safe working practices when working with computers.

- ensuring employees understand the organisation's ICT policies (e.g., acceptable use policies, etc.)
- the adoption of new working practices.

Training methods available

There are many different training methods available and which method or methods are chosen depends on a number of factors which include:

- the costs of the training
- the amount of training needed
- whether it is possible to allocate days out of work for training or whether the training is to be completed in addition to the normal work
- the existing capabilities/skills of the employees.

The training methods include:

- instructor-based/classroom training
- one-to-one training
- cascade training
- computer-based training (CBT)
- distance learning
- use of manuals/books/software guides.

Instructor-based/classroom training

This is a popular method for training a large number of users at a time and it involves an instructor/trainer delivering training material to an audience of employees. In many cases the training will include a computer workshop where the employees work through material for set tasks such as entering order details, etc.

One-to-one training

For most people one-to-one training is the best training method whereby an instructor sits down and shows one user how to use the new system. The trainer can work at a pace which is perfect for each trainee and the trainee can ask any questions which crop up.

The problem with this method is that it is very expensive as only one employee is trained at a time.

Cascade training

With cascade training one person is sent on a course or trained thoroughly on a one-to-one basis and this person then goes back to the organisation where they use their new skills and knowledge to train others. This saves the organisation money as only one person needs to be sent on the external training course.

Computer-based training (CBT)

Computer-based training (CBT) uses ICT systems for training in the workplace usually by making use of PCs or portable devices. It is important to note that CBT is not just about training people to use computers, although it can be used for this. It is about using computers to train people to do different tasks and also to train them how to react in different situations.

CBT can be used for:

- health and safety training – to teach people how to spot dangers in the workplace
- how to perform a particular job – for example, how to operate a piece of equipment
- induction courses – used to introduce new employees to the company or business
- instruction on how to use a particular piece of software.

Features of CBT

- It is highly interactive – users supply answers to questions and situations.
- It makes use of multimedia features.

Training materials are available for media players.

- It is used for tutorials – allows the user to learn something new.
- It uses models/simulations – so that the user can experiment to see what happens in different situations.
- It is used for revision – tests with interactive activities that allow students/users to assess their progress in the area of revision.
- Encouragement – it does not matter if a user gets answers wrong – they can try again and the answer is often shown after a certain number of attempts.
- Games to make learning fun – even the most serious topics can be made fun when turned into a game.
- Testing and assessment – here the user can take a test/assessment to see how well they have understood the learning/training. The results from the test/assessment are given immediately including information on what they did well and what they did less well.
- It can be used for learning at a distance – no need for formal learning with lessons in set places at set times, etc.

Advantages of CBT

- Employees have flexibility as to where and when they want to learn.
- Materials are provided in lots of different ways such as text, voice, video, animations.
- The material can be accessed using a variety of different hardware such

as laptop, PDA, mobile phone with MP3 player, iPod, etc.
- You can learn in many different environments such as in a car, while out running or walking, etc.
- Keeps people interested and motivated by the variety of activities.

Disadvantages of CBT

- The software is often complex and uses lots of animation and graphics which makes it expensive.
- Students often need the interaction of their colleagues in order to learn.
- Can present an opportunity for students to have a break rather than work on the CBT package.
- It is hard for trainers to gauge progress using some of the packages.

Distance learning

Distance learning is learning which takes place away from the confines of a traditional trainer in a room teaching a group of employees. Instead the learning takes place away from the trainer. In many cases distance learning makes use of videoconferencing so that the trainees can see the trainer and the trainer can see the trainees. Distance learning is ideal where the organisation cannot justify the expense of taking on a specialist trainer.

Distance learning can make use of all the latest ICT developments such as:

- e-mail – trainees are free to e-mail their trainers with problems they are having with the topic

If the solution is hard to use, then users can be in for long phone calls trying to get through to the help-desk.

Software manuals and guides can be used to learn new software.

- chat rooms – students can chat in real time amongst themselves or with their trainer in a group tutorial
- videoconferencing – allows a trainer to give a training session to trainees who may all be located in different places.

Use of manuals/books/software guides

Highly motivated users may find that the best way to learn about a new ICT system is to sit down at the computer and use manuals, books and software guides to help them learn the new system. This is a hard method for many people who would prefer to be trained by a person, as with this method there is no-one around to ask if you do not understand something.

This method is ideal for someone requiring knowledge in just a small area of the package – for example, a manager wanting to know about more advanced spreadsheet features such as pivot tables.

Support

Introduction

Ideally with comprehensive training staff would be completely competent users of the ICT systems. Unfortunately the time and money for this level of training to be provided could be prohibitive. This means that users of the system will need to be supported when they have problems and this support can be provided in a number of ways which are discussed in this section.

Support options available

Problems will always occur when people use computers and these problems can often leave the user unable to use the facility. With appropriate and proper training, the number of problems that can easily be solved by the user increases and this leaves only the occasional, more technical problems to be resolved. During the introduction of new hardware, applications software or operating systems, the number of problems encountered by the users increases, and for this reason many companies do not respond to every slight change in hardware or software the way that home users might.

There are many ways in which an organisation can deal with the problems encountered by users, and

Employees lose productivity waiting for help.

organisations use either one or a combination of the following methods.

Existing user base

If you are working in an office with other more experienced users and you encounter a problem with a particular piece of software, then it may be prudent to ask someone you work with for their help before approaching anyone else. It is reckoned that about 80% of ICT problems are solved by non-ICT staff. If the problem cannot be solved in this way then you can make a telephone call to a help-desk that may be in-house (i.e., within the company) or provided externally by the company who supplied the hardware or software.

Help-desks

In most large organisations user support is provided through the use of help-desks. Help-desks are usually manned by someone from the ICT department, although with the growth of outsourcing, the help-desk could be outside the organisation. Their purpose is to give expert advice to users regarding any software and hardware problems they might have.

By logging each call to the help-desk it is possible firstly to assess the performance of the help-desk and secondly to look at the frequency of user problems. For example, one particular problem might crop up time and time

Many problems with ICT systems can be solved informally by a colleague.

again and rather than just deal with these calls as they arise, it might be better to resolve them through changes in the operating procedures or by more training of the users.

Some companies have made use of intranets to enable the users to trawl through a knowledge base and therefore seek the answers to simple problems themselves without the need to consult a member of staff on the help-desk. Other companies use the web to send messages from users requesting help to the help-desk rather than use the telephone. Replies to the users' requests for help can be sent back over the web and this saves them time trying the help-desk phone number only to find that it is continually engaged.

In order to provide an efficient service to the users, the help-desk must be carefully managed to enable the users' problems to be resolved in the minimum amount of time. It should be borne in mind that many of the calls to the help-desk prevent the user from carrying on with the task they are trying to do, so the sooner their problem is resolved, then the sooner the user can return to productive work.

It is often advisable for the calls to the help-desk to be routed to certain people who have an expertise in a particular area. So a hardware problem should be directed at the person who knows most about hardware. Large help-desks are normally organised into teams with each team specialising in a different area of computing.

Details of those errors that occur regularly with a particular piece of hardware or software may be stored on a database so that the help-desk staff do not have to rely on their memory. These systems make use of a keyword describing the problem. A word is keyed in and if the problem is stored on the database, then possible remedies are shown.

Some help-desks make use of expert systems where fairly inexperienced help-desk staff can use a body of knowledge stored on the system and the system gives them a series of questions which they ask the users over the phone. The replies given are typed in and the system comes up with the best solution to the problem. After a while, the help-desk staff build up their experience and do not need to make use of the system as much.

When looking at how a member of the help-desk staff would troubleshoot a user problem it is important to bear in mind that in a large organisation the help-desk may not be in the same location as the user. This usually makes it impossible for the help-desk staff to visit the user to sort out their problem. Instead, most problems have to be sorted out over the telephone, which means that the help-desk staff usually have to ask a set of structured questions before they get to the actual thing causing the problem.

These questions will obviously vary from one organisation to another and in some cases the help-desk will have clear descriptions of hardware and software available to the user which will cut out some of these questions. Such questions will usually include the following:

- What hardware is being used?
- What applications software is being run? (This usually involves the version of the software being run.) It some cases the help-desk staff may have descriptions of all the software on the user's machine loaded into a database.
- What operating system is being used?
- A concise explanation of what the problem is and also what the user was doing prior to noticing the problem.
- The current state of the computer; i.e., whether the computer is displaying any error messages or has crashed, etc.

"Please listen carefully as some of our menu options have changed. For customer service, go fly a kite. For technical support, whistle in the wind until the cows come home. For repair service, wait for you-know-what to freeze over...."

What methods can be used to contact the help-desk staff?

There are various ways users can contact help-desks. They include:

- telephone
- voicemail
- e-mail
- company intranet
- Internet.

Because of the problems in contacting help-desks using the telephone, most help-desks allow users to send their problems in the variety of formats listed here. Sometimes the help-desk will send the reply back to the user in the same format in which it was sent and if the problem is vague, then it may be necessary for the help-desk staff to speak to the user. Since most users are connected to a network, it is usually possible for the help-desk staff to see the user's screen display on their own workstation so that they can see what they are trying to do. In some cases the help-desk staff can work at home, so this is a task ideally suited to telecommuting.

Help can be provided via the organisation's intranet.

Help-desk software

As you will have seen in the last section, keeping track of all the calls, details of users and their problems is a necessary part of the quality control for any help-desk. It is therefore not surprising that software tools have been developed to manage the calls and allow user problems to be solved in as short a period as possible.

Help-desk management software has the following features:

- There is usually a database at the heart of the software containing outlines of problems and their solutions, which lessens the need for the help-desk staff to rely on their memory.
- Since help-desk staff access the same database of solutions, they will all use the same consistent approach, regardless of the member of staff giving the help. This means that no matter which member of staff you use, you will still get the same answer to the problem.
- The system keeps track of the call until the problem is resolved.
- Once the problem is resolved, it is added to the database, so that if a similar problem occurs, then the same solution can be given to the user. This means that many of the calls to the help-desk are routinely solved in minutes rather than the 2 to 3 hours it used to take.
- The help-desk staff can call up the user's history of problems, which can help them give a level of help tailored to the user's ability. Repeated requests for simple help would indicate a novice user.

User support from software producers

Software producers provide user support via telephone help lines or over the Internet. Many software producers provide users with a free period of advice over the telephone and after

this period they usually have to pay for support. Help-desks are usually very busy just after a new version of application software or operating system has been brought out, since users may have queries which the manual or the on-line help does not deal with. As more and more books and training courses are developed and produced, the experience of the user is built up and they are then able to help the less experienced users without the need to resort to a help-desk.

It is important to determine in advance of buying software what sort of support is available, whether it is provided free and the period of this free support.

Many support problems arise when one company is taken over by another, since they may no longer want to support the older company's products. A similar problem can occur when there is a new release of software and the organisation is still running the previous version. Eventually the software producer may no longer support the older software and it will be necessary for the organisation to upgrade their version.

Support articles

Many users experience similar problems to other users, so many computer magazines from the supplier or articles in the computer press will address these problems and outline what the user can do to solve them. Also included in this would be the plethora of computer books that explain how to use a particular package. Many of these books are specific to a particular level, so if you are a very advanced user and want to develop applications using the software,

then there will be a book which will assume your prior knowledge, so that you do not waste time starting at the beginning again.

Many paper-based or on-line articles include a section called FAQ (frequently asked questions) and these deal with many of the problems users have and how they have got around their problems.

On-screen help

On-screen help is a feature of most software packages and its purpose is to supply the user with on-line help if they get stuck. In many cases the user needs to be quite knowledgeable on ICT to be able to use the help facilities, since they have to understand the nature of their problem and be able to describe it using a word or combination of words. Some packages make use of on-line tutorials which instruct users in how to perform certain tasks such as doing a mail merge using a word-processor. Many problems can be resolved using the on-line help and all users should be aware that this facility is available to them and how to use it.

The help-desk is an essential part of user support.

Specialist bulletin boards/blogs

Specialist bulletin boards/blogs are a useful place to go to for support from other computer professionals. Most staff will use the Internet on a day-to-day basis and it will be the natural place for them to look if they are having any problems with hardware and software. Since this advice is free and often impartial it is very useful. Many experienced computer professionals are keen to impart advice on problems that newer members of staff may come across.

Training and supporting customers

▼ **You will find out**

▶ About the interfaces available for customers

▶ About the relationship between the choice of interface and the business activities

▶ About managing the interface between the organisation and its customers

Introduction

Customers or other users outside the organisation often have to use an organisation's ICT systems. These customers need to be supported and in some cases trained to use the system.

If a system is to be used by customers and those customers are accessing the organisation's system via a website, then the user interface should be self-explanatory and as easy to use as possible.

The interfaces available for customers

It is important to realise that before a human–computer interface is designed, it is essential to understand the needs of the people who will be using it. Often their needs vary, since the interface will need to be used by people with widely different ICT skills and abilities. Sometimes the interface is to be used by a specific group of people

such as children, engineers, doctors or people with a specific disability.

Luckily the number of people who are unable to use a keyboard and mouse has diminished but there are many people around who have never used a computer. Any interface needs to support low levels of ICT skills so they can be used by almost anyone.

The main interfaces include:

• keyboard and mouse
• voice recognition systems
• touch screen.

When creating a good user interface there are a number of factors to consider which include:

• consistency of signposting and pop-up information
• on-screen help
• layout appropriate to task
• differentiation between user expertise
• clear navigational structure
• use by disabled people.

Cash machines need to be used by everyone, so great care is taken in designing the interface to make it as easy as possible to use.

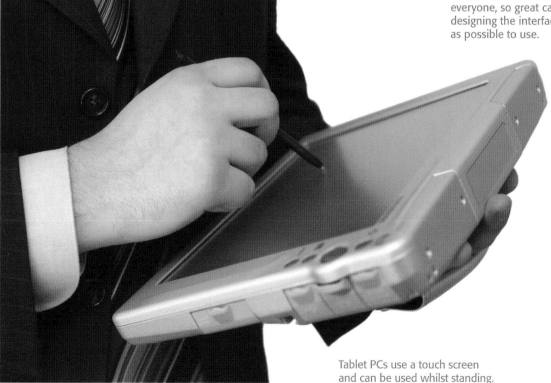

Tablet PCs use a touch screen and can be used whilst standing.

Training and supporting customers *continued*

The relationship between the choice of interface and business activities

There are many different interfaces available and which one is chosen depends on a number of factors such as:

- Whether it is possible or appropriate to train the user – if the user is a member of the public then training may be out of the question. For example, how could you train all the users of a petrol pump payment system or all the users of a cash machine?
- How complex the system is – clearly constructing the conditions for extracting management information from a huge mass of transactional data is not something people would be expected to perform without training.
- The money available for perfecting the interface – the costs of developing the interface can be divided among all the users.

Reading meters is prone to errors, so readings are entered onto a PDA which validates the data.

The type of business activity can also influence the choice of interface. Here are some examples:

- Meter readings – the interface needs to be used standing up and on the move. Keyboard input would be inappropriate and the interface must be capable of being used with minimal training because of the number of staff involved. Accuracy is paramount, so readings need to be verified and validated on the spot. A touch screen interface is used with a wireless connection to the main system, so readings are input directly so there is no need for re-keying.
- Taking customer orders/bookings – orders/bookings can be taken face to face or over the phone. The interface will involve the taking of information from the customer and keying it in by filling in an on-screen form. There are other interfaces that can be chosen. For example, the customer could fill in a paper order form and then send it by post, where it is scanned and read using optical character recognition.

Many orders are now made on-line, where the customer enters the details of the order and their own details including payment details. Because customers will use this interface without any training, the interface needs to be designed carefully. Most e-commerce sites allow users to customise the website, for example by increasing the font size, changing the colour scheme, etc.

- Processing questionnaires – many organisations need to assess customer satisfaction about products or services and they need to be processed in a cost-efficient and timely way. The main requirement here is that there should be little human involvement in the processing, other than batching the questionnaires. The interface must then be flexible and be capable of being used by anyone who needs to collect information in this way. Users may use this system as a one off, so it is hard to justify the cost of training to use the system.
- Management information systems – these systems need to be used by all levels of managers, many of whom may have limited ICT skills. The user interface needs to provide help to construct complex search conditions, so many of these systems guide the user through the steps.

Questionnaires completed manually should be read and processed by computers but with on-line questionnaires the data is in digital form ready for processing.

Managing the interface between the organisation and its customers

Customers often need to use systems that have been set up by other organisations and, as you have already seen, this is not simply restricted to websites. Because of the difficulties in training customers who are not within the organisation but still need to use the system as an integral part of their job, they need to have interfaces, training and support that will help them.

Managing the interface between the organisation and its customers would normally include:

- e-mail support – answering customer queries on getting the system to work
- user manuals – enabling customers to use the system on their own with little or no additional help
- feedback from users – this is important as users can give useful comment and feedback on how the user interface can be improved
- ensuring on-line help meets the needs of users – help is essential, especially for new users of the system. The help needs to be relevant to the task and there should be the opportunity for further support (e.g., phone calls to a help-desk or contact by e-mail) if the user has more problems.

Most software comes with on-screen help.

Copyright 2003 by Randy Glasbergen.
www.glasbergen.com

"Try our product for 30 days. If you're not completely satisfied, then just be grateful that you live in a country where people are still allowed to be dissatisfied!"

A user's satisfaction with the interface should be assessed.

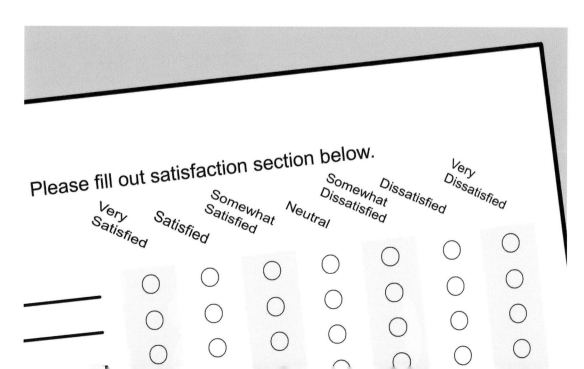

Questions

▶ **Questions 1** pp. 142–151

1 (a) By giving a suitable example, explain how different levels of staff within the same organisation require training to match job and role requirements. **(4 marks)**

(b) A car manufacturer has introduced a new ordering system for new cars. As all the dealerships are separate businesses, but will need to use this new system when placing orders, outline how the car manufacturer should train the staff in the dealerships. **(6 marks)**

2 Here is a statement which appeared recently in an article in the computer press on training methods:

'Computer-based training/computer-assisted learning is little more than an electronic page turning exercise that is hardly any different from reading a manual or book.'

From your experience of CBT/CAL packages, write a short piece in reply to the above argument, saying whether you agree or disagree with the statement and supporting your view with examples of CBT/CAL which you have used or seen. **(8 marks)**

3 You have been asked to advise an organisation on the introduction of a new software package.

(a) With the aid of **three** examples, explain why different users may require different levels of training on the new package. **(6 marks)**

(b) The users are given some initial training on the new software. After this initial training you advise that some users will require further training. Explain why this extra training may be needed. **(4 marks)**

4 A company needs to train users in the use of the company's new intranet. As well as being able to use the intranet, the organisation wants employees to be aware of the security and privacy issues involved in its use.

Discuss the methods that this company could use for the training of its employees. **(8 marks)**

5 Once users have been trained in the use of both the hardware and software for a new ICT system, they will still need on-going support.

(a) Explain one reason why this on-going support is needed. **(2 marks)**

(b) Discuss the support options that this organisation could use once the initial training in the new system has been given. **(4 marks)**

6 Explain, by giving a suitable example, why training needs to be specific to particular jobs and at different levels. **(3 marks)**

Activities and Case study

▶ Activity 1: Choosing the best training method

There are a variety of training methods that can be used depending on the task or skill users are trying to develop and which one is chosen depends on the ability of the user and the skills or tasks they are trying to learn. The training methods to choose from are usually from the following group:

- computer-based training (CBT)
- on-line tutorials or help
- step through guides
- a formal training course (i.e., one which is instructor led).

Here is a list of staff requiring training for a different purpose and your task is to pick a single method of training you feel would be most suited to their needs. When you have decided on the method, you should briefly explain why it is the best one.

1 John, who has never used a computer before, needs to use Office applications such as word-processing, spreadsheets, etc.
2 Kevin who has been using Microsoft Office for the last 4 years on a day-to-day basis is to install the latest version of the software. The user interface is quite different and he will need to learn quickly the similarities and differences compared to the previous package.
3 Sabrina works as a data input clerk taking customer orders over the telephone and inputting them with a networked computer. A major new system has been developed and all data input clerks (30 of them) need to be trained to use it.
4 Jackie has just graduated with a degree in Information Systems from a local university. She works in the computing department but finds her post as a junior programmer boring and she would like to build up her knowledge of HTML and website design.
5 Karl is a busy sales executive and is constantly visiting customers on their premises. He needs to find out about how to extract sales information remotely, as he would find it useful when he is away from the office.
6 The company keeps a lot of personal data on its system and all staff need to be trained regarding the implications of the Data Protection Act.
7 A user has forgotten how to set up a relationship in a relational database package. They have occasional problems but are on the whole an experienced user.
8 An experienced programmer who can program in three languages wishes to learn Java (another programming language) in order to improve their promotion prospects.
9 New employees are recruited at different times throughout the year. The company would like to provide a way of inducting the employee into the way the company works.
10 An organisation has a computer acceptable use policy which outlines those things an employee can and cannot do using the company's ICT systems. They would like all employees to be familiar with this policy.

▶ Activity 2: Troubleshooting printer problems

Imagine you are working on a help-desk for a large organisation. A user rings you to report a problem they are having with a printer, which according to them is not working. What general questions will you need to ask to enable you to sort out their problem?

(Remember that many novice users can make fairly obvious mistakes, so your troubleshooting should start off with the simple questions.)

Activities and Case study *continued*

▶ Case study 1 | pp. 142–151

Training methods

With the shelf life of most software packages diminishing all the time, barely have users learned to master the existing version when a new version is released. To narrow the ICT education gap there is now a huge and growing industry developed to help computer users close this gap. There are a wide variety of training methods and options to choose from covering formal instructor-led training, computer-based training, the use of step-by-step instructional guides, DVDs, and multimedia guides. There are also some firms offering training over the web.

The training method to use depends on a number of factors that include:

- whether the training is for a single person or an entire corporation
- the budget available for training
- the skill level of the student
- the subject matter of the training.

The nature of employment is changing. People now know that they are not going to work for the one company for their entire career, so individuals must take responsibility for their own training. There is no doubt that users are becoming much more sophisticated in their training needs. For example, a couple of years ago staff would be taught about how to boot up their computers and manage their own working area of the network. Now they are taught the latest sophisticated software packages or how to use the organisation's intranet. Managers are taught how to use management information systems to drill down into all the transactional data that the organisation has amassed in order to extract information about sale trends, profitability of particular customers and so on.

Although the costs involved in training large numbers of employees in an organisation are very high, the cost of not doing it can be even higher. For example, users who have not had proper training will experience more problems with hardware and software, leading to lost productivity and more expense in needing greater numbers of help-desk staff.

In the United States they call the peer support system the 'hey Joe' support system. Here a peer (a person you work with) is asked to help you with a problem, but the problem with this is that two people are now not getting their work done and if Joe does it the wrong way, we now have two people using the wrong method to solve the problem. In the meantime the help-desk staff, who are paid to sort out user problems, are idle because no-one has called them.

Other methods of training make use of the technology itself such as computer-based training, training over the Internet, interactive video instruction, and ordinary video instruction. This type of learning has the advantage that the user can set their own pace. There is also another type of training called JITT, just in time training, which provides simple training on a focused task on the user's computer. You may already have come across JITT if you are a user of Microsoft Office where Wizards are used to provide advice regarding how to perform a simple task.

1. Why might instructor-led training be more appropriate for staff who are beginners, whilst more experienced staff might use CBT? (2 marks)
2. In the passage above many types of training are mentioned. In fact most organisations use a variety of training methods when training their staff. What are the advantages in this approach to
   (a) the employee?
   (b) the organisation? (4 marks)

Exam support

Worked example 1

1 Many organisations use computer-based training (CBT) for the training of their staff.
  (a) Give **two advantages** and **two disadvantages** in using distance/on-line learning. **(4 marks)**
  (b) CBT packages are sometimes used with employees who have few ICT skills. Give **two advantages** and **two disadvantages** in using CBT packages with these employees. Your answers must be different from those for part (a). **(4 marks)**

Student answer 1

1 (a) There is no trainer around to make you look stupid if you get something wrong.
      There are ways in which you can move back to a topic you feel you did not understand.
      Learning is a social thing and you do not have the chance to interact with your classmates with on-line learning.
      There is no-one around to help you if you get stuck but if you had a proper trainer then they might be able to explain it a different way to help you understand.
  (b) The CBT package will not judge you if you make mistakes unlike a teacher who may think you are stupid.
      CBT packages cannot be used at home.
      The CBT package will make use of multimedia effects which means that it will encourage reluctant learners to learn because it will be fun.
      CAL packages are expensive because they take a long time to produce.

Examiner's comment

1 (a) The two advantages are sensible and well expressed, so full marks for these.
      Again both disadvantages are acceptable answers and are well expressed so full marks for these.
  (b) The first, third and fourth answers are justifiable reasons and they are all relevant to an employee who has few ICT skills.
      The second answer is incorrect as many CBT packages can be run over a network such as the Internet. **(7 marks out of 8)**

Student answer 2

1 (a) You can access the training materials from any computer, which makes it very flexible when you do the course.
      You can take the course 24/7, which makes it more flexible than traditional training sessions which have to be arranged according to a timetable.
  (b) You can learn at your own pace and not the pace of the rest of the class.
      CBT packages often make learning a game which is fun and keeps the employees engaged in their learning.
      The trainer could think you were learning on the computer when you weren't reading the information and simply guessing at the answers.
      There is no competition with your classmates to see who does best so this can de-motivate you.

Examiner's comment

1 (a) These two answers are very similar as they both refer to the fact that on-line courses offer flexibility (e.g., time and location). Students have to be careful they do not write an answer that is just slightly different, as marks will not be given for both answers. The answers to this type of question must be distinctly different. Only one mark is given here for one advantage. No disadvantages are given here. It seems likely that the student has forgotten to read this part of the question. It is always worth reading the question and your answer again at the end of the question to check for this.
  (b) All the answers here are correct so full marks for this part to the question. **(5 marks out of 8)**

Examiner's answer

1 (a) **One mark each for two advantages such as:**

Employees can work through the material at home or at work

Useful when employees cannot attend a training session because they are too busy

Employees become more responsible for their learning which is useful practice

Employees can repeat the training session if there is something they do not understand

Classes are able to be run with fewer trainees than normal

Classes can take place at any time – there need not be a set timetable.

One mark each for two disadvantages such as:

Employees need to be motivated otherwise they won't complete the tasks

Can be expensive

Lack of support and encouragement from a trainer

No encouragement or collaborative learning from others in the class.

(b) **One mark each for two advantages such as:**

Employees are able to work at their own pace

They do not have to worry about getting things wrong as there is no human to judge them

They can repeat parts many times until they fully understand them

The multimedia aspects of the software can be used to suit the different types of learner

Adds more fun to the learning process

Can use special input devices such as touch screens to help students who find it hard to use a keyboard and mouse

Learners can gauge their own progress.

One mark each for two disadvantages such as:

Lack of trainer encouragement

Employees may just think of it as a game and not learn anything

There is no collaborative learning

Does not teach them to interact with humans.

Summary mind maps

Training of internal or external users

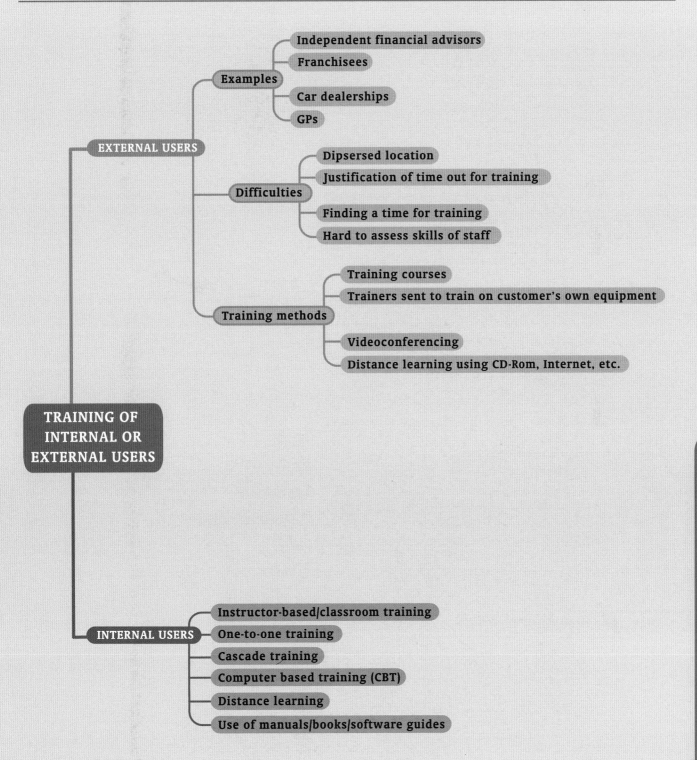

- **EXTERNAL USERS**
  - **Examples**
    - Independent financial advisors
    - Franchisees
    - Car dealerships
    - GPs
  - **Difficulties**
    - Dipsersed location
    - Justification of time out for training
    - Finding a time for training
    - Hard to assess skills of staff
  - **Training methods**
    - Training courses
    - Trainers sent to train on customer's own equipment
    - Videoconferencing
    - Distance learning using CD-Rom, Internet, etc.

TRAINING OF INTERNAL OR EXTERNAL USERS

- **INTERNAL USERS**
  - Instructor-based/classroom training
  - One-to-one training
  - Cascade training
  - Computer based training (CBT)
  - Distance learning
  - Use of manuals/books/software guides

Computer-assisted learning/Computer-based training

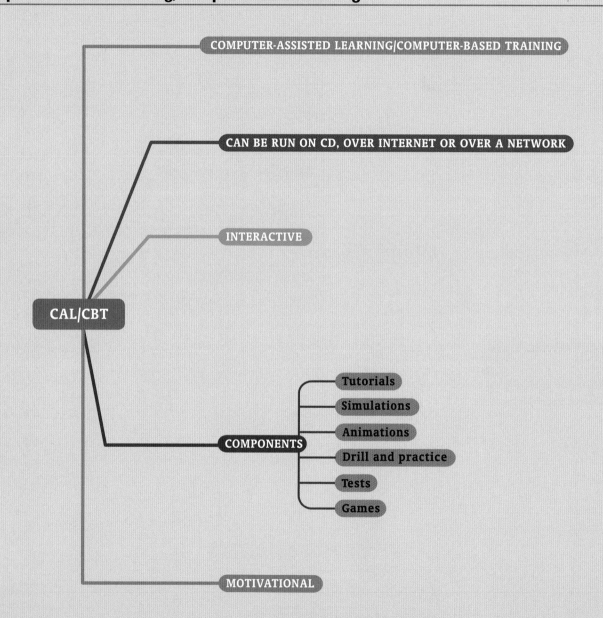

COMPUTER-ASSISTED LEARNING/COMPUTER-BASED TRAINING

CAN BE RUN ON CD, OVER INTERNET OR OVER A NETWORK

INTERACTIVE

CAL/CBT

COMPONENTS
- Tutorials
- Simulations
- Animations
- Drill and practice
- Tests
- Games

MOTIVATIONAL

TOPIC 12: External and internal resources

You may think that all organisations own all the computer equipment they use and they employ specialist ICT staff in their own ICT department, but this is far from the case for many organisations. There has been a trend over the last twenty years to concentrate more on the business issues in a company and use the organisation's staff for this. This means that many of the ICT facilities the organisation uses come from outside organisations. They basically contract another company to supply them with what they need.

Organisations make use of a large number of internal resources such as hardware, software, communications, consumables, facilities, power and people. All these resources need to be used carefully to minimise costs, so ICT is used to help with management of this. In this topic you will be looking at external and internal resources.

▼ The key concepts covered in this topic are:

▶ Using external services and business support

▶ Managing internal resources

CONTENTS

1 **Using external services and business support**..160
Outsourcing, offshoring, bulk printing and ways in which organisations can obtain ICT services from suppliers (contracting and leasing).

2 **Managing internal resources**...162
Planning the management and control of hardware resources, software resources, communication resources, consumables, facilities, power and people.

3 **Questions and Activities**...164

4 **Case studies**...165

5 **Exam support**...167

6 **Summary mind maps**...170

Using external services and business support

Introduction

Many companies do not have expertise in ICT and would find it difficult to recruit and retain staff with ICT technical skills. Some ICT staff such as systems analysts, programmers, testers, etc., are only employed when new systems are being designed and implemented, which means it is not financially viable to employ such people in small organisations. Instead companies prefer to leave certain tasks involved in the developing and running of ICT systems to external organisations which have considerable expertise in this area.

There are many aspects of ICT that can be taken over by specialist companies and many organisations choose this because it leaves them to concentrate on the part of the business they are best at. This section looks at the way some or all of the ICT services can be undertaken by external organisations.

Outsourcing

Outsourcing means subcontracting some or all ICT services to another company. Many organisations prefer to outsource their ICT requirements so that they are able to concentrate purely on the business

side of the organisation. The staff in the organisation can then simply get on with what they are best at and in doing so the organisation can concentrate on aspects such as marketing, sales, production, etc. The decision to outsource is a strategic one and will be made at director or similar level.

Outsourcing has the following advantages:

- It makes the best use of resources such as labour and capital.
- Other service providers often have more knowledge and expertise in the area being outsourced.
- It leaves the managers of the organisation free to concentrate more on business issues.
- The organisation does not have to worry about finding suitably qualified staff to work with ICT.
- The organisation does not have to worry about complying with the legislation for that part of the business – the outsourcing company takes care of that.
- In some cases the company does not have to purchase expensive hardware and software. They simply pay a fixed amount per month for the service.

Outsourcing can also have the following disadvantages:

- Outsourcing can mean that ICT people lose their jobs if an organisation decides to outsource.
- The quality of the outsourced service might not be as high as when the ICT was done in-house.
- The organisation has no control over the people employed by the outsourcer.
- It can compromise the privacy and security of the data held.

Offshoring (transferring part or all of ICT to another country)

Many organisations decide to outsource some or all of their ICT facilities offshore, which means they are undertaken in another country. India is often the preferred choice, as wage costs are much lower than in the UK and there are plenty of people there with suitable language and technical skills.

Offshoring can also refer to the situation where part of the ICT facilities, such as the help-desk, is relocated to another country.

There are two ways offshoring can be done:

- Where staff in the other country are still employees of the original organisation.
- Where an outsourcing company in a different country is used. In this case the staff are not employed by the original organisation.

Offshoring is popular with the help-desk and customer service areas of a business.

"**We found someone overseas who can drink coffee and talk about sports all day for a fraction of what we're paying you.**"

HELP DESK

Disadvantages of offshoring:

- Language problems – where the first language is different, there can be communication problems.
- Takes advantage of lower paid workers – many people think it is immoral to transfer work abroad to exploit low pay in other countries.

Advantages of offshoring:

- Lower costs – wages are lower in countries where ICT work is undertaken offshore.
- Suitably qualified people – it is hard to recruit experienced staff in ICT roles. Other countries often have a surplus of suitably qualified people.
- Employment opportunities – provides well paid employment for people in other countries.

Bulk printing

Some organisations need to regularly print and then post promotional material to a large number of customers or potential customers. Rather than go to the trouble of completing this process themselves, they can contract an outside company to do this for them.

Examples of jobs performed by these bulk printing companies include:

- bills
- mail shots
- promotional newsletters.

Ways in which organisations can obtain ICT services from suppliers

There are a number of ways that organisations can obtain ICT services from suppliers. Which one they choose depends on the initial amount of money they wish to spend. The two main ways are contracting and leasing and these are outlined here.

Contracting

Contracting is where you purchase either services or equipment and you sign a document agreed by both the supplier and the customer outlining the goods or the services provided. In the case of equipment such as computers, once payment has been made, the goods belong to the customer (contrast this with leasing in the next section).

Contracts normally specify:

- what the support companies expect of the customer and vice versa
- when the contract starts and ends, payment frequency and what happens in the event either party wishes to terminate the contract.

In some cases an outside organisation may supply all the ICT facilities to an organisation, so the only involvement the organisation has with ICT is as users of the facilities. All the hardware, software, communications, installation, maintenance, network configuration, backups, disaster recovery, user support, etc., are provided by the contracting organisation.

Leasing

All organisations need to buy hardware and software and when you are buying a large quantity this is a huge outlay. One way around this large outlay is to use leasing. Leasing allows organisations to have the hardware and software without having the high initial outlay.

Leasing is similar to renting in that you pay the leasing company the same monthly amount for the use of the hardware, software and communication links. The contract usually lasts between two and ten years depending on the useful life of the items being leased.

This means that you have the full use of the hardware and software but you do not actually own it. At the end of the leasing period you are given the choice of renting it at a much lower cost or to end the lease and maybe start a new lease with more up-to-date hardware and software.

The main advantages of leasing are:

- No large outlay – there is no need to have the money upfront to pay for the new hardware and software.
- Easy to lease – if you can't borrow the money to buy, you can usually still lease because the leasing organisation still owns the hardware and software as security.
- Budgeting is easier – the same amount is paid each month for a fixed period, so it is much easier to budget.
- Tax advantages – the rentals can usually be deducted from profits as expenses.

The main disadvantages of leasing are:

- No ownership – you never own the item, as the leasing company own the items during and after the lease.
- Works out expensive – it works out more expensive because you have to pay for the item and the leasing company's charges over the period of the lease.

© Randy Glasbergen
www.glasbergen.com

"Here's my report on the new budget cuts. To save paper and toner, I deleted all the vowels and punctuation."

Managing internal resources

▼ You will find out

▶ About planning the management and control of hardware resources, software resources, communication resources, consumables, facilities, power and most importantly people

Introduction

Organisations have many resources such as hardware, software, communications, consumables, facilities, power and finally people. To make the best use of these resources, and use them in the most cost-effective way, they need to be properly managed.

In this section you will look at the managing of internal resources.

Planning the management and control of hardware resources

Organisations can have huge amounts of money invested in hardware resources such as computers, laptops, servers and communication devices such as routers, printers, scanners, etc.

It is important for organisations to know exactly what specifications every computer in an organisation has. For example, the organisation may want to upgrade to the latest operating system and they will need to determine how many computers will run the new software without being upgraded and how many will need upgrading. The information can be used to determine what upgrading needs to be done and how much the cost will be.

Planning the management and control of software

Most organisations use networks, so it is possible for a network manager to keep track, using the network operating system, of the software users are actually using or have installed on their machine.

Careful management and control of software is needed for the following reasons:

- Software licences are expensive, so organisations do not want to pay for any more users than they have to.
- They need to ensure that they do not have more copies of the software than they have licences for, as if they are found out, they could be fined.

- They need to know exactly what software is stored on each computer to ensure that no illegally downloaded software is being used.
- Software will need to be upgraded, so it is important to know the details of what is being used by each user.
- Some specialist software (e.g., software to extract management information, project management software, budgeting software, etc.) is only used by certain staff, so it is necessary to restrict access to this software.

Planning the management and control of communication resources

As more computers and users are added to a network, the response time goes down until there comes a point when the network needs to be reconfigured.

It is necessary to carefully control what users do using their networked computers. Downloading large files (usually music or video files) from the Internet requires a large amount of bandwidth and this can degrade the speed of the network for other users. It is therefore essential to ensure that users are aware of this and act responsibly.

Users are allocated a certain amount of storage for their e-mails and they need to manage this storage area by deleting e-mails no longer needed and getting rid of spam.

Planning the management and control of consumables

Consumables are those items that get used up in the course of the organisation's business activities and that need constant monitoring and replenishment. They include such items as paper, envelopes, printer toner cartridges, removable magnetic and optical media and stationery.

It is important to manage and control these items as staff are likely to use many of them at home and may see it as a perk of the job to take some items home with them! It is also important to have a stock control system so that items are automatically reordered when low. It is best to have the minimum amount of stock but an efficient stock control system means that items never run out when needed.

It is essential that staff have all the consumables they need in order to be able to perform their job. They should not have to search around different departments trying to find a printer cartridge or a blank DVD to record on.

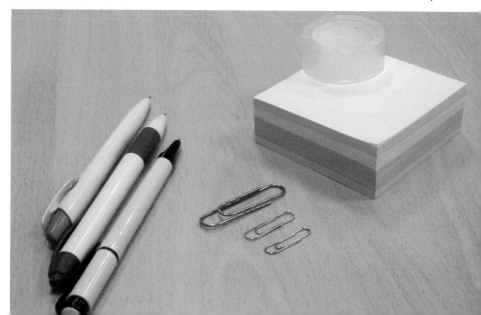

Consumables include items of stationery.

Ink-jet printer cartridges are an expensive consumable and staff should think if they really need a colour printout.

People are the most valuable of the resources an organisation has.

Planning the management and control of facilities and power

Power is an expensive resource and needs to be used wisely. Computer equipment contributes to greenhouse emissions when manufactured and when used so it is necessary to make sure that equipment is not left on any longer than is necessary.

Most organisations are environmentally aware and seek to reduce their carbon footprint and reduce energy usage and will make purchases with this in mind.

Planning the management and control of people (human resources)

People are the most valuable resource in any organisation and the ability to get the most out of each employee is a goal of all organisations.

ICT systems (called human resource systems) are used to maintain all the information held about employees so all managers can make use of the information it can provide.

Human resource systems can be used for:

- identifying the skills and knowledge required for each job
- storing information about the actual skills and knowledge for each member of staff
- identifying staff who need training in certain aspects of their job
- setting up appropriate training
- managing the training given.

ICT systems are used by managers to manage the staff under their control, for working out staff rotas, project management, budgeting, identifying who has had what training and so on.

Questions and Activities

▶ Questions 1 | pp. 160–163

1 A company is thinking of outsourcing its ICT facilities. Discuss the relative advantages and disadvantages of outsourcing. **(6 marks)**

2 Many utility companies (i.e., gas, electric, water and telephone) in the past produced and printed millions of bills that were posted to customers four times per year. Many of these utility companies now choose to outsource the bulk printing services to external organisations.

  (a) Explain what is meant by the term outsourcing and outline the benefits it might offer to a utility company. **(3 marks)**

  (b) Describe another function of their business that could be outsourced. **(2 marks)**

3 A company has the choice of buying a large network or leasing it.
Compare and contrast buying the equipment outright or leasing. In your answer you should explain the relative advantages and disadvantages of leasing. **(6 marks)**

4 Many organisation use offshoring, particularly for their systems development, programming and help-desk or customer support areas.
Explain what offshoring means and what the advantages are to the organisation. **(4 marks)**

5 (a) Give the names of four internal resources applicable to ICT that need to be managed. **(2 marks)**

  (b) Internal resources need to be controlled and managed. Explain, by giving suitable examples, why this is so. **(2 marks)**

▶ Activity 1: Outsourcing

Many of the jobs involved in ICT can be outsourced. Using the Internet and other sources of information, produce a brief document outlining the types of jobs which involve ICT and are popularly outsourced. In this document you need to outline:

• The details of the jobs outsourced.
• The details of the organisations involved.
• The reasons why the organisation chose to outsource the area of work.

▶ Activity 2: Jobs disappearing abroad

Many ICT jobs, particularly in call centres, are being lost to other countries, where the wages are less than they are here and it is easier to find staff having the necessary skills.

    You have been asked to produce a short magazine article of around 600 words on the jobs involving ICT that are being lost abroad.

    Before you start on this article you should do some research using the Internet. Good places to find suitable information would include the on-line newspapers and on-line computer newspapers/magazines such as *Computing*.

Case studies

▶ Case study 1 | pp. 160–163

Outsourcing payroll

Green Fingers Garden Services provides garden services to householders and employs around 120 staff who are paid on a monthly basis. Although the company use ICT extensively for garden design, purchasing of supplies, keeping details of staff (contact details, holiday rotas, qualifications, etc.) and customer invoicing, they have decided to outsource the payroll to a company called Payroll Services.

In their advertising material Payroll Services say:

'Our payroll services are designed to meet the requirements of the smaller business and will ensure that your employees are paid accurately and on time.' 'As well as calculating pay, we will make sure that you are kept up to date and compliant with all Her Majesty's Revenue and Customs (HMRC) procedures and regulations.'

The manager of Green Fingers Garden Services explains why they outsource the payroll:

- 'We are garden experts and administration is not our strong point so we leave it in the hands of people who are experts in this field.'
- 'Outsourcing frees up some of our time and allows us to concentrate on more productive things such as visiting our main clients.'
- 'We only have to pay a fixed monthly fee for the services, so we do not have to employ anyone nor do we have to buy any expensive payroll software.'
- 'The outsourcing company makes sure we comply with all the relevant payroll legislation and then sends us all sorts of management reports so we know how much money is going out of the business for pay.'
- 'Best of all we don't have to worry about backups for payroll as the payroll services company do all that for us. I believe they back up the data in multiple locations as they have branches all around the UK.'

1 (a) Explain what is meant by the word 'outsourcing'. (2 marks)
  (b) Green Fingers outsource their payroll. Describe some of the reasons why the managing director has decided to do this. (8 marks)
2 It is important that organisations are compliant with any relevant legislation.
  Explain how outsourcing can help with this. (2 marks)
3 Green Fingers has a small network consisting of eight computers. Discuss how they might make further use of outsourcing of areas of ICT applicable to their business. (5 marks)
4 Other than payroll services, outsourcing can also be used for other ICT-related tasks. Describe such a use and explain what advantages outsourcing gives to the organisation. (4 marks)

Green Fingers Garden Services wants to concentrate on its core activity.

Case study 2 | pp. 160–163

Why we decided on contracting

Williams and Partners are a large firm of solicitors who use the latest ICT throughout their practice. Until two years ago the practice ran all their own ICT services and they employed a few full-time members of staff who kept the network running, installed new software, dealt with user problems, etc. As the network got bigger and the practice opened several new offices in the town, things started to get more complicated. The existing staff could not cope with the increased demands and decided to leave.

The partners in the practice advertised for a network manager and some other ICT-related staff, but they had no luck finding anyone suitable at the wages they could afford.

One of the partners heard about contracting. She had heard that other similar practices did not get involved in the day-to-day business of keeping their networks running, supplying hardware and software as well as staff to deal with any ICT problems. This sounded ideal because they could concentrate on dealing with things they knew about – legal issues.

They contacted a contracting company who offered a full package which included:

- Support for all the existing hardware (PCs, laptops, printers, servers, etc.) – if any of these failed, they would be repaired or replaced.
- Support for all the software installed on the server (e.g., operating system, specialist legal practice software, Microsoft Office, antivirus software, etc.).
- Support in the form of network configuration and maintenance, telephone support, remote support,

software installation, replacement of hardware or components due to failure, disaster recovery, etc.

The contracting company set out in the contract:

- The payment and how long the contract covered.
- Response times – depending on the problem, the contract lays out times within which they would respond to problems.
- How disputes in the contract would be dealt with.

1 The firm of solicitors in the case study has decided to contract the running of their ICT services to an outside company.
 (a) Explain **one** reason why this company prefers to get an outside company to provide support for their ICT. (2 marks)
 (b) Explain what is meant by contracting and explain **one** disadvantage to the firm of solicitors in contracting. (3 marks)
2 Contracting is a popular way of providing support.
 (a) Describe **two** things an ICT support contract would typically cover. (2 marks)
 (b) Describe the reasons why an organisation would pay an outside organisation for these support services rather than appoint suitably qualified staff and do the work in-house. (4 marks)
3 Many organisations use contractors to provide ICT equipment, services or both. Discuss the relative merits of an organisation contracting their ICT equipment or services and explain what would normally be specified in the contract. (6 marks)

Exam support

Worked example 1

1   Many organisations choose to outsource some or all of their ICT facilities. Explain what the word **outsource** means and outline the reasons why they choose to do this. **(5 marks)**

Student answer 1

1   The word 'outsource' means getting someone from outside to do the job.

The main advantage of outsourcing is that you do not have to do the job yourself.

All the equipment to do the job is provided, so you do not have to pay for it.

If something goes wrong then it is their responsibility to fix it and not yours.

Examiner's comment

1   The definition of 'outsource' is far too vague and an example is not given that would have helped clarify the answer. Students at this level need to give a more than a 'man in the street' definition of any terminology, so this description gains no marks.

Again the reasons are vague but they have provided some answers and one mark is given for the final reason. **(1 mark out of 5)**

Student answer 2

1   Outsource means subcontracting a process in the business to an outside organisation that is better placed to carry it out because they have more expertise in that area of work. For example, network management could be outsourced, which would mean that the network would be provided but the company would not have to worry about configuring it, adding more computers to it, backing up all the data, dealing with user problems and repairing the network should it break down.

The advantages of outsourcing are:

You do not need to employ specialist ICT staff such as network managers.

The company can concentrate on business issues and not worry about ICT services.

The outsourcer is likely to have much more experience and can offer useful advice on technical issues.

The company does not have to worry about complying with the laws which apply to that part of ICT which is outsourced as the outsourcing company sees to that.

Examiner's comment

1   The definition of the word 'outsource' is very good and the student has added an example of a function of the business that could be outsourced which clarifies the definition further. This is good practice.

The advantages are presented as a list which is ok for this type of question but if the question had asked you to 'discuss', then this would not be acceptable.

The first point does not really state the advantage. They should have said that recruiting specialist ICT staff is difficult and expensive.

The other three points of advantages are well explained and gain marks. **(5 marks out of 5)**

Exam support *continued*

Examiner's answer

1 One mark for a correct description of the word 'outsource'.
   One mark for a sentence adding more detail or an example of a situation where outsourcing is used.
   Example answers include:
   Outsourcing is contracting with another company or person to do a particular function or task (1). An insurance company might outsource its network management function with another company providing technical support, network configuration, risk analysis and backup (1).
   Outsourcing means subcontracting some or all of the ICT services to another company (1).
   Three reasons for outsourcing should be given for one mark each. Examples include:

Many organisations prefer to outsource their ICT requirements so that they are able to concentrate purely on the business side of the organisation (1).
It makes the best use of resources such as labour and capital (1).
Other service providers often have more knowledge and expertise in the area being outsourced (1).
The organisation does not have to worry out finding suitably qualified ICT staff (1).
The organisation does not have to worry about complying with the legislation for that part of the business – the outsourcing company takes care of that (1).
In some cases the company does not have to purchase expensive hardware and software. They simply pay a fixed amount per month for the service (1).

Worked example 2

2 **Organisations use ICT extensively for the management of internal resources.**
  Name three internal resources and describe the way ICT is used for the planning, control and management of them. (9 marks)

Student answer 1

2 Three internal resources are:
  Computers
  Software
  People
  Computers – the computers need to be managed so that people are given the computer or computers that are necessary for them to perform their job.
  Software – organisations have to control the use of their software because the site licence may only allow a certain number of users of the software at any one time.
  Software needs to be managed so that certain software is only used by those people who need it for their job. This means that a person is allocated software according to their role in the organisation.
  People – people need to be managed and the work they do can be managed by the computer. Workflow management controls their work and can be used by managers to see how much work they are doing.
  Personnel systems hold information about each employee and this can be used to help manage them.

Examiner's comment

2 'Computers' is not an acceptable answer as computers on their own are very limited in what they can do. Hardware is the acceptable answer here. The other two answers are correct.
  The first statement on 'computers' is a bit vague – it would be better to have said that different people require a different spec of computer, based on their job. No marks for this part.
  The second answer on software mentions correctly control and management so full marks for this section.
  The third answer on people mentions control/management of work so one mark here. The last sentence is too vague to be allocated a mark. **(7 marks out of 9)**

Student answer 2

2 Human resources are controlled by the human resources department and individual managers. Planning is undertaken when ICT systems change to make the best use of the skills and knowledge of staff. ICT systems help manage staff by recording their details so that it can be seen what courses they have been on and what further training is needed.

Hardware resources are planned when new ICT systems are built and the specifications for each computer are determined based on the task being performed. Hardware needs to be controlled because network managers need to know which computers need upgrading for more demanding operating systems or applications software. Software resources need to be managed so that only certain staff have access to certain programs or modules of programs. For example, you would not expect staff in the order processing department to need access to the payroll program.

Examiner's comment

2 Before starting any question you need to check you understand what you need to write about. The key words in this question relate to planning, controlling and management. Try working out how the marks will be allocated, as that will give you an idea as to what to concentrate on. Here you could guess that there would be one mark for the names of the resources with two marks for any descriptions applying to planning, controlling or management.

The mark scheme could also be one mark each for planning, controlling or management. A good strategy would be to write the name of the resources and for each examples of planning, controlling and management.

This student has identified three correct resources so three marks here.

The answer on human resources is good as the student has mentioned planning and control/management.

The answer on hardware resources mentions two aspects correctly: planning and control.

The answer on software resources only mentions management.

This is a very good answer. **(8 marks out of 9)**

Examiner's answer

2 One mark for the name of the resource and two marks for each point made applicable to the planning, control or management of the resource. Examples include:

Hardware resources:
- Planning the purchase of new hardware
- Tracking for security purposes
- Deciding the type of computer needed by each member of staff
- Determining the usage of items of hardware
- Planning where is the best position for shared devices such as printers
- Keeping records of the specifications of all computers so that the costs of upgrading can be estimated.

Software resources:
- Controlling who has network access to particular pieces of software
- Ensuring that site licences are not being breached owing to too many users
- Checking which version of each software is being used for the purpose of upgrading.

Communication resources:
- Tracking personal and business calls to keep costs of calls down
- Monitoring of e-mails sent by staff for security purposes
- Ensuring users delete e-mail no longer required
- Ensuring users do not unnecessarily download huge files thus slowing the rest of the network down.

Consumables:
- For stock control so that important items such as paper and ink cartridges do not run out
- Keeping track of stationery so that staff do not steal it
- Ensure that costs are kept under control by giving each department a budget.

Facilities and power:
- Office space must be suitably allocated to the different departments
- Facilities such as power sockets, telephone sockets, suitable lighting, and adjustable blinds on windows must be planned
- Central ICT controlled temperature management ensures each room is not too hot or cold.

People:
- ICT systems are used by managers to allocate work to staff under their control
- Managers use ICT systems for working out staff rotas, staff holidays, etc.
- Human resources systems can plan staffing so that the staff are given tasks appropriate to their skills and training.

Summary mind maps

Using external services and business support

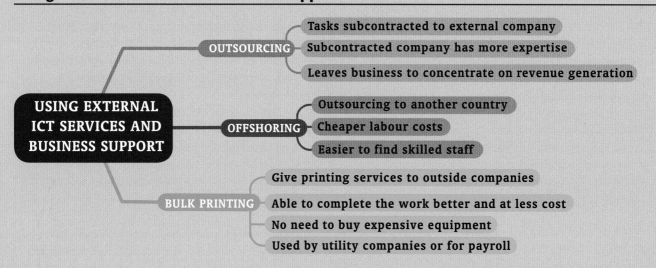

USING EXTERNAL ICT SERVICES AND BUSINESS SUPPORT

OUTSOURCING
- Tasks subcontracted to external company
- Subcontracted company has more expertise
- Leaves business to concentrate on revenue generation

OFFSHORING
- Outsourcing to another country
- Cheaper labour costs
- Easier to find skilled staff

BULK PRINTING
- Give printing services to outside companies
- Able to complete the work better and at less cost
- No need to buy expensive equipment
- Used by utility companies or for payroll

Managing internal resources

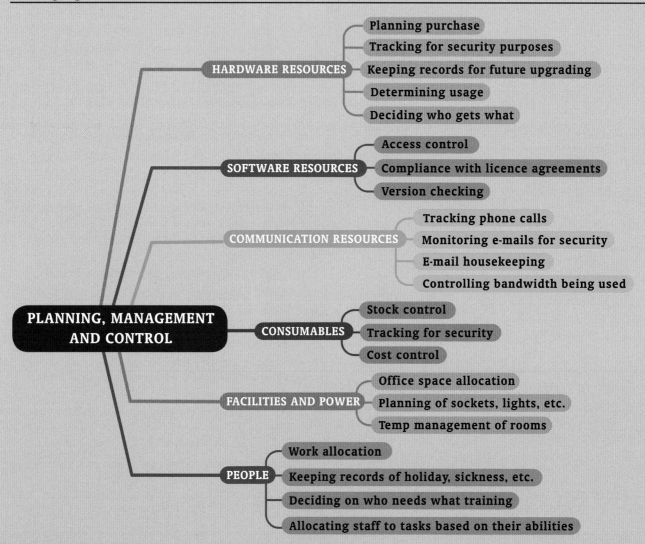

PLANNING, MANAGEMENT AND CONTROL

HARDWARE RESOURCES
- Planning purchase
- Tracking for security purposes
- Keeping records for future upgrading
- Determining usage
- Deciding who gets what

SOFTWARE RESOURCES
- Access control
- Compliance with licence agreements
- Version checking

COMMUNICATION RESOURCES
- Tracking phone calls
- Monitoring e-mails for security
- E-mail housekeeping
- Controlling bandwidth being used

CONSUMABLES
- Stock control
- Tracking for security
- Cost control

FACILITIES AND POWER
- Office space allocation
- Planning of sockets, lights, etc.
- Temp management of rooms

PEOPLE
- Work allocation
- Keeping records of holiday, sickness, etc.
- Deciding on who needs what training
- Allocating staff to tasks based on their abilities

UNIT 4: Coursework: Practical Issues Involved in the Use of ICT in the Digital World

In Unit 4, which accounts for 40% of the total A2 marks and 20% of the total A-level marks, you will be required to produce the solution to a problem of your choice. You are then required to produce a project report based on your practical work/investigation.

The project will be undertaken over an extended period of time and it is internally marked by your teacher/lecturer and moderated externally by someone appointed by the assessment board AQA.

▼ The key concepts covered in this topic are:

▷ Background and investigation

▷ Analysis and deliverables

▷ Design and planning for implementation

▷ Testing and documentation of the implementation

▷ Evaluation of the implemented solution

▷ The project report

CONTENTS

1 Choosing a suitable project 172
What problem do I choose?, tips on getting ideas for projects, possible projects, and working together, questions and answers on the project, some useful advice before you start the project, important notes about project work, the mark allocation for the main components of the project and things you should watch out for.

2 Useful project advice, tips and assessment 176
Frequently asked questions.

3 How the project is assessed 178
Background and investigation, analysis and deliverables, design and planning for implementation, testing and documentation of the implementation, evaluation of the implemented solution and the project report.

Choosing a suitable project

▼ You will find out

▶ About what problem to choose

▶ About tips on getting ideas for projects

▶ About possible projects

▶ About working together

▶ About questions and answers on the project

▶ About the mark allocation for the main components of the project

▶ About things you should watch out for

Introduction

Choosing the right project is essential for your success, so it needs to be given a lot of thought. If you get it right, you will be able to produce a project that is completed in the time allowed and you will be able to supply evidence of all the components for assessment. If you get it wrong, you could end up with all sorts of technical problems owing to the project being too complex, and the time spent sorting this out may come at the expense of evidencing all the components for assessment.

This section gives you important advice on choosing your project.

What problem do I choose?

Before you even think about a problem, you need to read through the whole of this topic, because only then will you understand what is required. You must choose a problem that will allow you to demonstrate all the components. You do not want the problem to be too complex, yet it needs to be complex enough to satisfy all the criteria.

The choice of a suitable problem is essential to the success of the project. You must not be too ambitious and should realise your limitations. You do not want to get bogged down in the complexities of software and you need to realise that you only have a limited amount of time to complete this project.

Tips on getting ideas for projects

Make use of contacts

Find out what you parents, relatives, neighbours, friends, etc., do in the course of their jobs, since they might be able to suggest an idea for you. If you are able to contact them to find out any information you might need, this will be a big help.

The best projects are the ones that use a real end-user and which continually refer back to the end-user for their reactions and input into the development. The end-user will need to be consulted at all stages in the project.

Real projects are often better than artificial ones

There is nothing wrong with creating a new system from scratch rather than improving an existing system. Many people start from scratch, so it is appropriate for you to design a system to cope with the many tasks they would have to perform. However, you will need quite a bit of prior knowledge of the type of business the system is for and there will no longer be an existing system to examine but there will be an environment into which the new system will fit.

Use reference material to help with ideas

A quick look through any magazines or newspapers will give you ideas about business, such as mail order businesses or e-commerce businesses, which advertise in such places. These all share common problems, so it should not be too difficult to think up a system for them.

Do not choose a system that is outside of your experience or about which you cannot easily find information

For example, you may choose to create a system to keep records for dentists, but unless you know or can find out about how dentists cope with their administrative tasks, then you could make things difficult for yourself and end up with a very unrealistic system.

Be realistic

It is important to be realistic about what you can achieve in the time. The better projects are usually the ones which comprise fewer tasks and which are better designed, documented, fully tested and evaluated and closely focused on the problem being solved.

Have lots of ideas initially

The best way to have a good idea is to have lots of ideas. When deciding on a project, you should have a few to choose from. You can then carefully go through what you have to produce and check how easy or difficult this could be. Also bear in mind your own strengths and weaknesses in using different pieces of software. During the project work is probably not the best place to be using and learning the software for the first time.

Use a real client if possible

Try to get a real client, as they will be able to help you by keeping an eye on the project development and they can supply you with feedback on prototypes (if applicable) and completed systems.

Keep referring to the document containing the allocation of marks for the project

A word of warning. Your choice of project is very important. Use the mark scheme in the copy of the AQA specification to see how the marks are allocated. Some projects are hard to mark because they do not easily fit the mark scheme. You would be best advised to not choose these projects but to choose a project with a discernable marking system.

Important note

This project work is A2 level and not AS level and therefore the level of complexity of any project should be higher.

Possible projects

For the project, you are required to produce a substantial project that involves the production of an ICT-related system. You will be given a large amount of time to complete the project, during which time you will learn new software skills and be able to use the knowledge you have gained by studying A2 Unit 3.

It is very important to note that not all ICT systems involve the use of a relational database. This means that you do not have to create a database for your project.

You can still, of course, produce a database if your user/client problem demands it.

You may prefer to produce one of the following ICT systems:

- A multimedia system for education, training, information, etc.
- An e-commerce site which allows the purchase of goods. If you choose this option, you will need to check the availability of suitable software.
- A user support system that can be used to log faults or errors for an organisation. You could model the system on the system used by your school/college and see if you could provide improvements to the system. You could, of course, create this system for an organisation that has no user support system at the moment.
- You could produce a security policy for an organisation. For example, you could produce a policy to specify appropriate use of an organisation's laptop computers and you could also devise a way of ensuring management of the organisation keep records of the specifications of these laptops, software installed on them, etc., and details of what data is stored and how any personal data is secured (e.g., encryption).
- A system that is used for communication in a department or organisation. This system allows students to communicate within the organisation and could contain a communal diary system, which would allow people to organise meetings and social events by knowing who is available and when.

- A system for evaluating new software for purchase or for evaluating the new hardware that forms a system. The system would include hardware, software, communications systems, consumables and services.
- A backup and recovery system and a disaster recovery plan for an organisation.
- A system for managing relationships with customers.
- A website, intranet or extranet.

Working together

When you approach your client to ask about ICT problems to solve, they may give you a list of things. You could therefore pick out a number of separate problems which could form many separate projects that could be completed by other members of your class. For this to run smoothly you will need a client who is very cooperative as it will take quite a bit of their time and they need to be fully aware of this at the time of agreeing to help.

It is important to note that although you will be working with the same client, you are in fact working on different problems. You can, of course, hold joint meetings, as you are effectively working as a team on different problems.

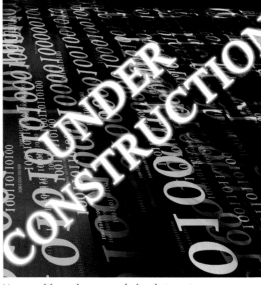

You could produce a website, intranet or extranet.

Why not try and set up an e-commerce site for a business?

You can work together on a project but the part you do will have to be a different part to others.

Questions and answers on the project

Do I need a real client and real users?

No you don't, but if you do have one it can be better because you are able to understand their requirements by interviewing them and you can also ask for their comments during the creation of the solution. It is also easier in some respects to produce your evaluation, as they will be able to make comments about your work.

Although you only need one client, it is desirable to have many users of your proposed system.

What is the best way to start?

Before starting on your project you will need to gain advanced skills and knowledge about any software you will be using. There is a tendency for projects to be developed in isolation and the only time the teacher sees

the results is when the project is handed in at the end. Your teacher should be kept up to date with the progress of the project so that if you are going off in the wrong direction, you can be stopped and put on course again. Too many projects are handed in that are inappropriate for the requirements of the A-level and by then there is no time to do anything about them.

Before you start the project work, your teacher may have given you booklets to work through with exercises to build up your knowledge of various pieces of software. You should make sure you know about the advanced features of these. One way to learn about such advanced features is to get hold of some of the more advanced guides to the software, particularly those guides that concentrate more on the development of applications. It is important to note that plagiarism is not allowed and is easily detected!

Some useful advice before you start the project

The following advice applies to all parts of the project:

- Do not waste time providing evidence that is not needed.
- Avoid cropping your work too much, as this sometimes destroys the evidence.
- Do not provide screenshots that are too small – the markers will need to be able to read them.
- You must produce proper design work – annotating (i.e., adding remarks) to implemented solutions is not proper design. Design must not be an afterthought.

Important notes about project work

Here are some important notes about the project work:

1 Your project does not have to be complicated for you to get a good mark.
2 Unlike in the past, there are many different systems you can develop, as you are not confined to creating a system based around a relational database.
3 Documenting your project is very important. It supplies your teacher with the evidence of your work and enables them to give your project an accurate mark.
4 Make sure that you check your work for grammatical and spelling mistakes. Do not just rely on the computer to do this. You should always proof read your work thoroughly.
5 You are not required to produce separate documentary evidence of the implementation, as this is provided through the testing evidence you produce and the final documentation of the solution.

It is best to have the software skills and knowledge in place before you start work on the project.

The mark allocation for the main components of the project

Below is a summary of the main components of the project and the marks allocated for each. In the following sections, you will be looking at each component in turn and then looking at the tasks and evidence you need to complete for each section.

Components	Max mark
Background and investigation	14
Analysis and deliverables	15
Design and planning for implementation	14
Testing and documentation of implementation	13
Evaluation of the implemented solution	7
The project report	7
Total	70

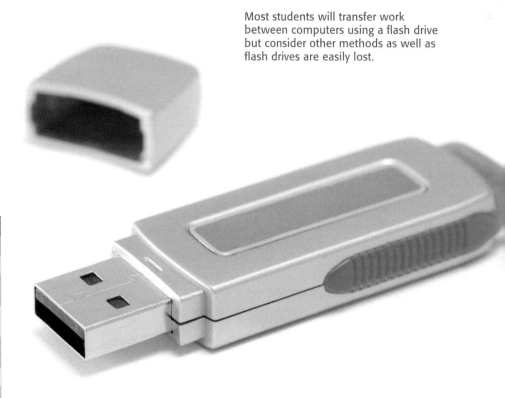

Most students will transfer work between computers using a flash drive but consider other methods as well as flash drives are easily lost.

Things you should watch out for

There are a number of things you should be aware of when working on your project and these are outlined below.

Plagiarism (i.e., copying)

It goes without saying that all project work must be your own work. It is no use copying parts of examples in text books or specimen project material supplied by the examination board, since your teacher will probably have seen it before and the moderator will almost certainly be familiar with the material. Also do not buy A-level projects off Internet auction sites such as e-Bay.

In cases where copying has been proved, the student could be disqualified from entering the examination in ICT and possibly any other subjects they are taking. Both you and your teacher will have to sign a declaration to confirm that the work you have submitted is your own and this is why your teacher needs to see you completing the vast majority of your work during class time.

Take regular backups

As Advanced Level ICT students, you should be aware of the dangers of having only one copy of your work. Regular backup copies should be taken and these should not be kept near the original. You may consider attaching the file containing your work to an e-mail and then e-mailing it to the e-mail address you use at home. This will ensure that you have a backup copy in a remote location. It is also a good idea to print out your work occasionally and keep the printout.

Pace yourself

There is a tendency amongst ICT students to get on with developing the system and to leave all the documentation to the end, when they hopefully have a system that works. This should be avoided and you should provide the documentation as you go along. If you need to make changes as you go along, then this is OK provided that these changes are explained along with the reasons for them. Time management is an important skill throughout life and you should manage your time and avoid attending school or college without having some idea as to what you hope to achieve during the practical sessions.

Document everything

Although the teachers/lecturers who mark your work will be familiar with the software you have used, the moderators may not have used it before or have a copy of the software themselves. This means that the moderators can only mark your projects on the basis of the documentation you have supplied. If, for example, you have included a very innovative on-line help system as part of a project, then the moderator would not know about it unless you have provided evidence in the form of screen designs and screen dumps. If any of the documentation is missing, then you will lose marks no matter how clever the ICT solution is.

Useful project advice, tips and assessment

Introduction

The project work is an important component of the A-level ICT so it is worth spending some time looking at some useful advice and tips.

Also included is detail on how the project is assessed.

Frequently asked questions

Here are some answers to questions students frequently ask about project work.

Who will mark my project work?

Your project work will be marked by your teacher and in turn a moderator will check that the work has been marked to a comparable standard to other schools/colleges. The moderator is normally a person with expertise in ICT (usually another teacher/lecturer) but they will not necessarily have any expertise in the particular software you are using for your project. What this means is that your work will have to be clearly explained and documented, so that they are able to see clearly what you have done and this will enable you to receive the maximum mark possible for your efforts. You may have done a spectacular project, but unless you have supplied proper documentation and evidence, you will only get a lower mark for it.

What software can I use?

It obviously makes sense to use the software that you are most familiar with, but this may not always be possible.

Any software may be used appropriately, but the software must be business quality and therefore not too simplistic. You will need to find out about the availability of software before deciding on the problem you want to choose for your project. Even if the school/college does not have the particular software you need, discuss it with your teacher/lecturer as they may be able to get it for you.

How much help can my teacher/ lecturer give me?

You teacher/lecturer should have given you enough practice at using some of the advanced features of packages to be able to identify those features that would be useful in solving a particular problem. Your teacher is allowed to use the project as a vehicle for teaching, so you will learn how to use the software but the teacher has to teach software in general terms, so you will have to adapt what you have learnt to your own solution. If your teacher has to directly help you because you are going completely off track, then they will record this on the assessment sheet, which may reduce the mark you get for your project.

You will probably use several different pieces of software for the production of your project.

Can I do the work at home?

Your teacher/lecturer must be able to supervise your work so that they can be sure that it is your own. You can still do work at home but enough of the work must be seen to be done at your school or college to satisfy the teacher/lecturer that it is your own work.

Can I do programming?

You can do a very small amount of programming as part of the project but for some students the nearest they will get to programming is to produce a macro or SQL instructions when extracting data. Please note that this is not a programming project.

Presentation of the projects

It goes without saying that all the project documentation should be word-processed and diagrams (usually screen dumps) should be incorporated into the documents. Although many of you will be able to produce 'glossy', high quality finished work, if there is very little evidence of analysis, design and testing, then you will not obtain high marks. In other words, the examiner will not simply be looking at the presentation of the project.

What software packages can be used?

You can use any applications software you require. Many projects will require the use of several different software packages.

What general points about documentation should I bear in mind?

All projects should have a signed cover sheet and a project sheet identifying the Centre, your name and the project title.

Make sure that your project report includes:

- A contents list
- Headers (suited to your project) and footers indicating the page numbers to which the contents refer
- Indexes
- Appendices.

What is the best way to keep the pages of my project together?

Projects must be securely bound in such a way as to reduce bulk and make it easy for the material to be marked.

When binding your project you should **not** use the following methods:

- Ring binders or lever arch files, since this makes the material far too bulky and causes storage and transport problems for both your teacher and the moderator.
- Slide binders which tend to inhibit the reading of the text or diagrams and which also tend to come off in the post or when being read.

Do not submit your project work in a folder like this.

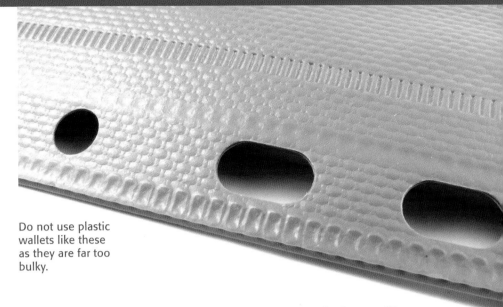

Do not use plastic wallets like these as they are far too bulky.

Do not put any of your material in plastic covers or plastic presentation folders. Your teacher may need to put marks or comments on your work and removing lots of pages from the plastic is time consuming and also annoying. In addition, the use of plastic covers makes the projects much heavier than they need to be.

It is best to use one of the following:

- A thin folder
- Punched holes with treasury tags.

You can use treasury tags to keep your work together.

Do I get marks for spelling, punctuation and grammar?

In order for you to get the marks for each component of the project it is necessary to convey meaning clearly. This means you must:

- use the spellchecker
- obey all the rules of punctuation
- proof read anything you have written several times before handing it in
- use the grammar checker
- get other people to look through your work to see if it makes sense.

You may be able to bind your work like this. Be careful though that the holes punched do not obscure any text or diagrams.

How the project is assessed

▼ **You will find out**

▶ About what you have to provide for background and investigation

▶ About what you have to provide for analysis and deliverables

▶ About what you have to provide for design and planning for implementation

▶ About what you have to provide for testing and documentation of the implementation

▶ About what you have to provide for evaluation of the implemented solution

▶ About what you have to provide for the project report

Introduction

In order to gain the maximum marks, you need to cover as many of the criteria given in the following tables as possible. Your teacher and the moderator will use these criteria to mark the various sections and components of your project. You should work through this and check that you have sections in your project corresponding to the sections and components in the table. You can also use the marks allocated to the components to work out how much evidence you should produce for each component.

Background and investigation

This phase of the project involves using investigation techniques (interviews, questionnaires, inspection of documents, etc.) to find out about the needs of clients and users for the new ICT system you will be developing.

Important note

It is important to note that much of the theory work you do in Unit 3: The Use of ICT in the Digital World is relevant to the project work you will be doing. Do not think of it as two separate things. Use the theory you learn in Unit 3 to help you with the project work.

Analysis and deliverables

Analysis and deliverables looks carefully at the existing or proposed new system and attempts to describe it in various ways. The scope of the system is identified, outlining what the system will do and what it will not do, and the benefits of the system are identified. The criteria by which the new system will be judged, called the evaluation criteria, are identified and agreed with the client. Those parts of the projects which can be handed over to the client in stages are identified and these are called the deliverables. The findings of the analysis are presented to the client in this stage.

Section	What the project report should include	Further detail
1 An introduction to the organisation	Name of organisation Type of organisation (commercial, public, etc.) What they do Indication of size Scale of operation (e.g., number of employees, sites, etc.) Name of the client and their position in the organisation and contact details	
2 A description of the current system (or existing situation) and its environment	Moving down in scale describe the system (or existing situation that needs the system) for the organisation Include information about the people and departments involved	This needs to describe how the system under investigation fits in the organisation
3 Identification of client and users	Who the client is Who the users will be	The client is the person who has asked for the new ICT system to be developed Users are the people who actively use the system – for your project you need multiple users
4 A business case (reasons) for change	Why the project is needed by the organisation	Need to state the business reasons for the project's development (e.g., to provide a way of enabling users to train on the new procedures and be assessed automatically)
5 Evidence of the use of relevant investigation techniques	You need to supply evidence that you have used relevant investigation techniques For example, you need to demonstrate planning, conducting, documenting, and evaluating meetings with clients You also need to show evidence of interviews, observations, research, etc.	Evidence of planning, conducting, documenting and evaluating meetings can be shown in the form of agendas and minutes for meetings You could record interviews and supply copies of questionnaires that had been completed
6 Requirements of the client	This needs to be a list of what the system is supposed to do Add details of the use of house style, usability, security requirements, etc. A brief cost-benefit exercise can be included here You should also specify any constraints (e.g., cost, using existing software, etc.)	The client requirements can be broken down in terms of deliverables – this enables the client to give you valuable feedback in the early stages of the project

Section	What the project report should include	Further detail
1 Statement of scope	How far reaching the system is What the system does and does not do Internal and external constraints such as hardware, software, format of external information requirements, staffing and environmental factors	Information may need exchanging with external bodies There may be legal restrictions
2 Description of the proposed system	Benefits of the new system Details of how it will affect the organisation	Benefits could include increases in accuracy of information, lower cost of processing orders, lower marketing costs, having a worldwide rather than just a national presence, etc.
3 Documentation of processes	This should be appropriate to the project	
4 Description of the users of the proposed system	Details of user skills are assessed to determine what user training is needed Levels of users who will use the system	This is needed to know what users need to be trained on and how much time is needed and how much it will cost
5 Evaluation criteria	Qualitative and quantitative evaluation against which the solution can be tested and evaluated Testing to ensure what has been produced meets the user requirements	Questionnaires can be used to assess how well the solution meets client and user requirements You can then summarise these
6 Agreed deliverables	Statement of what is to be produced and handed over to the client – this can be a prototype or partial system	Statement outlining what is to be delivered and when (i.e. the date)
7 Evidence of checking the findings with the client	Ensure that client/user understands findings	

Design and planning for implementation

In the design and planning stage, alternative design solutions should be considered and some indication should be given as to why any alternative designs were accepted or rejected. Draft designs are then produced, leading to final designs from which the solution can be implemented. Designs should be shown to the client/users for their feedback, which may lead to modifications. Implementation, testing and installation plans are drawn up and timescales for the implementation are produced. Training requirements are drawn up along with a testing strategy and test plan.

Section	What the project report should include	Further detail
1 Evidence of alternative design solutions	Need to provide evidence of other systems (maybe using different software) that were considered, along with reasons for rejection	Commentary of other ways of solving the problem: reasons for rejection of alternatives and why the final solution was chosen
2 Draft design work	Rough sketches of screens, interfaces, storyboards, etc.	
3 Final design work	Final designs from which solution is implemented	
4 Plan for implementation, testing and installation including proposed timescales	Plans, time charts (Gantt charts), diaries, etc.	Evidence that you have planned the project and have set timescales
5 Training requirements for the new system	Documentation for training the users	Questionnaires to determine user requirements, assessment of training needed, training plan, training notes, etc.
6 Testing strategy	Document setting out what testing is necessary, who will do it, when and where Description of any constraints on live testing that require a simulated environment to be used	Note that this is the strategy and not the actual testing which comes later
7 Test plan	This includes the tests that will be undertaken, what they are testing and the order in which they are to be completed	Again only the plan is needed, so no actual testing is included here

Testing and documentation of the implementation

This stage checks that the solution works as expected and supplies documentary evidence to this effect.

Section	What the project report should include	Further detail
1 Evidence of testing	If you cannot test in the intended environment, then testing in a simulated environment will be accepted provided that this has been explained and justified in the testing strategy Testing should concentrate on the testing of complete processes and the system as a whole Evidence of functional or unit tests, for example for validation or for the backing up of one file, is not required	
2 Evidence of client and/or end-user testing	This depends on whether the end-user is also the client	
3 Comprehensive documentation of the solution (that would allow the solution to be developed further) which is appropriate for the client/users	Documentation could be technical or user documentation depending on the individual project undertaken and the agreed deliverables	

Evaluation of the implemented solution

The evaluation of the solution needs to be critical, meaning that you should not sing the praises of the solution, as you need to identify things that need improvement as well as things that worked well. As well as providing the evaluation of the solution, you are also expected to comment on your own performance in producing the project. Again, this needs to be a critical evaluation.

Section	What the project report should include	Further detail
1 The solution should be critically evaluated in such a way to allow it to be used/maintained or developed further The evaluation should be appropriate for the client/user	A critical evaluation comparing the solution against the evaluation criteria and the client needs as defined during the investigation and analysis stages Evidence from testing should be evidenced	
2 An evaluation of the student's own performance	An identification of the student's strengths and weaknesses in the approach they have identified and how they would improve their performance for a similar project in the future	

The project report

The project report needs to be well structured and you are advised to structure the report so that it corresponds to the sections outlined in these tables. This will make it easier for you to check that you have included all the sections as well as for your teacher/lecturer and the moderator to mark.

Section	What the project report should include	Further detail
1 The complete work should be submitted in the format of a project report	The report should be well structured and should make use of the facilities available	The report should include the following: contents list, headers/footers, pagination, indexes, effective use of appendices and presentation techniques Appropriate use of technically accurate, illustrative and visual material for effective communication An appropriate style of writing should be adopted The standard of the student's written communication will be assessed in the report

Glossary

Analysis Breaking a problem down so that it is easier to understand and solve.

Back up Make copies of software and data so that the data can be recovered should there be a total loss of the ICT system.

Backup file A copy of a file which is used in the event of the original file being corrupted (damaged).

Bandwidth A measure of the amount of data that can be transferred using a data transfer medium.

Bluetooth A standard for sending data using short-range radio signals.

Bug A mistake or error in a program.

Business goals The long- and short-term objectives the business would like to meet.

Chief Information Officer The person at executive level responsible for making all of the strategy-related ICT decisions. They are responsible for the management, implementation and usability of all ICT in an organisation.

Compliance Conforming to a specification or policy, standard or law that has been clearly defined.

Computer Misuse Act 1990 The Act which makes illegal a number of activities such as deliberately planting viruses, hacking, using ICT equipment for frauds, etc.

Copyright, Designs and Patents Act 1988 The Act which amongst other things makes it an offence to copy or steal software.

Data controller The person in an organisation whose responsibility it is to control the way that personal data is processed.

Data Protection Act 1998 Law to protect the individual against the misuse of data.

Data subject The living individual whom the personal information is about.

Deliverables Parts of the project that are completed and signed off as being acceptable by the client/project sponsor.

Distributed computing Where a series of computers are networked together and they each work on solving the same problem. Each computer shares data, processing, storage, and bandwidth in order to solve a single problem.

Document management system (DMS) An ICT system which is used by organisations to keep track of electronically stored documents.

Encryption Coding data whilst it is being sent over a network so that only the true recipient is able to decode it. Should the data be intercepted by a hacker, then the data will be in code and totally meaningless.

Enterprise information system (EIS) An ICT system that supports a whole organisation rather than a single department or functional area within the organisation.

Ergonomics An applied science concerned with designing and arranging things people use so that the people and things interact most efficiently and safely.

Evaluation The act of reviewing what has been achieved, how it was achieved and how well the solution works.

External users People who use an organisation's ICT system but who are not actually employed by the organisation.

Extranet An external network that can be used by the customers, suppliers and partners of an organisation as well as the organisation itself.

File attachments Files that are transferred along with an e-mail.

Flash/pen drives Popular storage media which offer large, cheap storage capacities and are ideal media for photographs, music and other data files. They consist of printed circuit boards enclosed in a plastic case.

Footer Text placed at the bottom of a document.

Freedom of Information Act 2000 Act giving the right of access to information held by public authorities.

Grammar checker Used to check the grammar in a sentence and to highlight problems and suggest alternatives.

Hardware The physical components of a computer system.

Header Text placed at the top of a document.

Health and Safety (Display Screen Equipment) Regulations 1992 Regulations making it law for employers to take certain measures to protect the health and safety of their employees who use ICT equipment.

Health and Safety at Work Act 1974 Law making sure that employees have safe working conditions and methods.

ICT systems Hardware and software working together with people and procedures to do a job.

Implementation The process of producing the working version of the solution to the problem as identified by the client.

Information Output from an ICT system, or data which has been processed and gives us knowledge.

Information Commissioner The person responsible for enforcing the Data Protection Act. They also promote good practice and make everyone aware of the implications of the Act.

Input Act of entering data into an ICT system.

Input device The hardware device, such as a keyboard or a scanner, used to feed the data into an ICT system.

Input media The material on which the data is encoded so that it can be read by an input device and digitised so that it can be input, processed and turned into information by the ICT system.

Interface The point where two objects meet. In ICT this is usually between a device such as a computer, printer, scanner, etc., and a human.

Internal threat A threat to an ICT system that comes from inside the organisation.

Internal users Users of the ICT system belonging to an organisation who are employees of the organisation.

Internet A huge group of networks joined together.

Internet service provider (ISP) The organisation that provides your Internet connection.

Intranet A private network used within an organisation that makes use of Internet technology.

Legacy system An old system or piece of software that continues to be used because the organisation does not want to alter or replace it.

Linear methodology Systems development methodology where the project is divided into sequential phases where one phase is completed before the next one starts.

Log-in Identifying yourself to the network in order to gain access.

Log-out Informing the network you want to close access to the network facilities until the next log-in.

Macros Used to record a series of keystrokes so that, for example, your name and address can be added to the top of the page simply by pressing a single key or clicking on the mouse.

Management information system (MIS) An organised collection of people, procedures and resources designed to support the decisions of managers.

Methodology A collection of procedures, tools and documentation aids, which will help develop a new ICT system.

Milestones Points in a project which mark the ends of logical stages in the project. These are the points where the project is reviewed or part of the project is delivered.

Multimedia A means of communication that combines more than one medium for presentation purposes, such as sound, graphics and video.

Network A group of ICT devices (computers, printers, scanners, etc.) which are able to communicate with each other.

Network testing The actual measurement and recording of a network's state of operation over a period of time. It involves recording the current state of network operation to serve as a basis for comparison or control.

Networking software Systems software which allows computers connected together to function as a network.

Notification The process of letting the Information Commissioner's Office know that an organisation is storing and processing personal data.

Offshoring The transfer of business processes (e.g., programming, website design, backup, help-desk, etc.) to another country.

Operating system Software that controls the hardware and also runs your programs. The operating system controls the operations of handling: input, output, interrupts, storage and file management.

Operational tasks Those routine day-to-day tasks which keep the business or organisation functioning.

Outsourcing The movement of internal business processes to an external organisation.

Package software A bundle of files necessary for a particular program to run along with some form of documentation to help a user get the program started.

Password A series of characters which need to be typed in before access to the ICT system is allowed.

Personal data Data about a living identifiable person, which is specific to that person.

Podcasting Creating and publishing a digital radio broadcast using a microphone, computer and audio editing software. The resulting file is saved in MP3 format and then uploaded onto an Internet server. It can then be downloaded using a facility called RSS onto an MP3 player such as an iPod.

Policy A deliberate plan of action to achieve certain desirable goals or outcomes.

Process Any operation that transfers data into information.

Processing Performing calculations or arranging the data into a meaningful order.

Programmer A person who writes computer programs.

Proof reading Carefully reading what has been typed in and comparing it with what is on the data source (order forms, application forms, invoices, etc.) for any errors, which can then be corrected.

Protocol A set of standards that allow the transfer of data between computers on a network.

Proxy server A server which can be hardware or software that takes requests from users for access to other servers and either forwards them onto the other servers or denies access to the servers.

RAID (redundant array of inexpensive disks) A system used by networks to keep backups.

Relational database management system (RDMS) Database system where the data is held in tables with relationships established between them. The software is used to set up and hold the data as well as to extract and manipulate the stored data.

Relationship The way tables are related to each other. Relationships can be one-to-one, one-to-many or many-to-many.

Security Making sure that the hardware, software and data of an ICT system does not come to any harm.

Software Programs that supply the instructions to the hardware.

Software licence Document (digital or paper) which sets out the terms by which the software can be used. It will refer to the number of computers on which it can be run simultaneously.

Spellchecker Facility offered by software where there is a dictionary against which all words typed in are checked.

Strategic tasks Tasks undertaken by personnel at the top of a company or organisation such as directors and chief executives.

Systems software Any computer software that manages and controls the hardware, allowing the applications software to do a useful job. Systems software consists of a group of programs.

Tactical tasks Tasks completed by managers who look at how to achieve the objectives that the directors and chief executives set.

Test plan The approach that will be used to test the whole solution and consists of a suite of tests.

Thesaurus Allows a word to be chosen and the word-processor will list synonyms (i.e., words with similar meanings).

Transaction processing Processing of each transaction as it arises.

UPS (uninterruptible power supply) A backup power supply (generator and battery) which will keep the computer running should the mains power supply fail.

User log A record of the successful and failed log-ins and also the resources used by those users who have access to network resources.

Username A way of identifying who is using the ICT system in order to allocate network resources.

User testing A series of methods for testing an ICT system by collecting data from people who are actually using the system.

Videoconferencing ICT system that allows face-to-face meetings to be conducted without the participants being in the same room or even the same geographical area.

Web browser The software program you use to access the Internet. Microsoft Internet Explorer is an example of a web browser.

Webpage Single document on the World Wide Web.

Index

acceptable use policy 68, 69
access
    restrictions 23, 162
    rights 43, 60
    to Internet 2, 5, 43
accounts systems 25, 26
adaptive maintenance 132–133
alpha testing 124
analysis 76, 78
Apple 3, 4
approval to proceed 90
artificial intelligence 2
atomic attributes 110
attribute names 111
attributes of entities 108, 109, 110, 111
audits 69
autocratic management style 19

back office systems 26, 30
backup 128–131, 175
batch processing systems 128
batteries 4, 9
behaviour policies 60–61
beta testing 124
biotechnology 2, 3
black box testing 123
BlackBerry® 3
Bluetooth 2–3
British Computer Society (BCS) 79
budgets 44, 52, 76, 78, 79, 90, 161
bugs 61, 89, 92, 128, 132, 133
bulk printing 161

cables 61, 126
carbon footprint 8, 163
cascade training 144
changeover of systems 126
charging 4
chat rooms 6, 8, 145
Chief Information Officer (CIO) 44
classroom training 144
code of conduct/practice 7, 43, 68, 69
cognitive science 2, 3
collaborative working 27
commercial organisations 18
communication 2, 7, 23, 70, 79, 100
    between systems 23
compatibility 61
complexity of systems 78
compliance 52, 53
computer-based training (CBT) 144–145
Computer Misuse Act 1990 53, 60, 69
Connect2U 122

consumables 162
context
    diagram 106
    of systems 90
contingency plan 130–131
contracting 161
copyright 6, 23, 53, 60, 68
Copyright, Designs and Patents Act
    1988 53, 60, 68
corrective maintenance 133
costs of new system 87
crime 5, 8
cultural issues 8
customer involvement 77
customer relationship management
    systems 28–29
customer support 20

data
    access to 27
    collection 6
    confidentiality of 69
    dictionaries 110, 111, 127
    erroneous 88
    exchanging 23, 54
    keying in 23, 54
    modelling tools 106–111
    personal 6, 9, 22, 23, 24, 43, 69
    processing 2, 27, 69, 104
    recovery 130–131
    sink 106
    source 106
    storage 3, 53, 54
    store 106
    transfer 24, 78
    transmission 5
    type 111
    warehouse 127
data flow diagrams (DFDs) 106–107,
    108, 127
Data Protection Act 1998 9, 23, 43, 53,
    60, 69
databases 8, 27, 54, 88, 110, 127, 148
    linking 8
    structure 110
decision making 19, 27, 28, 29, 44, 54
decision support systems (DSS) 29
decision tables 102–103
deliverables of projects 76, 77, 79, 90
democratic management style 19, 42
denial of service attacks 70
design specifications 87
developments in technology 54

digital cameras/photography 2, 8
direct changeover 126
disabled people and ICT 8, 149
disaster planning 128, 130–131
disciplinary procedures 43
distance learning 143, 145
DNA database 5
document management system (DMS)
    26–27
documentation 127
DVLA (Driver and Vehicle Licensing
    Agency) 5, 22, 30

e-commerce 6, 30, 42, 52, 93, 142, 150;
    also see on-line shopping
economic issues 9
efficiency 24, 54
e-mail 3, 27, 30, 53, 60, 70, 145, 151, 162
employment, changes to patterns and
    procedures 7, 8
encryption 6, 23, 124
end-user
    involvement 76
    testing 88
enterprise information systems (EIS) 29
entity names 110, 111
entity relationship diagrams (ERDs)
    108, 110
entity relationship models (ERMs)
    108–109
environmental
issues 8, 61
policies 43
equipment policies 60

face recognition 5
fact finding 100
feasibility of projects/systems 86–87,
    90, 106
file conversion utilities 127
file sharing 5, 23, 27, 68
fireproof 128, 131
firewalls 23, 43
flash drives 69
flexible
    screens 4
    working 2, 6, 7
flowcharts 103–104, 127
foreign keys 109, 110
Freedom of Information Act 2000 53, 70
future of computers/ICT 2, 4
future proofing 54

gambling 6
games 6, 8
global positioning system (GPS) 3
grandfather, father and son principle
    128

hackers 23, 43, 70
hands-free 2
hardware
    cost 53, 61
    installation of 89, 126
    purchasing policies 61
    resources 162
    updating 53
health 8
Health and Safety at Work Act 1974 70
health and safety
    policies 61, 70
    training 144
help-desk 133, 146–148, 151
hierarchical structure 19, 42
hospitals 122
human resource systems 163
human resources see personnel

ICT
    future proofing 54
    impact of 6–7
    issues with 6, 8–9
    management of 42–44
    policies 6, 7, 23, 43, 54, 60–61, 68,
        69, 143
    poor systems 78–79
    projects 76–77, 86
    strategy 42–44, 52–54
    teamwork 77
    also see organisations
identity theft 6, 8
implementation of projects 87
industrial organisations 18
information
    collecting 100–101
    exchanging/transferring 23, 25, 122
    extraction 78, 79
    management over time 53
    needs 22
    patients 122
    presenting 27, 29
    sources 28, 29
    also see data
Information Commissioner 69
infringement of policies 61
Intel 3, 5
interface 4, 9, 127, 133, 149–151
    types of 150
interfacing 25, 52, 89, 90
Internet
    access 2, 5, 43
    browsing 3
    downloading from 5, 8, 68

interviews 100
iterative methodologies 92, 93
iteration 104

keying in data/information 23, 54

laissez-faire management style 19
laptops 2, 3, 4, 69
LCD (liquid crystal display) 4
leading questions 101
leasing 161
legacy systems 25, 52
legal issues 9, 44, 52–53, 60, 68–70,
    132, 143
licence 68
linear methodologies 92, 93, 112
link tables 110
local area networks (LANs) 19
log on procedures 43, 60, 69
logs 70

macros 127
management information systems
    (MIS) 27–28, 54, 78, 150
management styles 19, 42
manager involvement 76, 77
metadata 111
methodologies 78, 92¬–93
microchips 3, 5
milestones of projects 76, 77, 79, 90
mind maps xi, xii, 15–16, 38–40,
    49–50, 58, 65–66, 74, 83–84, 98,
    119–120, 139–140, 157, 170
mobile phones 2, 4, 7, 9
mobile working 2
MP3 players 4
multi-platform testing 112

nanometre 3
nanotechnology 2, 3
natural disasters 128
network tools 125
NHS (National Health Service) 122, 143

objectives of projects 76
observation 100
offshoring 160–161
one-to-one training 144
on-line
    booking 30
    essay banks 8
    help 151
    ordering 22, 30, 150
    shopping 8
on-screen help 148, 149
operational
    staff 100
    tasks 21
ordering systems 20, 122
organisation charts 101

organisations
    business strategy 44
    customers 20, 22
    ICT management 42–44
    ICT needs of 22
    ICT systems 24–30, 52–54, 89,
        100–101
    levels in 21, 44
    management styles 19, 42
    official/legal obligations 22
    scale/size of 19, 42, 61, 122
    structure of 19
    suppliers 22
    tasks performed in 21
    types of 18–19
outsourcing 160

parallel changeover 126
passwords 43, 60, 69
paternalistic management style 19
payroll 24, 25
peer-to-peer file sharing 68
perfective maintenance 132, 133
personal data/information 6, 9, 22, 23,
    24, 43, 69
personal digital assistants (PDAs) 2,
    3, 69
personnel 24–25, 29, 61, 79
phased conversion 126
pilot conversion 126
portability testing 112, 123
power resourcing 163
primary keys 109, 110
privacy issues 5, 6, 8, 9
process modelling tools 102–105
processing power 54
procurement 43, 54, 60, 61
professional standards 79
profit 18
project
    controls, establishing 91
    definition 86
    error planning 91
    managers/management 76, 77,
        90–91
    objectives 93
    plan 79, 90
    sponsors 76, 77, 90, 91
prototyping 113
public service organisations/
    authorities 18–19, 70

questionnaires 88, 101, 143, 150

RAID (random array of inexpensive
    disks) 128
records, inspection of 100
relationships between entities 108–
    109, 110
reliability of systems 123

remote working 2, 6
repetitive strain injury (RSI) 70
restoration 129
risk analysis 129
robotics 2, 3, 6

schools 28, 54
scope of projects 76
security
    of data/information 6, 23, 43, 69
    of Internet 43
    physical 43
    policies 43, 60–¬61, 69
    testing 124
    threats 60
selection 103
sequence 103
simulated environments 113
smart cars 5
social issues 6, 7
social networking sites 6, 8, 143
software
    faults 123
    help-desk 148
    installation of 89, 126–127
    purchasing policies 61
    tailoring to needs 122
    updating 53, 61
specification of projects 90
speed of transfer 9, 78
spiral methodology 93
SSADM (Structured Systems Analysis
    and Design Methodology) 106
stock control 6, 20, 21, 25, 26, 29, 30
storage capacity 9, 128, 162
strategic tasks 21
strategy, factors influencing 52–53
stress 7, 70
subject access 69
supplier selection policies 61
supply chain 25
symbols 104, 106
synonyms 111
systems
    analysis 78, 86, 100
    analysts 7, 78, 87, 90, 127
    building 88
    changing 126
    development 92–93

diagrams 87, 104
evaluation 92
feasibility 86–87, 106
functionality of 142
installation 89
interfacing 25, 52, 89, 90
investigation 86, 100–101, 106, 107
legacy 25, 52
loss 128
maintenance 89, 132–133
reliability of 123
requirements 87
resources 127
review 89
systems development life cycle (SDLC)
    86, 90, 132

tactical tasks 21
tasks 21, 24, 25, 27, 42, 44, 70, 77, 90,
    91, 92, 142
    allocating 91
    types of 21, 142
tax 22, 24, 52, 92, 143
teamwork 77
technical
    documentation 127
    issues/problems 9, 91
technology
    developments 54
    life cycle 54
Telecommunications (Lawful
    Business Practice) (Interception of
    Communications) Regulations 2000
    70
telecommuting 8, 147
terrorists 6
test harnesses 112
test plan 123, 127
testing 88, 92, 104, 112–113, 122–127,
    132
    functionality 127
    networks 124–125, 126
    techniques of 112, 123
timescales of projects 76, 77, 90
touch screens 4, 149, 150
training 6, 7, 18, 44, 60, 89, 127, 131,
    142–151
    external users 143
    methods 144

policies 44, 60, 61

unit testing 123
upgrading 53
usability testing 112
USB port 2
use policies 60
user
    documentation 127
    interface 4, 9, 127, 133, 149–151
    involvement 78
    requirements 87, 89, 90
    support 133, 146–148
    testing 88, 92, 113
usernames 43, 60, 69

videoconferencing 27, 143, 145
viruses 6, 8, 43, 60, 69, 70
volume testing 112

waterfall methodology 92, 93, 112
white box testing 123
wide area networks (WANs) 19
wireless
    energy 4
    networks 2, 9, 125
work, changes to patterns and
    procedures 7, 8, 54
workflow management systems 26–27

X-rays 122

Acknowledgements

Folens Limited would like to thank the following for giving permission to use copyright material.

p.vii, © This image is copyright of SnappyStock/Fotolia; © 2007 Ron Chapple Stock Inc./Fotolia; p.viii, © Andres Rodriguez/Fotolia; p.2, © Dana S. Rothstein/Fotolia; © Paulus Rusyanto/Fotolia; © Petar Atanasov/Fotolia; p.3, Iskin.com; iRobot Corporation; ©BlackBerry®, Rim®, Research In Motion®, SureType® and related trademarks, names and logos are the property of Research In Motion Limited and are registered and/or used in the U.S. and countries around the world; Henton & Chattell Ltd; © Mushakesa/Fotolia; p.4,Iskin.com; Glasbergen, p.5; © Intel Corporation; © zimmytws/Shutterstock © Kirsty Pargeter/Fotolia; p.7, © Levente Janos/Fotolia; p.9, © V. Yakobchuk/Fotolia; p.12, iRobot Corporation; p.18, © Cristian Ciobanu/Fotolia; © iMAGINE/Fotolia; p.19, © Tom Nance/Fotolia; © Jeff Dalton/Fotolia; © Scott Rothstein/Fotolia; © Johnny Lye/Fotolia; © gator/Fotolia; p. 20, © Peter Ivanov/Fotolia; © PArpad Nagy-Bagoly/Fotolia; p.21, Glasbergen; p.22, © dave timms/Fotolia; © Igor Krayushkin/Fotolia; p.23, © Saniphoto/Fotolia; © PNorman Price/Alamy; p.25, © JJAVA/Fotolia; p.27, © Dimitrije Paunovic/Fotolia; p.29, © ioannis kounadeas/Fotolia; p.34, Easyjet; p.35, TNT Holding B.V.; p.42, © JJAVA/Fotolia; p.43, © Rajesh/Fotolia; © maigi/Fotolia; p.44, Glasbergen; © Andres Rodriguez/Fotolia; p.45, Hampshire Fire and Rescue Service; p.53, © keki/Fotolia; p.54, © Lee Torrens/Fotolia; p.68, © Stephen Finn/Fotolia; p.69, © doug Olson/Fotolia; p.70, Glasbergen; p.76, © Philip Date/Fotolia; p.77, Glasbergen; p.78, © Rob/Fotolia; © Comp Image ID/Fotolia; p.79, Glasbergen; p.87, © Tombaky/Fotolia; © Roland/Fotolia; © Orlando Florin Rosu/Fotolia; p.88, © Leo Blanchette/Fotolia; p.89, © nyul/Fotolia; © Kirill Roslyakov/Fotolia; © PArtyom Yefimov/Fotolia; p.91, Glasbergen; p.100, © Roland/Fotolia; p.101, © Dominique LUZY/Fotolia; © Helder Almeida/Fotolia;

p.102, © Ronald Hudson/Fotolia; p.111, Microtechware@sbcglobal.net; p.112, © William Freeman /Fotolia; p.113, © Fredy Sujono/Fotolila; p.122, © Roger Bamber/Alamy; Smiths News; p.123, © Suprijono Suharjoto/Fotolia; p.124, © ktsdesign/Fotolia; © Kirill Roslyakov/Fotolia; p.125, © Mikhail Tolstoy/Fotolia; © rgbspace/Fotolia; p.127, © pressmaster/Fotolia; p.128, Glasbergen; p.129, © Tatyana Nyshko/Fotolia; p.130, © Yuri Arcurs/Fotolia;© Anyka/Fotolia; p.131, © Jean-Michel POUGET/Fotolia; © Spectral-Design/Fotolia; p.132, © Andrea Danti/Fotolia; © kentoh/Fotolia; p.133, © khz/Fotolia; © Alexander Kuznetsov/Fotolia; © Arpad Nagy-Bagoly/Fotolia; p.142, © David Hilcher/Fotolia; p.143, © Roxanne McMillen/Fotolia; © Jonny McCullagh/Fotolia; © oscar Williams/Fotolia; © Ptetrex/Fotolia; p.144, © Martinan/Fotolia; p.145, © Jaimie Duplass/Fotolia; © Aleksandar Radovanovic/Fotolia;© George Dolgikh/Fotolia; p.146,© Jonny McCullagh/Fotolia; © Arrow Studio/Fotolia; p.147, Glasbergen; © Olaf Bender/Fotolia; p.148, © treenabeena/Fotolia; p.149, © palms/Fotolia; © Anatoly Vartanov/Fotolia; p.150, © Alex Yeung/Fotolia; © Dominique LUZY/Fotolia; p.151, © vladislav susoy/Fotolia; Glasbergen; © Sharon Day/Fotolia; p.160, Glasbergen; © JJAVA/Fotolia; p.161, Glasbergen; p.162, © Alexander Kataytsev/Fotolia; p.163, © luchschen/Fotolia; © Roman Milert/Fotolia; p.165, © Horticulture/Fotolia; p.173, © Argus/Fotolia; © Giordano Aita/Fotolia; © Yuri Arcurs/Fotolia; p. 174, © dara/Fotolia; p.175, © cphoto/Fotolia; p.176, © Vieloryb/Fotolia; p.177, © Alex White/Fotolia; © Paul Gibbings/Fotolia; © Frolov Andrey/Fotolia; © Fedor Sidorov/Fotolia;

Every effort has been made to contact copyright holders of material used in this publication. If any copyright holder has been overlooked, we should be pleased to make any necessary arrangements.